VALLEY BOY

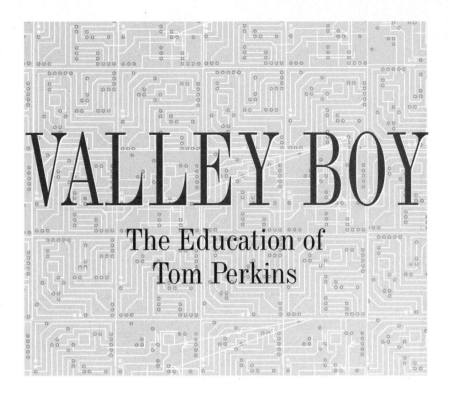

VALLEY BOY

The Education of
Tom Perkins

Tom Perkins

To Clent and Sharon with
best regards,

Tom Perkins

GOTHAM
BOOKS

GOTHAM BOOKS
Published by Penguin Group (USA) Inc.
375 Hudson Street, New York, New York 10014, U.S.A.
Penguin Group (Canada), 90 Eglinton Avenue East, Suite 700, Toronto, Ontario M4P 2Y3, Canada (a
division of Pearson Penguin Canada Inc.); Penguin Books Ltd, 80 Strand, London WC2R 0RL, England;
Penguin Ireland, 25 St Stephen's Green, Dublin 2, Ireland (a division of Penguin Books Ltd); Penguin
Group (Australia), 250 Camberwell Road, Camberwell, Victoria 3124, Australia (a division of Pearson
Australia Group Pty Ltd); Penguin Books India Pvt Ltd, 11 Community Centre, Panchsheel Park, New
Delhi – 110 017, India; Penguin Group (NZ), 67 Apollo Drive, Rosedale, North Shore 0632, Auckland,
New Zealand (a division of Pearson New Zealand Ltd); Penguin Books (South Africa) (Pty) Ltd,
24 Sturdee Avenue, Rosebank, Johannesburg 2196, South Africa

Penguin Books Ltd, Registered Offices: 80 Strand, London WC2R 0RL, England

Published by Gotham Books, a member of Penguin Group (USA) Inc.

First printing, October 2007
1   3   5   7   9   10   8   6   4   2

Gotham Books and the skyscraper logo are trademarks of Penguin Group (USA) Inc.

LIBRARY OF CONGRESS CATALOGING-IN-PUBLICATION DATA
Perkins, Thomas J.
Valley Boy : the education of Tom Perkins / Tom Perkins.
p. cm.
ISBN 978-1-592-40313-4 (hardcover)
1. Perkins, Thomas J. 2. Executives—United States—Biography. 3. Hewlett-Packard Company—
Management. 4. Novelists, American—20th century—Biography. I. Title.
HD9696.2.U62P47 2007
338.7'61004092—dc22
[B]   2007012507

Photo credits:
Pages x, 103, 118, and 130: KPCB achive; Pages 2 and 7: Associated Press; Page 24: Russ Fischella
Portraits; Page 25: Domkirkeodden; Pages 44, 65, 90, 164, 184, and 240: TJ Perkins; Page 73:
The Hewlett-Packard Company; Page 111: James Treybig; Page 152: Martha Swoop; Page 168: Rolex;
Page 169: Chris Gartner; Page 189: Greg Gorman and Danielle Steel; Page 210: R. Pieper; Page 230:
HarperCollins; Page 252: Perini Navi; Page 255: G. Dijkstra and Partners; Page 260: K. Freivokh

Printed in the United States of America
Set in Electra with Industrial 736 and Lord Swash
Designed by Sabrina Bowers

To Kathy, Richard, Chris, Gillian, Justin,
Brian, Angela, and Morena, with thanks

"I have observed that both optimists and pessimists seem to leave this world in the same way—but the optimists live better lives."
—SHIMON PERES

Contents

Author's Note   *xi*

Chapter One: *Sometimes in Cat and Mouse, the Mouse Wins!—Even If She Doesn't Play the HP Way*   *1*

Chapter Two: *Sailing Is Not Always Pleasure Boating*   *23*

Chapter Three: *Vindictiveness Is a Terrible Thing*   *43*

Chapter Four: *A Ferrari Is Not Necessarily a Wise Substitute for the Company Chevrolet*   *71*

Chapter Five: *Digging Up an Old Car*   *89*

Chapter Six: *A New Partnership, and a New Approach, Change the Venture Landscape*   *101*

Chapter Seven: *Coaching a Winning Team*   *129*

Chapter Eight: *If You Are Interested in Bare-knuckle Infighting, Join a Civic Arts Group!*   *147*

Chapter Nine: *In Ocean Racing, Preparation and Teamwork Make the Difference!*   *167*

Chapter Ten: *CELEBRITY WIRE 1 April 2007*   *183*

Chapter Eleven: *The Deal of a Lifetime Ends a Life*   *209*

Chapter Twelve: *The Best Ever Argument for Book Burning*   *223*

Chapter Thirteen: *The Man and the Myth*   *239*

Chapter Fourteen: *What if Orville and Wilbur Had Really Gone for Broke?*   *251*

A Final Word   *275*

Index   *277*

Tom Perkins in 1973 in the first Kleiner & Perkins office

Author's Note

If you are looking for something like *Investing in High Tech—the Seven Secrets*, I confess right now I don't have these secrets. You won't find checklists or tips in this book. But I have been privileged to be on the ground floor of Silicon Valley, and these are stories from that world. The building of Kleiner Perkins Caufield & Byers is such a story, and the creation of Genentech another. I will share some of this history, together with a number of other events in my life that are personal and not venture-oriented, like the toughest assignment I ever had—incredibly, it was for the San Francisco Ballet—and being tried for manslaughter in a backwater French town. You will see that I am both a passionate player, and one who is still learning.

In places I have changed names and identities to protect the innocent. (Or to shield myself from the wrath of the not-so-innocent!) But these tales are the truth, unvarnished, and as beautiful or as ugly as you may find them. The subtitle is a reference to *The Education of Henry Adams*. Adams was a self-proclaimed "boy of the eighteenth century" who was amused and bemused by the world about him, always learning, always finding more to learn. With a tip of the hat to that masterful autobiographer, this "boy of the twentieth century" will do his best.

So this book is an autobiography, but it does not remotely intend to include everything. It does not focus much on dates and numbers, nor does it follow the usual chronology. Others have done, and will do, a better job in documenting the history of the Valley. Rather, if we were together over a few dinners, or were traveling on a voyage, when it was my turn these are the stories I would tell. You won't find them elsewhere.

And, as I said in my soufflé of a novel, *Sex and the Single Zillionaire*, for better or worse, no "ghost" did the writing.

VALLEY BOY

Chapter One

Sometimes in Cat and Mouse, the Mouse Wins!—

Even If She Doesn't Play the HP Way

Most board of directors meetings are pretty dull, and the bigger the company, the more true this becomes. The Hewlett-Packard Company is very big, one of the biggest in the world. So, when in early 2005 the board unanimously voted to invite me back, I didn't anticipate much excitement. But I soon discovered that the old warhorse (me) was being summoned back for one final battle—and after the battle was won they found that the horse ate, as usual, too much hay and crapped, as usual, all over the landscape— But wait! I am getting ahead of the story.

My history with the company goes back decades, and later I'll get to my experiences working directly for Dave Packard and Bill Hewlett. Even though I had already resigned from HP three times, twice as a kid employee and once as a director, I loved the place. I had no thought of resigning, in May 2006, from the board in cold fury!

The day was typical Palo Alto beautiful, and the boardroom had its usual bland and modest look. But there were deep tensions around the table. We directors had been through a struggle that had left ugly wounds. I had originally joined the board in 2001 when HP acquired Compaq, a Kleiner & Perkins company on whose board I sat. The merger was a tough-fought battle, brilliantly waged by Carly Fiorina, HP's "celebrity" CEO.

Carly and I met for the first time just before the merger at that famous place for deal-making, the Village Pub in Woodside. Over dinner I agreed to join the new HP board if the merger went through,

Carly Fiorina, former CEO
of the Hewlett-Packard Company

helping to represent the Compaq shareholders, myself included, who would be traveling along with a couple of other original Compaq directors into the future of the "new" HP.

Carly is a star: an assured personality, attractive, and with a mind of the highest caliber. At that dinner I suggested that we establish a technology committee of the new board, like an audit committee but focused on the nearly five billion dollars per year that the combined companies would be spending on research and development. She loved the idea—an industry first—and made me the new committee's chairman.

The merger, which cost HP nineteen billion dollars, was the

biggest in high-tech history. Not only did Dave and Bill's heirs hate it—voting against the combination, losing a very close proxy war (during the battle, Carly made a rare public relations faux pas, demeaning Walter Hewlett, then on the HP board, by calling him just "an academic and musician")—but Wall Street hated it too, mostly. The family members didn't like the idea of diluting their ownership by issuing all those new shares to acquire Compaq—they thought HP could do fine on its own—and Wall Street was fully aware that virtually all big mergers in high technology failed. They weren't convinced that the synergies could be achieved. After 9/11, the stock really tanked.

But I had fought hard in favor, from the Compaq side, helping Carly as best I could. Around the world, where Compaq was weak, HP was strong and vice versa. The product lines didn't overlap much in their markets, either; even the personal computers (PCs) fit together seamlessly. Where HP was strong in the consumer market, Compaq was strong in enterprise. Of course, in PCs Dell was beating the socks off both companies over the Internet with the Dell Direct engine.

Carly was dauntless. As chairman and CEO she made Michael Capellas, the former Compaq CEO, president and chief operating officer. Together they set about untangling product road maps as well as the two vast marketing organizations, and they began to squeeze huge savings (measured in billions of dollars) from the overlapping operations and increased economies of scale. The downturn in the world economy following the terrorist attacks, however, slowed the overall markets and delayed the results Wall Street was expecting. Both executives were under immense pressure from employees, the investment world, and the board.

Mike and Carly started out working together reasonably well and their decisions were being implemented. I was surprised and pleased at how quickly the two organizations' cultures blended together, and after a short while it was hard to discern from which organization employees originally came. Plus, a number of the top jobs in the new company were held by executives from Compaq. It was almost as if giant, old, and ultra-conservative HP and the famous "HP Way" had experienced an injection of new "Texas hustle" DNA.

But the honeymoon at the top began to fade. In my opinion, Michael simply found it too hard to play the number-two role. Also in my opinion, Carly tried, very hard, to make the structure work. I spent literally hours on the phone and in person with Mike pleading to hold him in the job—hoping to convince him that he was a great "Mr. Inside" and that Carly was equally great in communication with the "outside world" of customers and investors—but I failed. He resigned after only about six months, having, however, laid much of the groundwork for the success that the merger has ultimately achieved.

The first inkling I had of the problem that I think ultimately led to Carly's departure was a discussion I had with her about replacing Mike with another executive to share her burden. She chose, rather, to assume many of his responsibilities herself, and while she always encouraged directors to "mix it up" in reviews of strategy and general matters, she made it very clear, in my view, that our opinions were less than welcome on operational and organizational specifics. Also, Carly was evolving a highly complex matrix-type organizational structure, which I thought unwieldy. People weren't clear on their responsibilities; if you could understand that organization chart, you'd find the recently solved Poincaré's conjecture in mathematical topology child's play.

Still, in the next three years, from 2001 through the end of 2003—when I did not stand for reelection to the board—much was accomplished. The technology committee became a major influence on policy. We established a program to license HP's patent and intellectual property portfolio to begin to achieve the sort of income IBM earns, from an only marginally larger portfolio. This potential, which had been ignored for years, might grow to hundreds of millions of dollars added to the bottom line annually in the not-distant future.

Probably more importantly, we encouraged management to develop the very long process toward additional and alternate sources for microprocessors—HP is the world's largest consumer of these devices—and thereby to siphon more profit into HP's earnings, and away from the primary vendor. This program was sometimes referred to as "Operation Hickory Stake," after my joking reference to that being the only thing through the heart of a blood-sucking vampire that might bring relief.

During 2004 I was not on the board. I didn't argue with Carly about staying on after passing the retirement age. She probably was experiencing "director fatigue" with me—she makes that pretty clear in her autobiography. And so I was unaware of developments between Carly and her directors. In October of that year a friend (from the original pre-merger HP board) visited me at my place in England, and we discussed HP in a general way. He asked me if I would consider rejoining, and I answered, sure, if the invitation was unanimous.

In December the invitation came. I checked with several directors, including Carly, and was assured by all that the board would be delighted to have me back. I attended my first meeting as an observer in early January, and when I walked into the room Carly gave me a big smile and a hug, welcoming my return.

Only during this meeting did it become clear to me that the board and Carly were in a struggle over the direction of the company. Much has been written about the events that occurred over the next few weeks. A lot of what has been written is incorrect, and how individual directors voted still must remain confidential. In my opinion, the last thing the board wanted was for Carly to leave. I believe the directors wanted her to succeed, but also wanted her to take more specific direction on how to reorganize the business and what to do about the various problems the company faced.

Prior to this meeting, a delegation of three board members had met formally with her to review some specific requests; I was not in this group. I was told that she "stonewalled" them. I don't have direct knowledge of whether she did or did not do so, but perhaps she reiterated her belief, as she had done with me three years earlier, that the board had no business poking into the specifics of management of the company. I am not sure that Carly, or for that matter any chief executive, entirely agrees what exactly should be the role of a board. Congress and the public probably think that it should be to insure that the company complies with the law. Of course that's important, but I am of the school that believes the board is also like the rudder of a ship: without its guidance things can go badly wrong. In my view the board must be actively engaged.

Around this time, accounts of the rift at the top appeared in the press, first in the *Wall Street Journal* and then in *BusinessWeek, Fortune,* and soon in many other media sources. The press was having a field day. The information certainly came from multiple sources, and probably from some directors themselves. Carly was, justifiably, very angry about the articles, a few of which seemed aimed specifically to undermine her position.

Finally a special meeting of the board was called, which I attended. Carly was there, I am sure attending reluctantly. We went to lengths to keep this meeting out of the press, even making reservations at the hotel under assumed names. The meeting was turbulent, I think all would agree. I believed that I had been brought back to the board—the warhorse—to stiffen everyone's resolve, and if Carly wouldn't budge on at least some of the changes the board sought, to take decisive action to find a new CEO. I concurred with that idea, and during the discussion it was evident that a majority, not counting my vote, agreed that this was the right course. There was less agreement on the timing. Finally, the decision was made to ask for Carly's resignation, and to appoint Bob Wayman, the CFO, as acting chief executive. Parts of this meeting made it into the press even before we returned home.

A director had resigned before this meeting for unrelated reasons, and another resigned shortly afterward, partly in disagreement with the decision. Among those who remained, deep disagreements lay just below the surface. It was necessary to elect a new chairman, to replace Carly, and to get on with finding a new CEO as quickly as possible. Director Pattie Dunn had, I thought, been particularly careful in being sure that the board followed all due process and procedure during these events, and I supported her election as chairman. She, Dr. Jay Keyworth, and I were appointed by the board to take on the responsibility of finding and recruiting a new CEO. We announced that the process might take up to six months. Among the three of us, we set a goal not to exceed six to eight weeks, hoping to minimize the period of uncertainty.

Pattie had been on the HP board for some years prior to the merger. She had an outstanding background in portfolio investment management with Barclays Bank with fiduciary responsibility for about a trillion dollars in investors' assets. Dunn had little experience in manufacturing, technology, marketing, human resources, or any operating aspect of a giant high-tech business. But she was helpful in the Carly situation by keeping everyone focused upon the

Patricia Dunn, former chairman,
at the congressional inquiry into the HP scandal

details of process; process and governance procedure became her chosen specialty. She seemed like a "neutral." Some might say that with twenty-twenty hindsight, she was not the right choice for the board to have made chair. Jay Keyworth, on the other hand, had been on the board for about twenty years, having been brought on by Dave Packard. He has a PhD in nuclear physics, had run the physics section of the Los Alamos Laboratories (where the atomic bombs are made), was science advisor to President Reagan, and was very instrumental in the Strategic Defense Initiative ("Star Wars"), which is frequently credited with helping to bring about the demise of the Soviet Union. Jay was deeply involved in all aspects of HP and was, in my opinion, the most important director.

With the help of a top recruiter, Andrea Redmond of Russell Reynolds, we three assembled our list of dream candidates. We were gratified to discover that a shot at running one of the biggest companies in America, even with the problems that HP exhibited of slow growth and low margins, drew most of our prospects out of the woodwork (on a confidential basis) to talk with us. The three of us devoted nearly one hundred percent of our time to the task, and after a few weeks we thought we had the perfect choice in our crosshairs.

Along the way, a friend of mine in the New York financial world asked me if Mark Hurd was on our list. My contact recommended him highly, saying that Mark had done a terrific job in turning around the relatively small (revenues of eight billion) NCR (formerly the National Cash Register company) to the immense satisfaction of "the Street."

We already had been flying around the country with our top candidates to introduce them to the other members of the HP board, wanting the directors' one hundred percent involvement in the decision. We were confident the top person we were focusing on would be our choice. I need to point out that two very strong internal candidates were on our list as well, and they also got our full consideration. I was comfortable that we already had the right choice for the job at the top of our short list, so it was almost with reluctance that I scheduled Mark Hurd for an interview in my San Francisco office. Pattie and Jay joined me.

Simply put, in the course of about one and a half hours Mark blew all the others out of the water. He had done his homework, and based upon public information and available SEC filings, he had analyzed HP's problems and prospects with an astonishing perception. Plus, he outlined a plan to fix things quickly and efficiently. When he left my office, the three of us just looked at one another and, virtually simultaneously, said, "He's our man!"

We quickly got him to the other board members and negotiated the contract. Mark was very exposed, as his board at NCR had no idea that he was considering HP. He was loyal to his company and his board, and he wanted to clear it with them in advance of any leak or disclosure. We just made it, by a hair's breadth—within hours of receiving the NCR board's blessing, his acceptance of the HP position was leaked to the press. A potential catastrophe was narrowly avoided, for Mark would not have accepted our offer without his board's okay. Leaks had, again, become a problem for us all.

■   ■   ■

Looking back now, I can only marvel at how quickly and effectively the HP board worked to find and hire Mark Hurd. He has accomplished much of what he set out to do. The merger has proven a strategic victory for Carly's vision, as implemented by Mark's management skills. Tens of billions of revenue have been added to the top line, and some new billions in earnings at the bottom of the P & L. The stock price has tripled from its post-merger low, becoming one of the fastest rising equities in the Dow-Jones index.

How then could this board, which to the outside world must have seemed invincible, eventually come to be, in my opinion, so dysfunctional and self-destructive? Well, probably much of it has been my fault. As I see it, some of the board's thinking was preoccupied by the cat and mouse game being played between Pattie Dunn and Tom Perkins until the final terrible explosion. Probably, the two of us could not have been more mismatched for roles requiring close cooperation.

I thought that Pattie should be an "activist" chairman, be deeply involved in the strategy of the company and take a very busy role, as I had for three New York stock exchange companies: Tandem, Genentech, and Acuson. So I persuaded my fellow directors to vote to pay Dunn an additional hundred thousand dollars on top of her normal annual fees (an industry record) to be an involved chairman. I was able to do this because Pattie asked me to become chair of the nomination and governance committee of the board—a key job with more than a little influence but, sadly, not enough influence.

Backing Pattie was, I think, an error on my part. Dunn, normally as quiet as a mouse, had a will of iron. Her vision, I soon discovered, bore little or no relationship to my own. Can the cat and the mouse productively coexist? I thought that she focused too much on the legal and compliance aspects of the business. In my opinion, the tired cliché is alive and well in many boardrooms: if the deck chairs are all in order, then all is well aboard the *Titanic*. There are plenty of consultants, advisors, and lawyers to opine on the deck chairs; you only have to ask—and at HP we heard from lots of them. The advent of Sarbanes-Oxley, a complex of disclosures and guarantees required by Congress after Enron and other scandals, may have encouraged thinking of this kind.

There has been much gnashing of corporate teeth and copious complaints about the compliance aspects of Sarbanes-Oxley (usually abbreviated as "SOX"). And in my view the new regulations are a huge overreaction to the problem—the simple step of requiring the CEO to sign the financial statements under criminal penalties is the strongest and most effective part of SOX. But corporate America has only itself to blame when Congress moves in to fix abuses. Unfortunately, the compliance aspects of SOX can, if permitted, come to dominate everything that a board does. And at the end of the day compliance doesn't add to earnings per share and a rising stock price. In my view it is bad news for the shareholders if a chairman's proclivities for SOX, that is for form over substance, become ascendant. What's most important is creating rising share-holder value.

The Dunn and Perkins meetings, both in private and at the board table, became increasingly rancorous, and maybe a little amusing to the other directors. I found that major disagreements always arose over the agenda. On what were we to spend our collective time? To Pattie, a discussion of the finer points of the company bylaws was quite productive, or so I believed she felt. To me, we never could have enough time to concentrate on direction: how to boost growth, improve profit, strengthen management, and how better to compete with IBM and Dell, two seriously tough challengers who would eat our lunch given the slightest opportunity.

Pattie told me that the technology committee was preempting the other board functions, which indeed it was, if strategy was considered a board function. We solved the problem by opening the committee to all board members, and all were interested in attending. Pattie and I had trouble agreeing on anything. I wanted to bring aboard new directors with entrepreneurial experience from the Valley; she opted instead for big company types who had names recognized on Wall Street. She told other directors that I was into "cronyism" from the Valley.

Some of our clashes were pretty funny. Pattie asked me for an advance copy of my novel, *Sex and the Single Zillionaire,* a satirical look at reality TV. I had a stack of them on my desk so, of course, I signed one and gave it to her. A few weeks later we were together at a cocktail reception for Stan O'Neal, the CEO of Merrill Lynch. As Stan and I were chatting, Pattie walked up and joined us. I asked her, "How did you like my book?" She literally couldn't answer. She just stood there with an incredible grimace on her face, and then she began to tremble slightly. After quite an embarrassing length of time, Stan poked me in the ribs and said, "Tom, I think you got your answer!" As far as I can determine, Pattie has a different sense of humor; the book is silent on the finer points of corporate governance, so she probably found it dull and a waste of time.

But all this was really superficial. The tensions on the board, suffice to say, were never smoothed or resolved from the time and trauma of Carly's dismissal. Maybe no one could have accomplished that goal. They were like rocks below the water, hidden, but dangerous at low tide. The tide went out in January of 2006.

There was another leak. This one was essentially different from all those in the past, which were entirely negative in their impact. This disclosure, to the computer site CNET.com, was extremely positive. It was obviously designed to give an upbeat spin to the style and substance of Mark as CEO and as HP's top strategist. There was no new information in the article, just a rehash of old press releases; nothing in the article was picked up and copied by other media. But it was sufficiently informed to have come only from a director. The article could have contained the director's name as source, it was so bland, but it did not . . . and it was unauthorized.

Pattie seized upon this event, as I was to find out. She made finding the "leaker" a major focus of her administration. Her e-mail to me on the subject said, "Bring out the lie detectors!" She discussed the disclosure and the idea of lie detectors with me, since I was chair of the nominating and governance committee and this sort of thing was technically under my purview. I volunteered to take a lie detector test, which I thought might be fun, or at least an interesting experience, which maybe I could use in a future novel. She seriously considered this idea, but her experts advised her that such tests were unreliable, so I didn't get the chance. Her decision might have been influenced by the bad press the lie detector testing of a director certainly would have had, should *that* news have leaked.

Over the next few months Pattie informed me from time to time that she was "working the problem." I didn't think seriously enough about what this meant. I assumed that she was sitting down with directors, one-on-one, and simply asking them about the leak. Now, looking back, I think that Dunn suspected that the CNET.com article could have only come from me, Keyworth, or director Dick Hackborn, the three directors most prominently involved in strategy. We were the kind of Silicon Valley "cronies" that I believe Pattie would have been happy to see off the board; we all had been trying to guide her in her new chairman's role. I think that she detested this guidance. Carly Fiorina has speculated that maybe she would use an investigation of the leak to get rid of one or more of us; maybe find a way to restructure the board more to her liking.

Around April, in a meeting at my office, she said, "I am getting close." For the first time I had a serious discussion with her about the leak. I remember saying that the last leak was absolutely benign, and that the leaker was perhaps misguided, but he or she was only trying to help, and that I didn't actually want to know who it was. I believed that all the board members were valuable; the leak had occurred months ago, and there had been nothing further; and—this was the most important point—if she found out who it was, that she and I would talk with the director "off-line," extract an apology and a promise never to do it again, and then we would move on. We would not present the name to the board; we would not, we absolutely would not, inflict further trauma on the already stressed directors. Pattie, I thought, agreed with all this.

So I let this quest for the leak slip from the forefront of my mind. Instead, I began to think of alternatives to Pattie as chairman, namely Mark Hurd. I had become convinced that HP could not succeed in the long run unless it had a chairman better versed in the strategic and operating aspects, as Mark indeed was. I stole a page from Pattie's book, so to speak, by using "the best governance practices." Borrowing a technique from the procedures at NewsCorp (I am on that board), I arranged for the directors to be visited by HP's chief legal counsel, Ann Baskins, to go over some routine governance questionnaires, one-on-one. One of the innocent questions was along the lines of, "Do you believe the board is properly balanced, and board responsibilities properly assigned?" I believed that I had sufficiently gauged enough of the board to know that they would tell the chief legal counsel that they were, to varying degrees, unhappy with Pattie as chairman.

The day of the next board meeting arrived in mid-March. It was in Southern California. I was HP's official governance guru, and I thought that there were enough votes to remove Pattie in a showdown at the conclusion of the annual agenda item on governance. She has subsequently revealed to the press that she was on to my plan.

Flying down to what proved to be the penultimate meeting for me, I was sure that with those votes in my pocket I could do the deed. But, while aboard the HP G-5 corporate jet (yes, directors do travel and live well), two board members, Lucie Salhaney and Jay Keyworth, talked me out of a high-noon shoot-out with Pattie. Their winning argument was, "Pattie knows that she doesn't have the support of the board. We can use this to change things; she'll follow our directions; we'll replace her with Mark at the next annual meeting and we'll get back to the business of making HP a winner. Don't rock the boat this way, at this time." Their reasoned arguments prevailed, and I did nothing. A mistake.

I did not expect the next meeting, in May, to be my last. I arrived early, and Pattie cornered me. She said that she had the goods on the leaker. When I asked how, I couldn't believe her response. Over the past many months, HP had employed a team of security experts. She took me into their room, where a table was filled with electronic gear, unfamiliar to me. Pattie said that it could detect the presence of "bugs" over a wide area, and even suppress them. She said that these experts, or others, had otherwise obtained all of the personal telephone connections for target board members for the period of the leak. They were tracing calls not just made from HP, but from the directors' homes, cell phones, and so forth. I was amazed! "How can this be legal?" I asked. She said that it all was quite legal, as long as the content was not transcribed—an assertion I immediately doubted. She said that she had definitively established the identity of the January leaker (the benign CNET.com leak). It was Jay Keyworth, but she had not established a connection to the malign leaks of the previous year. Those sources, which may be numerous, remain a mystery to this day.

Then she dropped the bomb. Ignoring what I thought was a firm understanding to handle this problem (assuming that it really was a problem) off-line, she told me that she had screened the information with the audit committee chair and that he recommended that the matter be put to the entire board, and that was precisely what she was going to do. Why? I can only suppose that, knowing my opposition, she just made an end run around me.

The meeting opened with her description of her investigation, which revealed her "proof." I was shocked. My good friend and stalwart director, Lucie, seemed quite equally shocked. Director Larry Babbio, whose own company, Verizon, was suing parties for using the practice (as I later learned), was silent on the point. Pattie and Ann brushed my concerns off. Lucie and I both thought that the magnitude of the investigation was completely out of proportion to the nature of the problem—if the disclosure even was a problem. Since there was no confidential information in the "leak," as I've previously mentioned, it would not have been surprising to have seen Jay Keyworth's name highlighted, as the source, in the article. Pattie then disclosed Jay's name as the "leaker" and distributed a yellow-lined copy of the offending article—which, with the speed of events, few, if any of the directors, took time to read.

Someone requested that Keyworth leave the room, and he, being polite, complied—but not before apologizing and saying, "I would have told you all about this. Why didn't you ask? I thought I was just helping the company through a rough patch with the press. Aren't directors supposed to do that?" Jay was the longest serving and most technically savvy person on the board, having had a hand in some of the most strategically important initiatives HP was undertaking. He had been asked to talk to the press on numerous occasions in the past by the company.

I expressed dismay that we were, in effect, staging a trial. A valued director was at risk of being destroyed, exactly the scenario I had discussed with Pattie and had sought to avoid.

But, after Enron—a company that behaved fraudulently, rather than stupidly—this is an age of corporate purity, purity at any price. The "sin" of the leak became the issue, not the content or intent of the leak itself, or the method used to discover the source. Form over substance. Keyworth was a director who most recently had tried to help Pattie and, ironically, he had been most persuasive in talking me out of my effort, planned at the previous meeting, to tank her, send her to the corporate bench, the sidelines, so to speak.

A motion was made to ask for his resignation. I was incandescent with anger. I felt betrayed by Pattie, and I said exactly that, in those words. (Did I have it coming?) I fulminated. I protested that any action should be postponed. I tried to get the board to "sleep on it": take the time to read and form an opinion on the alleged leak; postpone any vote until the next meeting. Pattie accused me of wanting to do a "cover-up." The debate continued for ninety minutes, but the outcome was nearly preordained. In today's world, Sarbanes-Oxley and corporate "goodness" will always prevail in such a trial. How can a director be faulted for doing the "right" thing? Just substitute box ticking for judgment; it's certainly easier. Why even have a board, these days? Just let the lawyers check off the boxes; take, always, the safest course; and maybe the lawyers will also check for *Titanic*-size icebergs as well? Increasingly directors are becoming "plug to plug" compatible—any director can serve on any board. Just comply with governance advice and don't worry too much about the actual business.

Two very new directors, with literally no experience in HP or Silicon Valley nor with the benefit of sleeping on it, were, I think, the swing votes when the motion was called with a secret ballot. (Secret votes are *extraordinarily* unusual in corporate America—this was the first in my experience.) The motion passed. Around the board table all the directors were watching me. I had been so passionate in my opposition to the investigation and to the motion to eliminate the director that I think everyone expected some further outburst. But, instead, I felt only a tremendous sadness—a profound disappointment. I knew without having to think about it that this was to be my last minute with this company, a company that I had helped to build and which I loved.

The HP boardroom is bland, monotoned, void of any decorative interest or distinctive feature—not even photographs of the founders. Without further debate, I stood, closed my briefcase, and simply said, "I resign," just those words. I left that nondescript room with its majority of cipherlike directors, as I now saw them, for the last time.

After I departed, Dr. Keyworth (who, along with Lucie, was one of the few admirable directors, in my opinion) was called back into the boardroom and asked to resign. He refused, rightly saying that the shareholders had made the election to the board seat and that the obligation to serve continued until those shareholders spoke otherwise.

Now, at this remove, I am more confident than ever that sub rosa surveillance of the board's communications was illegal. My opinion has been ratified by independent advice, including a prominent professor of law at a famous university, and by subsequent felony guilty pleas from the investigators. Legal or not, I found it all unconscionable, and I couldn't continue to serve on, or support, that board. Full stop.

Today I can only paraphrase Nathan Hale, the Revolutionary War hero, who said, "I regret that I have but one life to give for my country." I regret that I have but one HP board seat from which to resign. But at that, my last board meeting, the mouse certainly won the battle when the defeated cat resigned.

■   ■   ■

Still, cats have nine lives.

I tried to get the company, on a confidential basis, to correct the situation. The whole mess blew up in the press some months later. Keyworth had resigned and, of course, I was off the board, but leaks from directors continued to appear in print. Pattie took a major public relations hit for the spying on members of the board. She resigned from the company and was served with criminal indictments from the California attorney general. But by stepping down as chairman, she made it possible for Mark to take over that post, as I had planned. HP is back on track, and I have been hailed by many as a champion of corporate governance — what irony!

It was never my intention be a whistle-blower. In fact, I was not. In the three months after resigning, I attempted to get Pattie, lawyer Ann Baskins, and finally the whole board to write the minutes of the meeting to chronicle accurately what had transpired. All of them refused; the minutes simply continued to read, "After a discussion Mr. Perkins resigned." Then, when I discovered that my home phone records had been "hacked" and that the fraudulent practice of "pretexting" (a fancy name for identity theft) was used to get them, I formally asked the board to investigate itself, without the involvement of Pattie Dunn, and take whatever further action might be required. Again, I was stonewalled. The matter was referred to the nominating and governance committee, which reported to Pattie herself. My e-mails were not answered, my telephone calls were not returned. Had there been any reasonable response from the company during these months, all this would have remained off the public record. My communications to them were strictly confidential. Only when my lawyer insisted that I write to the Securities and Exchange Commission to defend my own name (as resigned chair of the nominating and governance committee, silence on my part could have made me complicit in any illegal activities) did I assume the risk that all this might become public. When the SEC on its own initiative notified HP of its inquiry, and HP finally came clean, a media firestorm ensued. To be fair, I had primed my editor friend David Kaplan at *Newsweek* to be ready with my side of the story, to counteract the spin I thought HP would use. As anticipated when HP went first, in the *Wall Street Journal*, I was essentially characterized as an angry old fossil with a vendetta against the chairman. (The "leaker," Keyworth, was almost literally thrown to the wolves — the press — by HP and was characterized as being responsible for *all* the earlier leaks, which was libelous, in my opinion.)

I am still to hear from Ann, who also resigned and pleaded the Fifth at the congressional hearing on HP. But Pattie, in defending her actions during Congress's inquiry, and Carly, in her self-vindicating book *Tough Choices* and its promotion, both gave me a thorough trashing in print, testimony, and over TV. What ever happened to my ol' way with the ladies? Their appearances on *60 Minutes* were an agony for me to watch. Pattie accused me of launching "a well-financed campaign of disinformation" — I didn't spend a penny, and offered "just the facts, ma'am." Carly castigated me numerous times on the air and in her book and largely blames me for her dismissal. Incidentally, the book is freighted with platitudes like: "I deeply believe that every person has more potential than they realize." Knowing Carly, she probably didn't permit any editing. She thinks that I feel guilty. She has been quoted as saying, "His head doesn't rest easily upon his pillow." I hadn't noticed.

It was the standard "shoot the messenger" approach from both of these women. The public whipping these two gave me kept my name in the limelight for weeks (and also revived sales of my novel, which sky-rocketed from oblivion to near mediocrity!). In another irony—sometimes I think that God is an irony junkie—*Business-Week* had me review Carly's book. I think I gave her an overall up-beat report, trying to overlook her unpleasant comments about me.

Following last November's election of a new California attorney general, a (somewhat confusing) settlement was reported between his office and the court. According to press accounts, the court dropped the charges against Pattie Dunn, while the three other HP defendants, after pleading no contest to a misdemeanor count of fraudulent wire communications, were told by the judge that the counts would be dismissed if they performed short periods of community service.

Pattie has subsequently revealed that she is fighting very serious cancer. This announcement trivializes our previous disagreements. I profoundly hope Pattie wins this battle, and I wish her, and husband, Bill, the best possible luck.

In *The Education of Henry Adams* the author pretty much sticks to chronology and avoids emotion. But this book flows more with mood than the calendar. We leave a chapter describing the world of power at the top of a giant corporation, and enter into quite a different realm.

At the front I offered a quotation on optimism, and surely that trait must apply to me. How could one be a successful venture capitalist and not have that outlook in spades? But there have been shadows in my life; it's not been all Silicon Valley sunlight. There's been cold rain and fog too.

In this next very personal chapter, I describe the greatest loss of my life, followed by my trial for manslaughter in a backwater town in France.

My education continues.

Chapter Two

Sailing Is Not Always Pleasure Boating

I'll talk about my wife of thirty-five years, Gerd Thune-Ellefsen, often in this book. Upon her death after a four-year struggle against cancer, I was so devastated that I had to leave our home, get away from my familiar surroundings, find something to help me overcome grief of an intensity I found nearly unbearable.

I needed projects. The first was the most important, creating something in Gerd's memory.

During her final illness, we never talked about the virtual certainty of her death. Both being such natural optimists, we always imagined another treatment, something, would turn up—it always had before. But one afternoon as I sat at her bedside, during the final week, I said, "Gerd, let's suppose that things don't work out as we hope. Would you like me to do the *Dom Kirke* project in your memory?" She answered with tears in her eyes that, yes, it would mean the world to her. We both knew that this short conversation would be our last communication about death, at least on this side of the grave.

Gerd was born and raised in Hamar, Norway, a charming place on the largest lake in the country. On a peninsula jutting into the lake, a hauntingly beautiful location, the Vikings had built their pagan temple. Later, one of the first Christian cathedrals (a *Dom Kirke*), among the largest churches in Scandinavia, was built on the site. However, during a war with Sweden, the church had been blown up and all that remained were the very picturesque ruins. Her

Gerd Thune-Ellefsen Perkins
circa 1988

home was nearby, and as a child Gerd played winter and summer among those ruins. They had become as familiar to me, almost, as they were to her.

On our last visit to Hamar, we were surprised to find the beautiful old walls covered by ugly sheds and tarpaulins, the government's solution to the problem of further rapid deterioration caused by the severe climate. An architectural contest had been held to design a *Vernebygget*, or covering, both to protect and to display the remaining vaults and arches of the old stone. It was an ultra-modern design in glass and steel, larger than but vaguely resembling the I. M. Pei design for the new entrance to the Louvre. The plan was to put it in place before the 1994 Winter Olympics; however, time and money ran out, and it was not started. This was the *Dom Kirke* project upon which Gerd and I settled that sad afternoon at her bedside.

She died on August 20, 1994, and during the first week of September I flew to Norway to meet with the mayor of Hamar. Gerd's brother, Arild, a lawyer, had arranged the meeting for me to discuss the project.

In the Scandinavian socialist paradises, private charity is essentially unknown. When the government allegedly provides everything, why spend your own money? So the mayor listened politely to my desire to fund the project, without for an instant believing a word I said. After tea had been finished, he began to make motions indicating that he had better things to do with his afternoon than spend it with a sentimental, nutty American.

I asked him to call the city's bank and open an account in the name of the project. He hesitated, but he did it. Then I telephoned my assistant, Kathy, in San Francisco, who was standing by, and gave her instructions to wire-transfer the millions required into the new account. Arild and I excused ourselves for an hour or so, and then

The Vernebygget *in Hamar, Norway,*
in memory of Gerd Perkins

returned to the mayor's office. As we entered, he burst into joyful tears and gathered me up in a strong embrace. The money was already in the account! He thought that he had witnessed a miracle. He asked for my conditions. They were simple — just get the project actually under way in three years, and put a little plaque in Gerd's name somewhere inside the new building.

Alone early the next morning, as I left Hamar, I saw the leading Oslo newspaper on the train station newsstand. The only item on the front page was my favorite photograph of Gerd, which Arild had given them to print. The headline was, "*Vernebygget* to Be Built in Memory of Hamar Girl." And that's what was done.

This brief task in Hamar — the finished building, for the record, is now known as the "Glass Cathedral" — hadn't lasted long enough to ease my depression. Something requiring more personal involvement was necessary.

Gerd and I loved sailing, and we had owned a series of increasingly larger sailboats. We had, together, sailed around the world over the course of four years, by commuting between work and home obligations and ports along our route. I made all the major passages, and she then joined me in the new places. I have always had a passion for boats and sailboat racing, and after her death I flew to Naples to see *Mariette*, a magnificent old schooner built in 1915 by the American yacht genius Nat Herreshoff. The yacht needed quite a bit of restoration, but it was not an impossible task, and I thought she could be a potential winner in the European classic yacht racing circuit. It would be a demanding project too, maybe therapeutic for me over the next many months.

The contract to buy her closed in January of 1995, and I immediately got involved with the work in an Italian yard in La Spezia. Just to get started, I carved scroll work for the bows and stern. I have always enjoyed working with my hands, and the design and construction of these scrolls drew me in. I spent most of that extremely hot summer practicing my Italian and working on *Mariette*, hauled out of the water in that little yard. The goal was to get her ready to enter the major races, starting with the premier Italian race at the end of August in Porto Cervo, Sardinia. By dint of incredible effort by my crew and me, we made it there in time to practice. *Mariette*, a yacht of some 135 feet overall, requires a racing crew of twenty-five minimum; thirty-five is better. We had a lot of practicing to do to understand how this magnificent creation could perform. Of course I wanted to win—rather ambitious for a newly restored machine with an untested crew. We arrived in Porto Cervo the week before the first race, and I was there on August 20, the first anniversary of Gerd's death.

I had been so much in mourning for her that the months of the year seemed to be merely weeks. This day I awoke after what had been another restless night with little sleep. I was experiencing re-curring dreams, always on the same theme—essentially, that she wasn't dead, that I was simply dreaming that she was gone. They were, of course, happy dreams, but the term "rude awakening" can't begin to describe my depression those mornings.

I am not a religious person, but that day in Porto Cervo I was drawn to a tiny modern church designed by the architect Michele Busiri-Vici. I walked up the hill from the boat to the church and entered. It was early in the morning and no one else was in the building. I sat silently in a pew, deep in depression, holding my head, with my arms resting on my knees, looking indifferently at the stone floor between my feet. The place was dark and quiet. As I fre-quently did, I began to converse with Gerd, imagining her responses. I asked the ageless questions: Are you still there, someplace? I love you so much. . . . Can't you give me a sign? . . . Is God really so cruel to take you from me forever?

There were tears in my eyes and I was staring blankly at the stone when there appeared a spot of sunlight right between my feet—this in a place with few windows and no light coming from them. The light was very bright, seeming to flood up directly from the dark floor. It lasted three or four minutes and then faded away.

Beyond the slightest doubt, I had her answer.

I had never in my life experienced a miracle. I studied physics and engineering at MIT; I didn't believe in miracles. In some kind of state of awe, I wandered around inside the church. There just wasn't sunlight from the windows. The door was solid and closed.

Finally, of course, I found the source. Busiri-Vici had designed a small dome high above the altar, and there were five small apertures at the very top, barely visible through the arch of the roof. The sun had been at exactly the right angle to cast a ray to exactly that place at my feet, at exactly the moment of my question. And in that instant I had a revelation. Of course, there will always be a physical explanation for any of God's miracles. . . . He can't make it too easy. There must always be reasons for doubt, as there must always be reasons to believe.

■   ■   ■

The race week, beginning a few days later, was marvelous for *Mariette*—strong winds, bright sunshine, close competition—and, gratifyingly, we were victorious! For our first regatta we were the overall winner. It was a high for us all.

We had agreed to do a demonstration match race before the trophy presentations scheduled for the night after the racing concluded. It was blowing about thirty knots, and we were up against *Astra*, a big J-class yacht from the twenties. (The Js are the largest-size racing sloops ever created—they are about 130 feet on deck with masts rising to around 150 feet from the water.) The race committee called *Astra* to see if they were willing to please the crowd and race in such strong conditions; they were not. They called me, and of course I said yes, being always ready for a tussle. That night, in addition to the ton of silver *Mariette* won on the water (class, daily, and overall), I received the most magnificent piece of silver art, the Torrini Trophy, a real masterpiece, for the match race forfeited by *Astra*—for which we never left the dock! Her professional captain, a hotshot racing specialist, was very embarrassed.

The next regatta was the Regatta Royale in Cannes, France. There we encountered much lighter winds and, for the first time, our really tough competitors, the J *Candida*; *Thendara*, a fast ketch; and, above all, *Altair*, a beautiful schooner designed by William Fife (the archrival of *Mariette*'s creator), which had dominated the classic yacht circuit for the past ten years. All these big wonderful boats were raced by their professional skippers. In contrast I raced my own yacht, calling all the shots in strategy and tactics and manning the helm throughout. We did well in the week, coming in third overall.

The most famous regatta for all classic yachts was next, winding up the season: the famous Nioulargue in St. Tropez. Over the years this race, which had started on a bet between two yacht owners to see who could race fastest from the water off a beach bar, the Club 55, and around the rocks for which the regatta is named, has become the big event in Europe. Spectator attendance has grown annually, and now numbers in the thousands. For St. Tropez it was the tourist bonanza of the entire year. Big regattas can be very dangerous events. There is always the possibility of collisions among the competing yachts, and, in a major contest like this, control of the hundreds of spectator boats is essential. Indeed the previous couple of Nioulargues had seen some serious damage caused by the chaos. Broken masts, broken bowsprits, and banged-up hulls had been commonplace, but no one had been seriously injured, so far.

But this was France! Independence, free spirits, and the contempt of officialdom are in the genes. The starts for the first two races were truly frightening. The spectator boats were like fleas swarming all around the starting line, and the line itself was a horror. One end was on the town's shore (so that the land-based tourists could have a great view), and the starting line was never properly perpendicular to the wind. A proper starting line is always perpendicular to the wind, so that no yacht has an upwind advantage over another. This careless organization forced all the yachts to the favored windward end, which might be the shoreward side or the outlying buoy in the bay, depending on the wind direction. Such a casual approach compounded the danger of collision. Further, not all the spectator boats were motorboats, so dozens of relatively uncontrollable small sailing yachts were close to the action. Somehow, I managed to have two good starts for the first two days, and we won one race and came in third for the other. We were leading the regatta on points.

The next day was a "lay day" with no official racing, but yachts were encouraged to challenge their key competitors in private contests. *Altair* challenged us, and of course *Mariette* accepted. It was raining and very windy, with poor visibility over the course within the small bay of St. Tropez, but how exciting it was! The two great schooners both had perfect starts, and we were off on the most exciting race of my life. The yachts never were more than a boat-length apart over the full twenty miles of the course, with two up-wind legs and two downwind legs. Finding the turning marks in the rainy murk was tough. I used every trick in my book of yacht racing experience to win. I tried false tacks (that is, pretending to tack—or come about—but not completing the maneuver), hoping to mislead our opponents into making a real tack in the wrong direction. I shouted misdirections to my own crew, wanting the opposing skipper, Steve Hammond, a professional, to overhear and make an erroneous response (but Steve was too smart to fall for that sort of thing). Then I pulled out a final trick of mine, slightly overstanding (that is, not tacking when I could have) the finishing line's outer buoy, which under the racing rules forced Steve to sail along with me, as I was blocking his path to the finish; this tactic (probably frustratingly obscure to a nonsailor) gave me the victory by one quarter length. Both yachts' crews cheered each other, and the race was replayed endlessly in the bars that night by the seventy-some sailors aboard the two yachts. I too took my fair share of the Champagne.

Disaster struck the following morning.

The previous three days of racing had the whole town at a fever pitch. There were only two more races to go to decide the regatta winners. Although hundreds of smaller boats were racing, it was the big classics, about fourteen yachts—our group—that were the focus of everyone's attention. Literally hundreds of observer boats, power and sail, were around the starting line, many with professional photographers aboard. Several helicopters were roaring overhead, making it hard to communicate with the crew on deck.

As always, Tom, my professional captain, who sailed the boat in my absence, acted as sailing master to get the maximum speed from our complex of sail choices. Also as usual, I acted as skipper, calling the shots at the wheel. Again I was the only owner at the helm of his own yacht.

The wind was brisk at about thirteen knots, and to slow down for the prestart jockeying for position, I had ordered the main and fore sails to be sheeted in—not the optimum trim but safer prior to starting. The safety and yacht-racing rules are both complex and extremely important. In the chaos that morning, I was keenly aware of both my right-of-way opportunities and my obligations to keep clear. Decades of yacht racing had made these rules second nature to me.

At five and a half minutes before the start (as displayed on my racing stopwatch, which counts down backward from ten minutes), we were already racing. I was heading toward the shore end of the starting line, which obviously could not be rounded, as the shore-end flag was about fifty feet on solid land, and my *Mariette* was on the port tack—this is not the right-of-way tack, as all racers understand. I would be passing safely between two right-of-way yachts on starboard tack, *Altair* and the huge *Candida* sailing toward me away from the shore. This was all normal prerace jockeying, very safe as long as everyone understands and obeys the rules. My plan was to turn (tack about) at the land end, and then come back to the favored end of the line—the seaward end this day—on the controlling (starboard) tack. I thought that my timing was spot-on and that when the cannon fired we would achieve another perfect start, at the right place and going full speed.

While I was concentrating on the positions of our competitors and setting up the start, my crew of thirty-three, plus six guests, were busy shouting at the spectator small craft to keep clear. Particularly annoying and dangerous were the photographers, who love to position themselves under the bow, out of sight, to snap a spectacular shot of the bow wave rushing toward them and the bowsprit and rig towering overhead. Usually at the last moment the spectators would veer away. For the races of the three preceding days I had at hand an electric megaphone, useful in adding my own imprecations. But this day Tom had removed it to keep, you know, the "ugly American" from being rude to the civilized French.

I became aware of the crew shouting in particular excitement at a small sailboat, also on port tack, coming toward us on a course that would surely lead to a collision. Another nut out to watch the start, I thought. But the boat's skipper wouldn't tack or bear away to keep clear, even though either maneuver was easily possible for him, and as the shouting increased I looked for the megaphone, missing from its place. I saw the man at the tiller look directly at me and shake his fist in defiance. He wasn't going to alter course! What was he thinking? He couldn't possibly be racing—race committees never set a course to take small boats through the starting line of big boats.

For safety, I had the engines ticking over in neutral, and I threw them both into full reverse. But even while deliberately trying to sail more slowly than optimum, we were still doing ten knots—the engines began to slow us, but not enough! I was in an impossible position. Roaring toward us on either side were two huge yachts, both with right-of-way. I couldn't turn in either direction without hitting one of them, and a collision between yachts of this size at these speeds would bring down masts and certainly kill a number of sailors. I began to steer toward *Candida*, trying to get away from the oncoming small yacht. I came within six feet of the big J boat, her own crew of about forty shouting at me, in pure panic, to bear away. I thought it would be all right, for we had slowed down to about six knots, and I thought the small yacht would just clear our bowsprit. But a wire staying her mast on her port side snagged the end of our spar, and the wire didn't break. Rather, it pulled the little boat directly under our still-moving bow. The small yacht capsized, and it sank in roughly two seconds. We could see three of her crew members swimming. I killed the engines to avoid their being injured by our propellers and threw them a life ring as we glided past, over the spot where the little yacht had sunk.

This was an accident with at least a thousand witnesses. Nevertheless, I radioed the race committee, saying that there had been a collision and that *Mariette* would be withdrawing. We motored away from the starting area and began to take down our sails, a forty-five-minute business involving the whole crew. I heard on the radio that the race was canceled, and then some minutes later the shocking news: a navy diver had found the body of a drowned crew member of the little boat.

From the earlier noisy scene of frantic activity, a silence descended over the water. I tried to pilot *Mariette* back into her berth in the inner harbor, as I usually did, but found that my hands were shaking so badly, and my mind was so overwhelmed, that I couldn't do it. Tom had to take over. When we arrived, I was met by armed members of the Coast Guard, and I was arrested for manslaughter.

During the next eight hours I was confined aboard a French Coast Guard vessel while the Coast Guard conducted its official investigation into the accident. I saw about a dozen witnesses come and go to be interviewed, but I was not aware of what they were saying. Meanwhile, the skipper of the small boat, of the six-meter class, was trying to become my friend—he was also being held for manslaughter—and it was weird. He had ignored all the sailing rules, all the safety rules, and above all just plain common sense and had, in effect, killed his friend. Now he was offering me cigarettes, coffee, and companionship. I am no shrink but I couldn't help but think that he was not just crazy French, but literally insane. I am of that opinion still.

Around ten o'clock that night, after gallons of coffee but no food, I was the last to be interviewed. The Coast Guard had a very prominent French yachtsman, an important guy still connected with the America's Cup, on hand to act as my translator. It was only then that I discovered the name of the drowned man, a prominent physician from Nice, age fifty-three with a wife, a grown daughter, and a son in his late teens.

The officers were most polite, and I quickly got the impression that they fully comprehended everything I was explaining. One even corrected me when I omitted a small detail in the diagram I was drawing. Clearly they understood the nature of the accident, and the fact that I had done everything possible to prevent it. I was excused at around midnight, but before I could return to *Mariette* and collapse, I was summoned to a meeting of the race committee's jury, who wanted to do their thing as well. Instead of ignoring them, I foolishly complied, trying, I suppose, to clear up everything that night.

The race jury exists to settle disputes involving the racing rules.

This thing was way over their heads, but I soon discovered that it had indeed been a race! The little six-meter was racing; the committee had actually done the unthinkable and had given the little boats a course directly through the starting line of the big yachts—an unimaginably dangerous thing to do. The six-meter was leading the early starting fleet by literally a mile, so it was not obvious to anyone that two fleets were converging on that short line. The tourist board apparently liked plenty of action to be seen from the shore, and they got it that day. My French is abysmal, and I had trouble understanding the points being made—such as, that I was within the ten-minute starting time, therefore, technically, I was racing too. The jury never got any of the details right, and I just walked out at about one o'clock that morning in a state that would look phlegmatic on a zombie.

The next morning someone showed me the front page of one of the Paris tabloids. It carried a huge, frightening photo of *Mariette* striking the little boat. The headline said, "Monster American Yacht Kills French Doctor!"

I assembled my whole crew inside *Mariette*'s beautiful Edwardian saloon, with its rich walnut reflecting the sunlight streaming through the open overhead hatch, gleaming with its polished brass fittings. All racing had been canceled for the balance of the week and I wanted to caution my crew against talking about the accident. I wanted them simply to stick to the exact facts and not offer opinions. I was just winding up when word came that the doctor's widow was on the dock, wanting to come aboard.

His widow! My mind raced. What if she became hysterical, violent? But there was nothing I could do other than to bite the bullet and invite her aboard.

To my surprise, two charming, attractive, middle-aged women stepped onto the yacht. Through my fractured French and their skeletal English, I understood that one was the wife and the other the mistress, or as the French say, the *courtesan*, but to this day I have never been clear on which one was which. They were not violent; rather, they hugged me! It seemed that they had driven from Nice immediately upon hearing the awful news, arriving in

St. Tropez to do their own personal investigation into the accident. Quickly they had determined, from talking to the surviving crew members of the six-meter, that the skipper had been at fault, reckless, and that he had been entirely responsible for a tragedy that they knew I had tried hard to avoid. The little boat's crew had told them that I was distraught—which was certainly the case—and they had come to comfort me, and to put my mind at ease. I swear, if I ever slight the French again (and they *do* give reasons to do so, almost daily), God should strike me down after this display of thoughtfulness.

They said that "their" seventeen-year-old son loved to sail with his father, and could I take him aboard *Mariette* as a crew trainee? I said of course, though later my lawyers blocked me from carrying out my promise. They also encouraged me to return to St. Tropez to race again, for "their" man had loved the racing so much in the area. We had coffee and cookies, but I couldn't persuade them to stay longer. Clearly they were in deep mourning and shock over the accident that had taken the physician so abruptly.

On Saturday morning, which was the scheduled prize-giving day, we all climbed the hill to the old fortress overlooking the town. It was a glorious morning, but somber because of the accident. Most of the hundreds of sailors had formed their own opinion and were not openly hostile to me, but still, I had the big boat, and I was a "rich American," never a good thing if one is European and stops to think about it. The prizes were duly awarded, starting with the smaller boats. At the end, the big boat first prize was awarded to *Mariette*, based on points before the remaining races were canceled; it was a silver tray. I accepted the trophy and made a little speech.

The crowd became stone silent as I said that I would have given anything to reverse time and undo the accident. When I said that I had had a "sympathetic" meeting with the doctor's family, and that the family hoped that we would return to St. Tropez to race again, there were tears as well as cheers from the sailors present. My comments wound up the program and the committee released one hundred white doves, which fluttered skyward in an unforgettable moment . . . once again, death transformed by a miracle of beauty. Then a French "oom-pah-pah" brass band struck up, beer and fried sausages appeared, and spirits rose. Following this, I was hugged by dozens of sailors, some of them pretty tough, in gestures of friendship.

I left France when the police gave me my passport back, a couple of weeks after my arrest. I was there for the drowned man's funeral in Nice, which I attended with many of my crew. I met his children that day for the first time. My heart ached for them.

■ ■ ■

Danielle Steel says that one day she will base a novel upon my manslaughter trial. Arrested and tried in a foreign court in a language you don't understand, by judges indifferent—or worse—to justice, represented by an inappropriate lawyer with the negative outcome preordained; she says it has a great plot line. I don't think I'll read it. I lived it.

The trial was exactly one year from the date of the accident, in the provincial town of Draguignan. There had been much advance publicity, and the prosecutor vowed in print to see me put in jail. Only I and the race committee chairman (a woman) were charged with the crime; the committee chair was charged for the idiotic courses that virtually guaranteed accidents. But the victim's family was so incensed that the six-meter skipper was not charged that they brought their own suit against him. So, in the event, the cases were combined and all three parties were charged. For good measure my captain, Tom, was included as well.

I took these matters seriously, and took the step of hiring a brilliant man, the best marine lawyer with criminal case experience in France. That was a terrible mistake.

Also, I hired a firm of private detectives to help gather data that might help. The accident had been witnessed by hordes of spectators on the shore, on spectator boats, on competing yachts, and overhead in helicopters. The private eyes did a great job, collecting some fifty photos from many angles, which showed the whole process of the accident in intervals of about ten seconds. The photo record was really astonishing. It demonstrated without the slightest doubt that the six-meter was in violation of every safety, yachting, and common sense rule, while *Mariette* had done everything she could do, short of causing an even bigger accident, to avoid the smaller boat. Plus, we had experts lined up to testify on the rules, all totally exonerating my boat of responsibility. So I felt pretty confident walking into the courtroom the first morning of the trial. Danielle (whose first language is French) was at my side to whisper the translation into my ear. No one ever identified her as a celebrity; she was simply taken as another of my hired guns. This was still early in our relationship, long before we married.

Those of you who have read *The Wind in the Willows* would have immediately identified the three judges—they were Mr. Toad, Water Rat, and the Mole. Mr. Toad was essentially blind. His glasses made Coke-bottle bottoms look thin. He scanned any paper handed to him at a distance of one inch, literally, and when he peered into the courtroom, it was obvious that he saw nothing at all—not promising for the blow-ups of the accident photos I had present on easels. The Mole, like Mr. Toad, never said a word. Water Rat ran everything, so I'll now, properly, promote him to chief judge.

Within minutes, I saw that I was doomed.

The prosecutor, the chief judge, and the two other defense lawyers (one for the committee, and another for the small boat's skipper) all seemed to be buddies, old drinking friends who had grown up together in this dreary place. My Parisian lawyer, a man of unquestioned excellence, was in the boondocks here in his fancy powdered wig and black cloak; he was an outlander, a pariah, an abomination—beyond the pale in this regional court. My guy could hardly get a word in. I would have been smarter to have hired the local barber to represent me. I am serious, because as far as I could determine, matters of law were not considered in this court. It was chaotic in the extreme. Someone would make a point, and the others would rush forward to the bench and shout at each other (incidentally, no court reporter was present) for quite a long time until the chief judge sent them back. The cycle was repeated endlessly.

I became ever more bewildered as Danielle translated. The chief judge ruled that no technical terms would be admitted into discussion. So *port* and *starboard* became *left* and *right, windward* and *leeward* became *north* and *south, overtaking yacht* became *behind boat*, and so on. Needless to say, any expert's testimony was rendered gibberish by this ruling. The confusion was compounded by the testimony of the racing jury (from the night of the accident), who never had the facts right in the first place; who, squidlike, added their own ink of confusion; and who refused to comply with the *right* and *left* nonsense.

My lawyer was not permitted to let me testify or show and explain my photographs in any meaningful detail, which sat for the full two days on their easels, waiting. As the farce dragged on, it dawned on me that the fix was in. This was best understood when the chief judge beamed approval at the prosecutor's interchange with a beribboned officer from the French Navy:

"*Monsieur le Capitaine.*"

"*Oui?*"

"Did this accident occur within a mile of the French coastline?" (One end of the starting line was in the damn parking lot!)

"*Oui.*"

"Were the boats traveling at a speed in excess of five knots?" (Sure we were—hell, we were *racing.*)

"*Oui.*"

"But is this not a violation of the French law?"

"*Oui!!!*"

Hard to believe, but by day two I had lost interest in my own manslaughter trial. Day two was devoted entirely to speeches from all the lawyers. They really orated. Little reference was made to the accident, but much poetry was read. The *Willows* judges slept through most of it, and I finally asked Danielle to stop translating.

Not at all to my surprise, I was found guilty. But I had company—so were my captain, Tom; the six-meter skipper; and the committee chair, to boot. Jail sentences were suspended, and ten-thousand-dollar fines assessed; of course, I paid Tom's.

The lessons learned in my continuing education?

A couple of things. Most important, I'll never take our American system of justice for granted again. As slow and as frustrating as it may be, it is fundamentally fair. At least you can present the court with your own defense, and by law the court must listen. It is the jewel of our system, and must be protected. For a while afterward I even thought of renewing my long-lapsed membership in the ACLU . . . but I didn't.

Another lesson: even though France is no third-world country, life is cheap there. My lawyers and my insurance carrier told me many times that my financial liability would be a fraction in Europe of what it would have been had the accident occurred in America. In the civil case that followed, I thought that the poor physician's family was beaten down by the lawyers. Like, perhaps, most Frenchmen, he hadn't declared his full income, so when a few years of his earnings were awarded by the court, it wasn't much.

When it was all over, and too late for new guilt or new blame, I called his wife and had her open an account in their son's name to help with his education. I wired the funds in.

My lawyer assured me that I was an idiot.

Well, the previous chapters have been about an individual at the top of his game. But how did it begin, during that period in the sixties when Silicon Valley, venture capital, and megamillions were all in the future? What drove this young man to achieve his first millions— back when, as they say, a million was a lot of money?

Chapter Three

Vindictiveness Is a Terrible Thing

The loft above the glass-blowing laboratory on University Avenue in Berkeley was divided into three areas, with flimsy partitions separating them. At one end, a really tough young giant of a man, an African-American artist, was manufacturing enormous papier-mâché gorillas, painted in glorious psychedelic colors. The colors were appropriate, because the other end of the loft was occupied by the laboratory of recreational drug pioneer Augustus Stanley Owsley III, who was heavily into the production of LSD. This was before it was illegal to make the stuff, and before he went to jail for failing to "notice" the change in the law. My space was in the middle.

Mine was perhaps the most exotic of these three pretty weird rooms. It was filled with frosty tanks of liquid nitrogen that exuded a steady stream of cold white fog, big transformers, and electronic and optical apparatus of all sorts, and it was noisy from the constant clatter of the vacuum pumps. Most important and most prominent was the orange light brightly glowing from the prototype plasma tube we were hovering over. The place looked like the set for a remake of a Frankenstein movie, if the producer hadn't many extra dollars to spend on décor. But at two o'clock the morning of July 7, 1966, it was the center of the universe for me. That's the date I first got my laser invention to work, and at the instant that first piercing, intense, red beam flashed through the vapors of the nitrogen, I felt exaltation—the highest high I have ever experienced.

Driving back to our little rented brick house in Palo Alto at four

Tom Perkins in 1965 while chairman
of University Laboratories Inc.

in the morning, my head was still spinning from my Archimedes-like *eureka!* moment. I stumbled into the bedroom, not wanting to wake Gerd, but she was sitting in bed with the light on, smiling at me. She said, "Wonderful that your laser works, but don't undress, *Elskling*. You are driving me to the hospital right now—I am going to deliver a baby!" And so, in less than twenty-four hours, the laser company and our beautiful daughter, Elizabeth, were both born.

I have frequently called myself a nerd, and certainly that lab in Berkeley was a nerd's lair, but I think nerddom was sort of forced upon me. As an only child who moved around the country many times before high school, I was always lonely. I arrived late in my parents' lives, and they let me know that, all things considered, it would have been better if I hadn't been born. My father had a quaint way of putting this: "Why did we ever whelp this pup?" he would ask my mother when my behavior fell anywhere short of perfection. Dad had been a star baseball and basketball player thanks to his six-foot-six-inch height, which was unusually tall for his day, and he was very impatient with me that I lacked the coordination to be a hoop star or a natural batter. His teaching technique was to call me "sissy" when I flinched at the basketball when he bounced it on my head or when I "swung the bat like a girl," missing his fast pitches. He gave up on me early.

But, in the late forties, when I didn't know any better, our meager family life together seemed normal. Spam, margarine, Wonder Bread, and lime Jell-O—with the "treat" of canned salmon in a baked loaf on Fridays—was all right with me. And radio provided plenty of entertainment. To be fair, both my parents had been devastated by the Great Depression. It left its debilitating malaise on them. Dad was fearful of risk and endured years of unhappy employment, never once trying to escape his low-level white-collar job as a fire-risk assessor for a Midwest insurance company. Mom was obsessed with money. She was a brilliant seamstress and made the latest styles of women's clothes to sell, copied from magazine photos. When things went wrong for her emotionally, as they frequently did, she was given to the high drama of threatening suicide. I'll always picture her standing in our little kitchen with a butcher's knife pressed against her wrist. As a kid, I found these scenes absolutely terrifying.

There was never enough money. I responded to Mom's pressure with a series of after-school jobs: paper routes, grocery-bagging, lawn-cutting, babysitting, and so on. I suppose that I should be grateful for the work ethic driven into my subconscious, except for the fact that it's never permitted me not to feel a little guilty, even now, if I'm not grinding away. I do thank Dad, however, for my love of automobiles. I'll always remember him polishing the long series of Plymouths that he owned, waxing them over and over until the polished steel showed through the thin paint. My grandfather, on Dad's side, came to live with us, but he too was the unhappy, silent type. I remember, though, him telling me that his father had taken him to a political rally in Illinois, and Granddad—when he was a nine-year-old—had shaken Abraham Lincoln's hand!

In my teens I wasn't much good at sports, except for swimming. A distant relative had forced me to learn to swim when I was one and a half years old. Her technique was, essentially: learn, or I'll drown you. I learned, and apparently folks came from all around to see the miraculous swimming baby. I eventually became a swimming champion, but at White Plains High School, in suburban New York's Westchester County, our football team was everything, and we didn't have a pool. I wasn't a jock, so I retreated into studies, after-school jobs, and—well, becoming a nerd. It started as a protective cover and gradually took over my life. I became fascinated by physics. I spent my pocket money on science stuff. I made Tesla coils, Hilsch tubes, photoelectric cells, and such. My interests brought me to the attention of Mr. Wilson, the physics teacher. I can truthfully say that he was the first person in my life to pay me any serious attention. Dear Mr. Wilson, cancer took him many decades ago, and he never got to see the blossoming of this particular nerd.

One of my jobs was assembling kit television sets to sell in the neighborhood. They were clunky things that you filled with mineral oil in front of the tube, making a lens to magnify the tiny picture. My kits worked better than others', and upon graduation I planned to make a career as a TV repairman. That future looked pretty good to me. Mr. Wilson, who was one of my TV customers, refused to accept that plan. He insisted that I apply to college. But my parents had never gone beyond high school, no one in the family ever had; there wasn't money for it and they saw no need. Mr. Wilson came to my house one night and talked seriously to my parents. He would help me apply, help me get a scholarship—with that, and with my working and borrowing from the school, if my parents could chip in a little, it could happen. He made the sale, and my dad kicked in two hundred dollars (which he demanded, and got back from me, the day of my graduation). I was accepted at both Harvard and MIT, choosing the latter as it offered the larger scholarship.

How quickly one's life can change.

In a matter of days after arriving in Cambridge I went from being a nerd in a school of jocks to being a jock in a school of nerds! During the freshman orientation weekend, I had a go at joining the swim team, and my time for the fifty-yard freestyle came within a jaw-dropping second or so of breaking the pool record. The coach promptly signed me up with great expectations, and my teammates dutifully elected me captain of the freshman team that same day.

Then I met my roommates. MIT was still recovering from World War II, and about twenty of us freshmen were housed in a single big room in a ramshackle temporary building where we would all sleep and study together. You have seen cartoons of these guys in *Dilbert* and other comic strips. Thick glasses, pudgy, puffy faces, pocket-protector plastic pen holders, and, above all, each one carried a long slide rule in a tan leather case mounted to his belt. I couldn't believe that I fit into this bunch. After about the fifth one asked me if I would be joining the chess club, I panicked. I walked over the bridge into Boston, where I knew there was a row of fraternity houses on Beacon Street. I had heard that they were having something called rush week, during which they signed up new pledges, and that the best house, with the best athletes and the best school grades, was the D.U. house. I found the place and liked the guys, some of whom were vets attending MIT on the GI Bill. I was pleased to find out that living there would cost me only about sixty percent of the dorm rate, and I couldn't believe my luck that they wanted me to join. I did join, and never slept a night with the chess-club stalwarts.

If you want a great tale of university life, read Tom Wolfe's excellent *I Am Charlotte Simmons*—you won't find stories like that at MIT. But I had four good years, mostly because of the fraternity, and in my senior year I finally did break the pool record. I held it for fourteen glorious, golden, marvelous, shimmering days, until some kid from Yale, in a regional meet, broke it again. *Sic transit gloria mundi.*

A month or so after breaking the record, I flunked the final medical examination to become an ROTC lieutenant upon graduation (and maybe get the GI Bill to pay for graduate school). I was called up by my draft board to become a private in the army instead. At this time Truman's war in Korea was raging. Some months later, at an army processing center in Oklahoma, I failed the medical again for the same reason. A congenital heart murmur runs on the male side of my family; it's fatal, and it killed both my father and my grandfather in their eighth and ninth decades, respectively.

So, you will be denied my military memoirs. Interestingly, although many American families have had a son, brother, or father in every one of our many wars, the Perkins family has not, going all the way back to the Revolutionary War. This mostly is true, I suppose, because we Perkins males don't seem to reproduce very often, or maybe it's that our wives and mothers have been exceptionally prescient in when they give birth, dodging our country's bellicosity that seems to arise each generation.

I had two more years of school to go after graduation. Harvard Business School was a snap, a breeze; I didn't realize it at the time, but after MIT, hell, *everything* is a breeze! The best part was that thanks to Uncle Sam's defense policies, the government, indirectly, paid for most of my time at Harvard Business School.

But I couldn't just go directly to Harvard. After graduation from MIT I was totally broke, even worse, deeply in debt after getting my degree in electronics from the Institute, and I needed a job that would pay as much as possible as soon as possible. I found it with the Sperry Gyroscope Company of Great Neck, Long Island. They were desperate for engineers who would be willing to labor in inhospitable places around the world to keep their stuff working. In my case, I signed on to keep advanced radar-controlled gun sights for jet fighters running in Turkey. The location was awful, but the pay was great.

After a minimum of training, I found myself in Eskisehir, in the desert between Istanbul and Ankara. The poor Turks had received these extremely complex systems from NATO a year earlier, and they couldn't figure out how to use them. Turkey had come in last in the previous NATO gunnery competition. The pilots were just sticking chewing gum on their windscreens to use as a sight, because our fancy computer-based system wouldn't work—and remember, this was before Bill Gates was born, so it couldn't, as is normally rational, be blamed on Microsoft. I had a full-time translator, Ziekie. I worked hard, first to get everything running right, and then, with Ziekie, to train the pilots to trust our system. I was twenty-two years old, and during a week when I hadn't shaved I looked at least sixteen. It took some persuading to get these pilots to believe in me—they were the toughest, most macho guys I have ever encountered. But over the months, things began to click. At the next NATO competition, I wasn't sure who was more proud when *my* pilots won, the pilots themselves or Ziekie and me.

I had been living in a small hotel on next to nothing. Everything was so cheap and in those days I was naturally frugal, but for some reason the home office wasn't reimbursing my expenses. I started to worry, and cut back. I found that I could really save the company quite a lot if I was particularly careful. As I recall, I was coming close to getting my living costs down to about eleven dollars a week toward the end. Still, they didn't pay.

Finally I had a trip back to Great Neck to oversee some engineering revisions. I met with my boss, a guy I had met only briefly before. He said, "We are having some problems with your expense reports. I have them all here." My heart sank. I said that I had been careful not to live too high. He replied that they were full of errors and omissions—I started to tremble. He explained, "I have over a hundred guys like you around the world and their expenses average around three hundred and fifty dollars a week. Yours are only running at around fifteen."

"Well, Turkey is very inexpensive," I said. He handed me my pile of reports, maybe one and a half years' worth. "Review these," he instructed. "I am sure that you will find that you have omitted *at least* two hundred dollars of items per week. Please correct them."

I got it. I was able to go to Harvard a year earlier than I had planned. But, in a long career, I have never had another job that had anything much to do with the government.

Why did I want to get an MBA from Harvard so badly? Because, frankly, at MIT I discovered that I just wasn't smart enough to be a theoretical physicist, which was my first and truest love. I'll never forget a class in thermodynamics, or maybe quantum mechanics, where five of us were taking the final exam. There was just one problem on the paper to solve. Four of us simply stared at it for a while, signed our names, and left. The fifth guy came up with a unique solution, so elegant that I think the professor published the answer in the *Physical Review*. That's when I decided to become an electronics engineer, and then a businessman.

Probably I made the right choice. At Harvard I got the first inkling that my instincts were tuned for business. I'll spare you the story of being placed on social probation at Harvard for breaking a rule against after-hours parties in the dorm—there were women involved. And how in the second year my classmate friend and I rented a small place on Inman Street where we made our own rules. Many years later he took making his own rules a little too seriously, I guess, and wound up in federal prison for fraud. I'll, rather, talk about studies.

I took the famous course of Professor Georges Doriot, universally called "The General" because he had been Quartermaster General in the U.S. Army during World War II. He was the star on the B-school faculty, even though he disdained the school's pioneering case method of teaching, in favor of pure lecture. His subject was called manufacturing, but really he tried to imbue a way of thinking, both about business and about life. His allure was enhanced by the fact that in addition to his position at Harvard, he was chairman of American Research and Development—the first really full-time venture capital company. They had financed Digital Equipment Corporation (DEC), whose newly introduced minicomputer was revolutionizing the industry. He also was on DEC's board.

The General opened his first lecture to a packed room of some eighty students by teaching us how to read a newspaper. He said it shouldn't require more than four minutes. He held aloft a copy of *The New York Times* and challenged the class with the question, asked in his wonderful rich French accent: "Gentlemen, which of you can tell me the most important section—the one I read first?" A few of the daring risked answers: "The headlines?" "*Non.*" "The business section?" "*Non!*" "The stock market tables?" "*Non! Non!*" The room was silent, then filled with guffaws and titters when I raised my hand and said, "The obituaries!" The General commanded silence, and then he announced that I was the most astute man in the room, that great things could be expected from me. He then made the point that obituaries were the only true news, and the only thing that the papers rarely lied about. When I graduated he asked me to be his assistant for a year. It was considered an enormous honor to be the annual pick, but my eyes were aimed on California, and I turned him down. Some years later he asked me to come back to Boston to run American Research and Development, but by then my roots were too deep in the Valley, and again I said no.

While at Harvard I worked part-time at the Cambridge-based General Radio Company (GR). They were an old company, and at the time they were the premier manufacturer of electronic test and measuring instruments in the world. The products were mounted in beautiful French-polished wooden cases and the panels were in the highest quality finish black-crackle paint. During the summer between my two years at the B-school, GR gave me the assignment of measuring the quality and the accuracy of competing instruments from an upstart competitor called the Hewlett-Packard Company in Palo Alto. The HP products didn't look nearly as elegant, but they sold for a fraction of the price. I had used the GR instruments in laboratory work at MIT and I had a deep respect for the company. My instincts were to prove that the HP products were just cheap junk. But try as I might, and being exceptionally careful, I proved the opposite. In every case, the HP gear exceeded its specifications and, indeed, was more accurate than the lovely GR counterparts. I gained a great respect for the California company, and when it came time to think about a job after graduation, I sought them out.

Dave Packard answered my letter, and he invited me to come down to New York during the IEEE (electrical engineers) convention. I took the train, and located the 67th Street Armory, where exhibits of equipment were being held. To my surprise I found Packard and Bill Hewlett personally assembling their booth. The GR executives wouldn't have dreamed of doing that! They let me pitch in to help, and while we were getting everything set up, they interviewed me. When I left, Dave said that I would be receiving an offer. I was so impressed by these guys that I didn't talk to any other potential employer, and that day we established an association and friendship that endured through the decades, until their deaths. This is, maybe, the best place to confess that Dave Packard was my mentor, an inspiration, and, I am sure, the father I so desperately needed. He taught me everything I know about entrepreneurship, and was the most important influence in my life. Dave was a giant, and the proof is, probably, that there are many dozens of others who feel just as strongly about him as I do.

■   ■   ■

I drove with my girlfriend, Sally, across the United States to California in the summer's heat in my beat-up Jaguar XK-120 hardtop coupe. British cars were never intended for that sort of thing, and I had to change the water pump seal three times, I think, before we made it. By the time we arrived, I could do the job in under two hours. We explored San Francisco for a few days, and were astonished at how the temperature had dropped from around 110 degrees in Sacramento to a shivering 60 degrees in the city of fog.

The following Monday I reported for work, armed with my MBA degree. I expected to be running the place in no time. Dave welcomed me warmly, but said that I was about the first MBA type they had hired, and that the other managers were uncomfortable with the whole idea of MBAs. The company was booming but had revenue of only about twenty million dollars per year at the time. He said that he would like me to get to know the business from the ground up. They didn't have a personnel department then ("People are too damned important for a personnel department," he said), so he would oversee my training, and I would start in the machine shop. That day I became a somewhat incompetent, but rather well paid, machinist.

Dave knew what he was doing. I needed to lose most of my

MBA arrogance and prove myself in the nitty-gritty of making a quality product that customers would pay for. And also I needed to prove
that I could earn the respect of the HP "family" in doing so. But
Harvard had not prepared me for some things, such as the wrath of
the shop foreman who gave me the dressing down of a lifetime for
forgetting to remove a lathe chuck wrench when I shut the machine
down for a coffee break. (I could have killed someone, had I started
the thing up with it still in place.)

Sally had returned east, and I was frequenting San Francisco
some nights and most weekends, driving up from Palo Alto, where I
had a tiny place. I got to know a very nice crowd, and I met a terrific
girl, Ellen Davies. Ellen and I began to see a lot of each other. I
knew, in a vague sort of way, that she came from wealth, but it wasn't
obvious from the apartment she shared with two of her friends, and
I didn't think much about it. After a couple of months, I was surprised when she asked me to have dinner at her parents' place. I arrived at a luxurious penthouse atop one of the highest buildings in
the city, with a staggering 360-degree view. Mrs. Davies was extremely kind. Mr. Davies owned American President Lines, a steam-
ship company, which I believe was only the tip of the iceberg of his
fortune; he was not present. I was surprised to note that the table was
set for only two, and when Ellen excused herself, her mother and I
sat down to dine.

We were served by a discreet staff. What was going on? It took
until after coffee at the end of an extremely strained dinner conversation for me to find out. Mrs. Davies (now of Davies Symphony
Hall fame), in the most delicate of ways, pointed out that the family
had a certain "social position"—she made a slight wave of her hand
to take in the splendor of the surroundings as she said this. And that
it was very difficult to bridge differences in "backgrounds." And
that Ellen had acquainted Mr. Davies and herself with the fact that
Ellen and I indeed came from very different backgrounds—and the
gap would be unbridgeable. Then, with a steely look hitherto unre-
vealed, she said, point blank, that Ellen would no longer be dating a
machinist!

I left. In the elevator, I couldn't resist looking at my fingernails to see if I had scrubbed the day's oil entirely away. I had. They were clean. But I never dated Ellen again.

Hey! It was the fifties. That's the way things worked back then.

After the summer in the shop, I apparently made the grade, and Dave gave me a job working for Noel Eldred, head of sales for HP. Back then the company didn't have its own sales force; manufacturers' representatives were used around the world. My region to manage was California and bits of the desert. The sales representative was Norman B. Neely, who had built a large, top-flight organization that at the time nearly rivaled HP itself in importance. HP was the biggest line the firm represented, and the Neely team was very proud. Mr. Neely let it be known that no twenty-some-year-old kid with an MBA was going to supervise him. All the representatives sensed that eventually HP would be replacing them with internal people, and I was seen to be the tip of this arrow. Fortunately, I figured this out in advance of my first meeting with Norm Neely in his North Hollywood headquarters. He was too smart to be openly hostile, but the resentment was evident. However, I presented myself not as trying to tell him anything at all, but rather suggesting that he should use me to get things done inside HP—I would, in effect, be his organization's internal representative. And that's exactly what we did. Eventually his people trusted me enough to listen, a little, to the ideas my bosses wanted me to deliver, and my region was doing very well.

In those early days at HP Dave and Bill were in the habit of inviting guys in management on a weekend down to their jointly owned spread, the San Philippe Ranch. (It's now semi-surrounded by the city of San Jose, and is worth billions.) We would spend the weekend playing poker and castrating sheep. I can't say that it was much fun, certainly not for the sheep, or for me. I'll never forget losing the better part of a month's salary to Bill Hewlett over the poker table. I couldn't afford to lose five minutes' salary in those days, so it was a very hard lesson indeed.

While dealing with Neely, as a side job I reorganized the sales order processing for the company, which had become almost impossibly cumbersome. For all this I got some nice kudos, but after a couple of years I still wasn't running the place. Like many an MBA before and after me, I got restless and, rather stupidly, I quit HP to join Booz Allen Hamilton, the big consulting firm, in their San Francisco office. It was a prestigious outfit, and my base pay was about double what HP was providing.

Consultants are the butt of many jokes—maybe the best is "a consultant is a person who borrows your watch to tell you what time it is"—but I never had to work harder in my life than I did for the twelve months I worked for Booz. The San Francisco office was small, and the firm's clients tended to be small as well. My assignments included helping the Harry and David ("Fruit of the Month Club") company of Medford, Oregon, to rationalize their orchards and to devise an exit path from their hugely money-losing travel trailer business. The son of the founder, the late David Holmes, was the first to manufacture the beautiful trailers from fiberglass, but the costs were so high that a market was not available. The other members of management had hired me just to carry the bad news to him, their boss.

Another client, a wealthy farmer in California's Central Valley, hired us to find five new ventures for his five sons-in-law. I did find businesses, but the client kept the best ones for himself.

I thought the managing partners, my bosses, competed by promising to deliver the moon to the clients in as short a time as possible. I had moved into a great apartment in Sausalito but was on the road so much that I rarely was there to enjoy it. As I recall, I had about twelve assignments—all solo jobs—in that frantic year. I quickly decided that I wasn't cut out to be a good consultant. I had trouble delivering the promised strongly worded recommendations based upon the scanty research I had the time to do. But I did learn the tricks. As in most things, twenty percent of the time delivers eighty percent of the answer. In my last few jobs I even felt some pride in my work, but I realized that leaving HP had been a mistake. I called Dave to see if I could come back.

He said that I could, but maybe I should take a look, instead, at a company being put together in optics. He and Bill would be investing personally, along with the early Palo Alto venture capital firm of Draper Gaither and Anderson (DG&A) and a handful of other top HP executives, in a start-up to be called Optics Technology Inc. (OTI). The new company would be headed by Dr. Narinder Kapany of the University of Chicago, and Kapany needed a business person to run the commercial side. Dave suggested that I consider the job.

I flew back to Chicago and was blown away by Narinder—what a guy! He had a PhD in optics and had written numerous scholarly papers on "fiber optics." I believe he even coined the term, and he had dozens of ideas on how profitably to "exploit" modern optics. He was a Sikh with a full beard and requisite turban, and he had a great sense of humor and an infectious booming laugh. After an interview with the key partner, Don Lucas, at DG&A, I was offered the job, at a fraction of my Booz pay but with cheap stock that would make me rich if we hit it commercially in our "exploitation." I took the bait and signed on.

Ultimately, years after the demise of OTI, fiber optics became very important. Fiber use ranges from imaging bundles used in medical endoscopes and industrial camera probes to communications: virtually all high speed data transmission over long distances is via optical fiber today. But we had little or nothing to do with fiber optics' final success.

From my perspective, over the next four years Dr. Narinder Kapany and I developed what is fortunately a rare thing in life: a mutual hate for each other of near biblical proportions. Years afterward, I told anyone who would listen that I wanted engraved on my tombstone: "I still hate him." Perhaps it's time to cancel that request. . . . I'll start to think about it, one of these days.

To get OTI under way the backers purchased a small optical components company in Belmont, south of San Francisco, both to house our new venture and to provide a modest source of revenue. The company manufactured optical thin-film coatings for a scattering of customers. These films, sometimes called interference filters, are used in some optical components to restrict the light to certain narrow bands. I set about trying to build from this base, and Narinder and his team of about a dozen researchers, mostly associates of his from Chicago, set about trying to raise money from the government to fund various ideas that might lead to products. From the very beginning it was evident to me that Narinder and I had entirely different philosophies on how to build the business. I wanted to spend our own resources on developing proprietary products to sell. He wanted the funding to come from the government. It might have been a good idea if he could have carried it off, but the contracts that were obtained rarely were sufficient to fund much product development, and there was always a shortfall of contracts—our capital resources were gradually consumed in supporting the researchers.

Meanwhile, with virtually no budget, I tried to standardize some products we could produce and sell routinely. I was able to deliver boxed sets of optical filters using the technology we had inherited from the little Belmont group. I found a steady, if modest, market for these filters in university and other optical laboratories around the country to be used to calibrate optical instrumentation. Also, I was able to "productize" that group's own monitoring equipment for measuring the thickness of films as they were being deposited. I found a market for these things in the wider world.

The products from Narinder's group were highly specialized, and I was unable to sell them at all broadly. One was a fiber-optic camera for scanning the innards of nuclear submarine reactors. Alas, the navy only needed one of these. Another was a ruby-laser microscope for punching holes in biological cells—not much demand for that. Still another, a huge machine to test the resolution of lenses, was a one-off. Kapany was a pioneer in fiber optics, and the products we know today, such as flexible endoscopes in medical practice for looking around inside the body, were still years in the future. OTI was unsuccessful in developing any commercially important products using that technology. The fiber-optics manufacturing equipment was never developed to the point of making the fibers inexpensively enough for practical application or wide commercial use.

Meanwhile, on a sales trip back to Cambridge, at MIT I encountered Professor Ali Javan, inventor of the helium-neon continuous gas laser. This was the first laser to produce a steady beam of light—a huge advancement from the earlier pulsed ruby laser, of Ted Maiman at Hughes Research. I was in his laboratory trying to sell optical components, and he showed me the thing, one of the most important inventions of the twentieth century. For the first time continuous light of a very pure color, and coherent in phase-like radio waves, was available. This invention opened the door to the host of applications in communication, entertainment, medicine, and the military that we know today. I'll never forget seeing a running laser for the first time. That shaft of intense red light was unforgettable! But the device itself was a "kluge," as we called complicated, expensive, and unreliable things in those days. His laser had a quartz plasma tube mounted on about a two-hundred-pound granite optical bench (to minimize vibration) and external mirrors, aligned by microscope drives. By just resting one's hand on the granite, it could be bent enough to stop the laser action. A tiny fraction of a degree of misalignment was too much.

I thought that if we could, somehow, make lasers like this available there would be a good demand for them; they were just so exciting. I believed that every lab would want one, simply to play with—revolutions in optics are pretty rare, but this was a big one. Another engineer and I scrounged around inside OTI and, for next to nothing, made a poor man's version of the Javan device. (In those early days, no one worried about patents on lasers. MIT basically gave away the idea. Decades later, "laser patent wars" loomed over the industry and were hard fought; this was far in the future, and by then I was long out of the laser business.) Our device too was a kluge, but we offered it for a few thousand dollars, and sure enough orders started to roll in. To stimulate sales, I knocked out a textbook on my Sausalito kitchen table at night, *Experiments in Physical Optics Using Continuous Laser Light*, to help boost sales into the university market. The book (now out of print) was published with considerable fanfare by OTI. It incorporated ten experiments a student could perform with one of our lasers to demonstrate the underlying principles of light—diffraction, interference, the concept of coherent-path-length, and so forth. The book was well received, and my side of OTI began to prosper.

And my personal life took a huge lift (which lasted thirty-five years) when I met Gerd through an OTI contact. Dr. Buzz Kramer was a young San Francisco ear, nose, and throat specialist who had been sought out by Narinder for advice on making a fiber-optic endoscope for examining ENT problems. A flexible fiber bundle can carry an image if the fibers are aligned end to end, so that the picture emerges as from a mosaic—but if the fibers are not perfectly aligned (and tens of thousands of them are required), if they become scrambled, just light with no image at all emerges. Nothing came from this, as OTI couldn't make an image-carrying fiber bundle for less than the cost of the Great Pyramid. (That's an exaggeration—OTI couldn't have made one for any price, at the time.)

Optics notwithstanding, Buzz and I became friends. We both worked Saturdays, so we decided to drive up to the Sugar Bowl ski area in the Sierras for a single day of Sunday skiing. It was great on the slopes, and I spotted a most beautiful girl—Gerd looked like Ingrid Bergman all her life. Buzz said, "I met her last week—I'll introduce you." He had met her at a party just some days before. We skied down the mountain and joined her for a good lunch on the porch of the lodge in the bright sunlight. I couldn't keep my eyes off Gerd. She was stunningly beautiful, fun and full of life. Her Norwegian accent, which she never lost, was charming. It turned out that she had been in America for less than a month, and although she had a job as a receptionist in the personnel department at the Bechtel Corporation, she wasn't planning to stay in San Francisco much longer.

You nonromantics may cringe, but there really is love at first sight. At least there was for us. She accepted my invitation for a sail on my racing boat, which had coincidentally been built in Norway, and had a great time. It turned out that she and her brother had been Norwegian snipe sailing champions a few years earlier. From that day on the bay, we dated nonstop until that just became silly, and then we simply lived together—very modern, but scandalous still in the early sixties. Boy, did that perception of scandal change fast!

Gerd's U.S. sponsor was a lawyer contact of her father's who was a top attorney in Norway, and the sponsor was, coincidentally, the mayor of Sausalito, where we were living. After about a year we decided to get married and I sought out a pretty little local church to do the service. It's hard to believe now, but the pastor insisted on a private interview with each of us to discuss the birds and the bees — he became embarrassed when we didn't become embarrassed in listening. Just a handful of friends, two couples actually, attended but it was the happiest day of our lives. To this day I carry a snapshot of Gerd standing on the balcony of my apartment overlooking the bay, radiant in a huge stylish hat. There was no time for a honeymoon, however, as OTI needed all my effort.

The company had developed a decent product, finally, from Narinder's group — a ruby laser photocoagulator. This was a device for eye doctors to use in "stitching" detached retinas back in place. It replaced a giant machine developed in Germany using conventional light. Our thing worked pretty well, and in those days the FDA was reasonably lenient in permitting new devices for trial use by doctors. So we sold a number of the instruments, and to the best of my knowledge there was never a serious mishap in their use. However, I believe that we never broke even on the research costs, and we needed many such products for success.

Narinder and I had never had a comfortable relationship. I suppose there was simply too much rivalry between us. The investors were anxious for commercial results, profits, so that the company could be listed — that is, taken public with an initial public offering (IPO) — thus they might recover their investment with a nice upside. But the continuing struggle between my "commercial" profitable products, as shoestring as they were, and the prestigious but money-losing handful of products from the "research" department, became ever more rancorous. And Narinder aspired to a better address than our humble location in the back alleys of Belmont. What better address than the Stanford Industrial Park? The same place in Palo Alto where HP was located! After a major piece of lease borrowing, a location in the park was achieved, and we moved.

It didn't make sense to me; I didn't see how we could afford it. I had hired some really good folks to help with the commercial side;

a young guy, Dick Jaenicke, was a superstar on my staff, but it seemed our results were always vitiated by the money-sucking research department. Narinder was given to making extravagant promises, I thought. In my opinion, he loved to be the up-and-coming science hero, and he had great access to, and coverage by, the press. To me it all seemed to be a castle in the clouds, and I began to discuss OTI with Dave Packard. I asked for his advice, and it was pretty simple: "Just get out," he said.

Things fell apart rapidly after the move to Palo Alto. I tried to make peace with Narinder and invited him and his very charming wife, Satinder, to dinner at our apartment. Tor, our son, had been recently born, and Gerd and I were feeling solid and confident in the world. The evening was a disaster. Too much was drunk by Narinder and me, and the personal insults exchanged, humiliating me in front of Gerd, could not be smoothed over with copious apologies during the following weeks.

About this time Narinder announced the invention of "color translating radiography," color X-ray, in short. He had filed for a patent on the idea, but little had been done to prove the principle in the form of a working device. There was nothing to see, even though a friendly reporter described the colors as being "as vivid as those in a stained-glass window." I don't know what the reporter thought he actually saw, but I saw red. I decided to quit by asking the board to choose between Narinder and me. There was never much doubt of the preference of Don Lucas, the venture capitalist from DG&A, who strongly influenced the board; they picked the glamorous and charismatic Dr. Kapany, and I was out.

Over the next many months, the market became very hot for IPO technology stocks, in one of its endless cycles, and OTI indeed did become a public company. The stock rose very nicely (I had surrendered all of my stock back to the company, and never made a penny), but not too long thereafter, the company faltered after a number of acquisitions, and it ultimately simply passed out of existence. Dr. Kapany has subsequently had a distinguished career according to the information provided in his Google biography. He and I have never spoken again.

I returned to HP, but lasers were never far from my thoughts. I believed that if some way could be found to make continuous lasers as simple and as reliable as lightbulbs, big markets awaited. Dick Jaenicke, who had remained at OTI, and I got together from time to time to kick ideas around. Gradually we evolved an approach that might be the breakthrough required.

The Javan design had several problems. The cost, of course, was too high, but the root of all the problems lay in the fact that the laser's mirrors were external to the discharge tube. If some way could be found to put the mirrors inside the tube, everything would be enormously simplified, the reliability would skyrocket, and the cost would plummet. But how could one align the mirrors inside the plasma tube during its manufacture? That was where a new idea was required. Eventually Dick and I thought we might have a solution, but the idea existed just on paper. We would have to run extensive experiments to prove the concept. In looking back, I think it's amazing that I proceeded. I had a full-time job at HP; our second child, a baby girl, was due in a few months; and I didn't have much money — only what Gerd and I had saved for a down payment on the house we were renting and hoped to buy. I am sure that I was driven by my loathing for Kapany and OTI. I wanted to succeed, sure, but more important, I wanted to defeat them, to drive them out of the laser business. This is one of my ugly truths: vindictiveness is unattractive, but very powerful!

In order to proceed I had to evolve risk-reduction and cost-saving strategies, which proved typical of those I would use subsequently in many venture situations. First, I had to persuade Gerd to let me stake our life's savings in a risky laser development program. I had prepared quite a long train of argument for her. But after only about thirty seconds, she said, "Sure." Her faith in me was total. More vital, I had to get Packard's permission to moonlight, notoriously, on an idea that in no way would benefit HP. I explained the idea to him with a small technical sketch. Dave was one of America's truly great entrepreneurs, and he admired that kind of thinking in others. Plus he didn't think much of the OTI bunch either, and I am sure he didn't object to my desire to stick it to them. So he said okay, with the proviso that I didn't let it get too much in the way of my HP work.

My small racing sailboat, upon which Gerd and I had had our first date, an International One Design (IOD), was built in the thirties and kept afloat by dint of my constant weekend effort at the shipwright's crafts. Another IOD owner, Henry Rhodes, was a guy I saw around the yacht harbor. He was a skilled glassblower with his own shop on University Avenue in Berkeley. Henry worked mostly for the University of California, and he was expert in blowing quartz and Pyrex, the materials I thought we would need. I approached him with my idea, and proposed a deal: if he would make all the experimental models we required, and would then, if we were successful, provide the first one hundred tubes at materials cost, he would own, in return, one-third of the company. I made a similar arrangement with Dick, who got a third in return for agreeing to run the company if the invention worked. I, of course, had the remaining third in return for the idea, the money, and my work on nights and weekends. There were no others involved, and no additional capital.

Henry was a glassblowing genius, and he quickly produced a series of tubes, beginning with the design I thought most likely to work. Unfortunately, all these initial designs failed. I couldn't get the mirrors adjusted as he sealed off the tubes. There was no laser action. After about a dozen failures, we had our breakthrough moment with a design involving spherical rotary glass vacuum joints, with the mirrors deposited on the flattened inner face of the joint. The things carrying the mirrors looked like a child's glass marbles with two flat surfaces on either side. It was thus possible to adjust the mirrors while the tube was still on-line, before the tube was sealed off containing its own internal gas reservoir and electrodes. The design had the further advantage of being entirely symmetrical, and it was made in low-temperature-coefficient Pyrex, which insured that, once set, the mirror adjustment would never change.

The above is all preamble to the *eureka!* moment described earlier. But getting the Lasertron, as I named the device, to work was, of course, only the first step in building the business.

I had only enough cash left to buy parts for the first twenty-five lasers and their housings and power supplies. I needed to sell them instantly to provide the cash to get the fledgling company, University Laboratories, Inc. (ULI), off the ground. To this end I wrote an ad to run in *Physics Today* featuring the new product and incorporating a coupon, with which the prospective customer could "reserve an instrument from current production." We got several hundred replies, and Dick followed up quickly to convert these into actual orders. The Oakland branch of a major California bank would lend us money against the receivables when we shipped the lasers.

But we couldn't get any of the first production run tubes to work. Everything seemed normal, but within an hour or so the laser beams would just fade away. Meanwhile the prototype was blazing as strong as ever. Dick worked frantically to solve the problem. Everything was done over, and done over again, but the tubes just always died. Dick called me to Berkeley after my day at HP and I hurried, knowing how desperate we were. Rather than repeat the process again—I was confident that Dick and his technician had done everything right—I just asked questions. Had the mirrors (manufactured by an optical company in Santa Rosa) been delivered with the required reflectivity graphs, showing that they peaked at exactly 6328 angstroms? Indeed they had; they showed me the graphs. Was the helium-neon ratio exactly the same as on the prototype tube? Yes, it was. Well then, what had been changed? Nothing.

While I may have blown that physics final at MIT, I still had some of the analytic ability the institute so proudly claimed its graduates learned. I just sat pondering the data, and concluded that the only explanation had to be that, somehow, the mirrors changed wavelength when they were placed in the near vacuum of the plasma tube. It was too late to call the supplier, and since it was a Friday, no answers would be available until the following week. I asked Dick to try bleeding pure oxygen into the system. He threw up his hands in disgust, but he did it. Slowly the lasers began to operate again, steadily gaining intensity. We left them on the system with the decision that if they were still strong on Monday morning, we would ship

The advertisement for lasers
that launched University Laboratories Inc.

them. They were, and we did. Later, Dick found out that the mirror vendor had omitted a small (but important) final "oxygenating" step in the processing before shipping them to us. That was the only small problem we ever had with this excellent supplier.

As we began to ship these ULI lasers in the hundreds, Optics

Technology sued to try to shut us down. They accused Dick of steal-
ing customer lists—we just had our coupons—and, incredibly, the
laser wavelength itself of 6328 angstroms, which was determined
either by God or Albert Einstein, take your pick. As I recall, I agreed
to pay them two weeks of Dick's salary at OTI, and they went away.

A much bigger problem was brought about by our success. A
rapidly growing company needs cash to fund growing inventory, receivables, and an ever-expanding workforce. We needed money, and
a visit was arranged from the bank to Henry's shop, where we were
making the laser tubes; it was now the primary activity of his many
glassblowers. Henry was a political liberal, very far to the left even
for Berkeley, even in the 1960s. Dick and I begged him to clean up
the place before the visit. I arrived with Dick and the bankers to find
that Henry had strung a huge banner across the entire back wall of
his place. It said FUCK COMMUNISM.

We borrowed against our skyrocketing receivables until one day
the manager of the branch called me at HP to say, "No more money!
No more money until you put some equity under the company. No
more!" I didn't have any more equity to put in. I was stumped. So,
innocently, I called the bank's senior executive vice president at the
San Francisco headquarters, who was in charge of public relations,
and explained our wonderful growth and so forth. He said, "Lasers,
huh . . . I have a daughter who has a science fair project due on
Saturday, and she hasn't—" I cut him off and asked, "How many do
you need?" On Monday the branch manager called me back to say,
"I don't know what you did, or how you did it, but I am supposed to
lend you more money!"

Regardless, the picture was clear—I needed venture capital. At
this time, though, there wasn't much professional venture capital
available. But our growth and profits were impressive, and I was able
to persuade some fellow executives within HP, who had a sort of
investment club, to invest. Some risk money was offered from the
local brokerage firm of Davis Skaggs, and finally we raised some
money from one of the first true VC firms, Sutter Hill. In total
around two hundred thousand dollars were committed for about
twenty percent of the company. This restructuring was also an op-

portunity for Dick and me to buy Henry out. He wanted to buy a bigger yacht and just sail away. Between us, Dick and I borrowed (on the strength of our ULI stock) eighty thousand dollars for Henry's third. He was fully aware of the valuation we had just achieved, and that we might, someday, hit it big, but the allure of the yacht was just too much. I, too, know that feeling.

With the equity in place we were able to expand into new quarters in Berkeley, install our own glassblowing equipment, and set up true production lines. Along about this time we hired our first laser PhD to carry us into newer types of lasers at different wavelengths and powers, but all with our intrinsic simplicity and reliability advantages. The most important development was the invention of our DialGrade product line.

One of our salesmen had the idea of laying sewer pipe by shining a laser through the sections to keep them straight—just center the red dot on a plastic target at the end of the pipe and keep digging! This would be a perfect laser application. After all, our tubes were waterproof and rugged. We took one of our Lasertrons and mounted it in a metal housing, painted yellow so it looked at home on a construction site among Caterpillar machines, ran it from a car battery, put a dial on the top so that one could "dial the grade," or the desired slope of the sewer line, in degrees and fractions of a degree, and we were in business. Our cost was around three hundred dollars—we sold it for five thousand dollars, and the contractors were able to pay for it in the savings on the first job—the survey crew was eliminated. We followed with additional products for construction: vertical lasers to align the rails in elevator shafts, rotating laser beams to align hanging ceiling acoustic tiles, and spinning beams for horizontal and vertical reference. One sees these devices still in use around the world, even after all these decades, and they are always painted "our" yellow, though now made by many competitors. My ULI was on a roll, one of the hottest new companies around, and it was becoming a problem.

It was a very high-class problem. I was chairman of a rapidly growing company that had every prospect of making me a multimillionaire, however, it needed much more than the nights and weekends I could spare from HP. But I didn't really want to quit HP—I had made that mistake once before—and I was running the fastest-growing part of the company. I began to discuss my problem with George Quist, of the top San Francisco investment banking firm of Hambrecht and Quist. Originally I thought of taking ULI public, but George had a better idea. His firm had floated a laser company called Spectra Physics. That company was very long on science but seriously short on profits—ULI was just the reverse. George suggested that I let Spectra acquire ULI. It would give me instant personal liquidity; I would become a major shareholder; and I would go on the board of the combined companies. Moreover, I wouldn't have to quit HP to do it all.

Dick and I agreed to the merger. On the day the final papers were signed, I was walking out of my lawyer's building on the way to lunch. I spotted a quarter on the sidewalk and stopped to pick it up. My attorney said, "Tom, today you made a couple of million and a quarter." Within a few months Dick retired. He told me later that the only problem in being retired at twenty-five was that all his golf and tennis friends were in their sixties.

Adams was a scholar and minor diplomat, noted for being extraordinarily well connected politically in Washington and Europe. He drew his lessons quietly from the finest of teachers. Mine were more workaday but nevertheless very good.

The previous chapter overlaps with this one in time. The following pages cover the other half of my life during the sixties. While I was active with the laser company, things were very busy for me at Hewlett-Packard, ultimately leading to the path of venture capital.

Chapter Four

A Ferrari Is Not Necessarily a Wise Substitute
for the Company Chevrolet

In the five years I was away from HP the company had changed tremendously. Upon my return from management consulting and Optics Technology, I found a big company with revenues of hundreds of millions of dollars annually and lots of MBAs. HP now dominated the test and measurement market, was branching out into medical instrumentation and, importantly, all the sales representative organizations had been acquired, so the firm had its own marketing arm for the first time—although the former reps pretty much operated autonomously as before. The company was organized into divisions, and Dave spotted these divisions around the country where they could be close to local engineering schools. This strategy worked, and HP was able to replicate the university/company culture that had so characterized the original HP/Stanford relationship. The division general managers (GMs) were the crown princes of the company, and all were successful to more or less the same degree, as all were essentially in the same business (there are not profound differences between microwaves and volts—from a distance); all sold through the same organization; all paid their technical people about the same, and so forth. It was reasonably easy for Dave and Bill to manage all this with their famous "management by walking around" technique—wherever they went, it all looked familiar—and they presided over a money-making machine.

But Messrs. Hewlett and Packard were restless and driven men.

Their aspirations always reached beyond the present success. Their partnership at the top of HP was, in my opinion, totally unique in America. The entrepreneurial ideas and the skill to implement those ideas flowed down from the top. Sure, innovation was encouraged throughout the company, but the big steps were always taken by Dave and Bill.

I was fortunate to have come knocking on their door, after bolting from OTI, at such a time of change. Bill was in the process of organizing what was to become the famous HP Labs. He had decided that leaving all the engineering scattered among the dozen divisions (eventually there were seventeen) wouldn't lead to breakthroughs in technology that could lead to new businesses. The GMs weren't encouraged to take those kind of risks (although some did: the Laserjet printer was a huge success that originated at the divisional level). In addition, Bill wanted his personal "hobby shop" near corporate headquarters. Dr. Bernard Oliver, the HP vice president in charge of engineering for the whole company, would be the director of the labs.

The late Dr. Oliver was truly a genius. His mind ranged over vast fields of math and physics—he had been a superstar at Bell Labs, where legend is that he did the math for Claude Shannon, of Shannon's theorem fame, before Hewlett snagged him for HP. But he was totally undisciplined. If the prospect of building devices to communicate with dolphins captured his fancy, that's what he did for months on end. Or perhaps, instead, listening in on alien broadcasts from outer space. When something technical caught his imagination within HP, he worked on that too. His plusses so overwhelmed his minuses that Dave and Bill indulged all his non-HP-specific projects his entire career. But all agreed, particularly Barney himself, that management was not his forte, and that he would need help in first pulling the labs together, and then in running them. Dave and Bill decided that I might succeed as his assistant, as administrative manager of the labs. Some reporters have erred in describing this era of my life. I never was "in charge of" the labs, just as I never later "started" the HP computer business. I think Dave and Bill were counting on my restlessness and ambition to help push through the difficulties that the labs would encounter throughout the organization.

Basically, the problem was that the cost of the labs would be borne as a "tax" upon the operating divisions. Any money the labs spent was not available to be spent by the general managers in their own engineering departments. And, they would have little or no say in the lab's projects. "Taxation without representation" led to the Boston Tea Party, and those same feelings were strongly evident within HP. So, in addition to pulling things together for Barney in terms of space and people, an important aspect of my job was to coordinate with the divisions, trying to gain their goodwill and key them up to accept, and put into production, the inventions that would be flowing down from the labs. This was a most unpopular mission in the beginning, and I was seen to represent corporate

Bill Hewlett and Dave Packard in 1959

encroachment on the rights of the divisions. Those battles are now long forgotten, and may be seen as part of the never-ending cycle between centralization and decentralization that occurs in most large and growing companies over time.

Dave and Bill were right in needing the labs to pioneer new directions for HP. Bill made the first big move by pushing the labs into the development of the desktop calculator through his personal involvement in the invention of the first practical read-only memory, which made the new complex algorithms of the machines possible. (Bill Hewlett was a man who solved Bessel functions in his head, just for fun.) The desktop calculators were a breakthrough and became an enormous success for HP when transferred to a division for manufacture. That product alone validated the whole concept of the labs, I thought. Then Bill, even more aggressively, pushed the development of the handheld calculator. This was during the era when slide rules costing around fifty dollars dominated, absolutely, the engineer's world. The handheld device would cost hundreds of dollars.

The top management in marketing were appalled. They thought the little calculator would find no market, and they hired the Stanford Research Institute to do a market study to prove their point. The study was duly presented to Bill Hewlett (I sat in on the presentation) and it was, put politely, extremely negative. At the end, Bill just smiled and said, "Well, I guess that gives us the go-ahead." The product, the HP 35, was a stupendous success worldwide—and today a good slide rule will cost you a fortune because of its antique rarity.

It was Dave Packard who pushed the labs into the diversification that led to HP's computer business, now the largest in the world, edging toward one hundred billion dollars annually including printers as peripherals. Dave was intrigued with the possibility of using computers to control instrumentation. He had made a pass at acquiring the Digital Equipment Corporation (DEC) from Professor Doriot, who was chairman of the DEC board, but the asking price of twenty-four million dollars seemed too high, and Dave decided to do it himself. So, like Bill, he initiated the development of a computer in Paul Stoft's group of electronic gurus in the labs. In due course the "machine" (which is what we computer nerds invariably call these things) emerged. It was named the HP 2116, and it was transferred into the Palo Alto division to be manufactured and sold. This product was a credit to the company. It was built to the temperature and vibration standards of HP and was virtually indestructible at a time when the products of IBM and DEC weren't so reliable. It had four thousand bytes of magnetic core memory, a fast enough input/output (IO) channel, and everything needed to control instruments, plus it was priced competitively. This was an emerging market for minicomputers — DEC was doing well. The Palo Alto division offered it for sale, and during the first full year . . . not a single one was sold!

Dave's anger was legendary, and pretty frightening. As his temper frayed during the course of a day, he would gradually roll up his shirt sleeves, and by the time they were above his elbows it was smart to steer clear. Also, his pace of cigarette smoking so increased that he seemed to nearly chew them. When Dave called an all-day meeting to find out what was wrong with the computer, some one hundred of us attended, not without trepidation. It was a long meeting, and his shirt sleeves were rising. The engineers had dozens of ideas of what was wrong: there weren't enough index registers, the IO should be faster, the memory was too small, and so forth. I knew little about computers, except that they were complicated and that the sales force that sold all HP products from the company catalog was probably as ignorant about them as I. Toward the end of the day, when Dave's frustration was peaking as the alleged technical shortfalls of the product were still being compiled by the technical guys, he asked: "Tom, you haven't said anything—what's your opinion?" I answered, "Well, Dave, when everything else fails—try selling!" All I got back was an angry snarl. But the next day he dropped by to ask me what I had meant. I said that I thought the salesmen were intimidated by the computer, that maybe they were afraid to show their ignorance in front of computer-savvy prospects, and so they simply sold other things to make their quota. He just walked away, with no further comment.

A week later I got a call from Margret, Dave's secretary, saying that both Mr. Packard and Mr. Hewlett wanted me to join them for lunch. This was not long after my laser company was beginning to ship in some quantity; I wondered if they were pissed off over my shameless moonlighting. Were they going to fire me?

We met at the Palo Alto Club, an exclusive place in a former residence on a quiet street. I had never been there. Both Dave and Bill talked about all kinds of things going on in the labs, and neither made any mention of the laser company. At the end of the lunch Dave asked me if I would be game to take on the computer problem. They wanted me to become the marketing manager for the Palo Alto division. Our lunch had been a job interview for the most promising but worrisome thing on their plate. I was tremendously excited!

And so began the most challenging episode in my business career. It changed me and it changed the company, beginning a process of many decades that can only be said to have ended a few years ago, when the computer side of HP finally spun out all the noncomputer businesses into the company called Agilent.

The Palo Alto division was managed by Dr. Jack Melchor, a former entrepreneur and later a successful venture capitalist. The regular business of the division was customized measurement systems involving multiple HP products, but the computer preoccupied everyone's attention. I took myself at my own word and decided that the computer itself was fine and didn't need to be changed, but that everything about its marketing was wrong and had to be changed, and changed as soon as possible. The most important thing to be done, I thought, was to get people in the field who understood something about computers. I approached Noel Eldred, who was still the overall boss of HP marketing, about hiring a number of DEC salesmen to scatter within the sales force (essentially the same old representative organizations) to act as specialists. They would be a source of knowledge to support the regular salesmen.

Noel was only a year or so away from retirement. He looked me squarely in the eye and said *no*. He was not about to preside over the creation of a sales force within the sales force—he thought that every division would want the same thing. He said that, frankly, he wouldn't permit me to make his remaining time at the company a misery. And so began a process of my going to Dave to get permission to override and circumvent the fundamental structure and backbone of the corporation. It happened with advertising, public relations, trade show promotions, personnel, and manufacturing as well. I became extremely unpopular with the managers of the conventional side of the company, for getting my way so often for things that they wanted to do as well but were not permitted to try. But, in what seemed to be no time at all, the changes began to work. The computer business began to take off as the sales specialists gained the confidence of the salesmen, and the latter were delighted to discover that their customers loved the HP computer products. The business began to grow at a compound rate of about thirty percent a quarter—growth like that doesn't take long to become important, especially when the gross profit was above seventy percent. Those early months were frantic. My boss, Jack, suffered a minor collapse, perhaps an anxiety attack (having me as a direct report was *not* the cause . . . I think), and he needed some rest, so Dave made me the GM for what quickly had become the computer division.

Even Dave and I clashed. The business was entirely different in so many ways from the instrument business. We were trying to get customers to buy our computers to use in their own systems to resell to third parties. That is, we were trying to penetrate what is called the original equipment market, or OEM. But to do so we had to offer discounts off our list prices. This was a practice that HP had never done. Dave Packard considered it illegal. During a meeting with Bill when I made a case for granting discounts for OEM volume, Dave became very angry and stormed out of the room after turning me down flat. Hewlett said, "Well, Tom, what are you going to do now?" I replied that Dave was wrong on the law and that I'd be back to make a stronger case. Backed up by expert legal opinion and examples from the industry, I returned, and Dave signed off on the idea as if we had never discussed it previously. That's the way Dave was. He never resented a challenge—rather he encouraged it—and disputes never became personal, or even remembered.

I think it's fair to say that my vertical support, upward to Dave and Bill and downward to the people in my exploding division, was excellent. But my horizontal support among my peers, the other GMs, was beyond terrible—they hated my guts. Even four decades later, when the prospect of my joining the HP board first emerged, some of them came out of retirement to lobby against the idea!

I was on a roll, though. We entered the market of making time-share computers (central smart computers that divide their resources, simultaneously, among a network of dumb terminals) against IBM, with a product we sold for a fraction of the IBM price. The old guard panicked. IBM was a major customer for HP instruments—Perkins had to be stopped before the relationship was irredeemably wrecked! Dave was persuaded to tackle me on the matter. After sternly reminding me of the importance of friendship with IBM, he got around to asking how we were actually doing in that new time-sharing business. I showed him the order book, several million dollars of equipment with a margin of seventy-five percent. He stood up, gave me one of his rare but marvelously charming smiles, and said that he thought it would be "all right to continue."

During this time of rapid growth for computers and indeed for the whole company, the "crown prince" division GMs became ever more predominant, but there remained the original vice presidents at the top, who had previously held most of the power. Noel Eldred still had marketing, even though I was evolving my own sales force— but Noel and I got along very well at last. The official title of vice president for manufacturing resided with Ralph Lee, but all manufacturing had devolved to the divisions, and Ralph had little to do but interfere with the GM's lives, which he did incessantly. He had opinions on everything. The traditional advertisement for an HP product was simply a photograph of the product and a dry list of specifications. I joked that if HP were to produce sushi, it would be promoted as cold dead fish. So, my ads for computers were very different: one showed a picture of a crate on a receiving dock, with the headline "Some computers are delivered, others are abandoned." The copy stressed that with HP the customer got installation and continuing service. Ralph was so offended by this ad that he tried to kill it, but I prevailed.

He too, managed by wandering around, but he had no sense of the dynamics within a division, at least not mine. One day he wandered in while I was holding a staff meeting, wanting to have a private meeting with Roy Clay, my software manager. I refused to let Roy leave my meeting. Ralph was furious, and fought back by demanding that I surrender my company Buick for a lesser Chevrolet, he had the power to do that.

I had become independently wealthy when I merged my University Labs into Spectra Physics. This was in the mid-sixties, when HP represented the very best in solid middle-class American corporate culture including the perquisite of a company-provided automobile. A GM's car depended upon the size and profitability of his division—cars ranged from Buicks through Chevrolets and down to Pintos. After Ralph's revenge over my company car, I stuck my finger right into the eye of this culture by taking some laser money and buying a Ferrari! The grinding of teeth overcame the grinding of gears when I parked it in front of headquarters. How stupid I was! How wonderful it felt!

My colleagues, the other GMs, were not above revenge. The company had annual off-site meetings where socializing occurred. Skits were performed, which really were extremely funny, and a photo gallery was always included in which cartoonlike word bubbles allegedly revealed inner thoughts. I'll never forget a shot of me that everybody found hilarious. I was sitting at the head of a table, leaning back in my chair with a supercilious look on my face as I listened. All my direct reports were there around the table in very serious discussion. The bubble over my head said, "How did I ever get mixed up with this bunch of middle-class nonentities, anyway?"

I attribute this piece of wit to Al Bagley, who was GM of the counter division—we are still friends.

My direct reports were far from nonentities. Virtually all of them had very distinguished careers in the Valley after moving on from HP. Bill Davidow, my marketing guy, became VP for marketing at Intel. Roy Clay, our software guru, is still CEO of his own instrument company. Bill Abbott, the manufacturing czar, became executive VP of Acuson (a KPC&B company), and so on. We'll hear much more about Jimmy Treybig, the peripherals manager, a little further on.

All of my people detested the interfering Ralph Lee. He was a scourge of the whole organization. I conspired with John Young, who was running the microwave division, as big and profitable as mine, to visit Dave together and beg him to get Ralph to lay off. Dave didn't do much about the interfering, but the fact that he listened to the two of us without exploding let us know that he understood our feelings.

■   ■   ■

One day in early 1969, Bill Hewlett's voice came over the company's public address system. This had never happened before. He asked for all the machines to be shut down and the production lines halted, as he had an important announcement to make. We were all stunned when he told us that Dave would be leaving the company to go to Washington to become deputy director of defense in the Nixon administration. This was disturbing news. "Pappy," as some old hands still called Dave, would be leaving the family, and Bill, who had to the best of our knowledge never actually run anything, would be taking over.

In the early months of Dave's absence, things didn't change much, or maybe I didn't notice because the computer division continued to rocket forward in its growth. We were hiring dozens of new employees each week. For quite a while Gerd and I hosted a get-acquainted reception at our home a couple of times a month, so that my managers and I could get to know the new faces. Few of these new people transferred in from "old" HP, and we began to develop our own very aggressive culture. We seemed always to need more space, and finally (over Ralph Lee's objections) the company acquired a vast place for our headquarters in Cupertino. It was some one hundred eighty thousand square feet—we filled it within a year. The software programmers didn't like to wear shoes, so when Ralph refused to approve paying for the carpet they wanted, I provided it from my own pocket. This was a time during which the whole company was prospering, and the competition for resources was heated among the seventeen division managers. Dave made decisions rapidly, but Bill was far more deliberate. I became particularly outspoken at corporate meetings, and I wondered if Bill resented my growing impudence and impatience. When he called me up to his office, about a year after Packard left, I thought that there was better than an even chance that he would fire me.

Instead, he asked me to move up to the corporate headquarters, take an office just outside his door, and as he put it in the most flattering way: "Help me figure out how to run this place." He went on to say that if I didn't want to give up my division, now the largest in the company, I didn't have to, but that he would really appreciate my direct help. I asked what authority I would have, and he made it clear that it would be a staff job, but that he would implement any good ideas. What would be my title? "Invent one," he said. After sleeping on it, I decided to try the new job and I gave myself the title of Director of Corporate Development, which could mean just about anything.

Having been a management consultant, I understood the powerlessness of a staff job. If you picture a dog lying on its back, legs in the air, in abject surrender before the other dogs in the pack, you will get some idea of the posture I felt I needed to adopt. I knew that my erstwhile "colleagues," the division managers, would resist my ideas almost viscerally. But that wasn't the real problem. The real problem was that I didn't have truly significant ideas to implement. I had been vociferous in my hectoring complaints about Bill, but now that he was asking me to help, my slate was pretty blank.

Bill was an entirely different kind of manager from Dave. Dave was a natural leader, an entrepreneur who always seemed to know what to do next, who maybe had a grand strategy, or maybe not. Dave had grown the company from the famous garage in which it started to its then-current size of hundreds of millions of dollars annually. Bill was much more intellectual in his approach. He wanted a structure and a philosophical underpinning in place for the future. I'll be forever grateful for everything Dave taught me, but it was Hewlett who wanted, and got, me to focus on how to get from hundreds of millions to billions. During the brief three years with Bill alone at the helm of HP, the company transitioned into the really big leagues. He would have done it without me, but I helped a little, I think.

I had left my division, pressure cooker–like in its intensity, to move into a serene atmosphere up at corporate. Here, my in box was perpetually empty and the few obvious things for me to do, like organizing the budgets for Bill's review, looking into the potential for some HP Labs ideas (classical market research), and attending to the mechanics of a couple of small acquisitions then in the works, left me plenty of time for the larger mission — if I could define it. Bill was not one for anything the least fuzzy or not fully cooked. He was a guy who, when handed a paper containing any sum of figures, no matter how unimportant, would seize the paper and mentally check the arithmetic before the discussion could begin. I have seen him do this a hundred times, and heaven help if there was an error! Whatever I came up with had to be solid — bear in mind this polymath had an IQ in the stratosphere. In his calm, apparently open and friendly way, Bill could be more terrifying than Dave at his sleeves-rolled-up, cigarette-chewing, storm-mode peak.

So when a brochure crossed my desk with the headline "How Do You Allocate Resources Among Competing Corporate Entities? What Is the Best Strategy for Building Businesses — How Do You Decide on Which Ones Not to Feed?" I thought that it was addressing me personally. The brochure was from a new consulting company called the Boston Consulting Group (BCG), and they were offering a free weekend seminar to interested managers. Boy, was I interested! I flew back to the next session.

Those of you who have been in the management racket for more than a little while will be amused that anyone would pay serious attention to the ideas of "cash cows" and "stars" and the concept that everything should be based upon rates of growth and market share. But back then these ideas were really fresh, powerful, and true, and to me that weekend was a revelation. It seemed to be a reasonable system that could apply to the complexity of HP. The ideas took hold in my mind; they seemed to offer the theoretical framework for what Bill was asking me to do. I worked up a presentation on the theory itself and then its application to HP, using internal market share data; it took a couple of hours to present it to Bill, one-on-one. He loved it! In no time he had me present the theory to the executive council, and soon it seemed we had a rational process in place to modify our budgets and strategies. The entire budgeting process became infected with this thinking. My efforts had the power to influence the flow of resources into promising areas and to diminish the hold of the older, stagnant businesses on the overall plan. In the following two years the ascendant BCG methods saturated HP; I think they had a tremendous positive effect on the company's growth. But, as in many religions, the converts at the lower levels took the gospel too seriously, and distorted the ideas to suit their own needs. Eventually, after my departure, BCG became discredited within HP, but the "snake oil" worked pretty well for Bill and me in those early heady months.

One Saturday morning in late 1971 I was working in my office when, to my astonishment, Dave Packard walked in and sat down at my desk.

I had seen him a few weeks earlier in New York, when he had flown up from Washington to attend some social/political event, and he had invited John Young (years later to become president of HP) and me to drop by from our meetings to have a drink in his hotel room. He was in a tux, and I had never seen him looking so fancy, but he also looked exhausted, really devastated. This was during the height of the Vietnam War, and John and I were amazed as Dave told us in detail how he had to become directly involved in managing that horror. Like civilians before, he found the military bureaucracy intractable—we were astonished at his stories of deploying troops and planning battles. He was officially upbeat, but we both concluded that his heart wasn't in it.

Now, instead of being at his desk in the Pentagon, he was in my office asking me to find the last five days of the *Wall Street Journal*. I found them, and we averaged the price of HP stock for that last week. He muttered something about my keeping mum about his visit, and he disappeared.

Some weeks later it was announced that Dave would be returning to HP, and the mystery of his visit became clear. When he left to go to the Pentagon, all his HP stock had been put into a trust, so that any profit on his holdings while he was in the government would be given to charity upon his return. The stock price had declined in the intervening years but had been rising recently. The five-day average established the price for his return—his timing was nearly perfect in that there was very little profit to be given away. Why did he worry about something like that, when later he donated billions to his charitable foundation? I don't really know, but I suspect that there were two reasons: first, I think he was disillusioned, totally, by the war, and second, I think he had an early whiff of what was soon to become the Watergate scandal. I just think that he wanted to keep his stock and not have to surrender any to pay for those two things. Dave would never talk much about his Washington years, but I believe they had a profound and depressing effect upon him at the deepest level.

After Dave was back, he called me into his office and told me that Bill thought that I had done "a damn fine job," but now he, personally, would be helping Bill, and the two of them would find another part of the company for me to run. I knew that all the local divisions were headed by capable guys, and that the prospects were very strong that I would have to move to some outlying division, maybe in Colorado, maybe back east. I thanked Dave for his vote of confidence, but I told him the next day that I was going to try my hand at venture capital.

And so I resigned for the second time from the Hewlett-Packard Company. Two more of my resignations from that company were still to come, many years later.

Shall we take a little break from work and have some "car talk"? Cars have been a lifelong passion of mine.

Chapter Five

Digging Up an Old Car

The Ferrari I mentioned buying earlier was an extremely rare 500 Superfast model, one of only twenty-eight made over a period of about four years, and it was absolutely gorgeous. The original purchaser was Dr. Alejandro Zaffaroni of Syntex, the birth-control pill pioneering company. I bought the car from Alex for a surprisingly low price, and I soon discovered why—at anything over room temperature the thing boiled like a tea kettle. It was a puzzle, because as the four-hundred-horsepower engine warmed up, an electric fan turned on to cool the radiator. It was only when I got down on my knees to look into the sharklike snout of the car that I discovered that the fan was trying to blow air in the wrong direction, that is, out the front of the car, fighting the natural incoming breeze from the speed. Boiling was the inevitable result. In custom-made cars like this, bad things can happen. The fan assembly was too big to be turned in the proper orientation, so I had to rewire the motor, making it run in the opposite direction, and also to turn the fan blades around on the shaft. Then the car worked perfectly and never overheated again. I kept the Ferrari for years, and it triggered a passion for collecting that has only recently abated.

Over the next twenty years I assembled one of the best collections of classic sports cars in the world. Most collectors specialize in a particular brand ("marque," to use the car nut's term). Germans, for example, love to collect Mercedes-Benz. But my collection was eclectic. I went after the crown jewels of each producing nation;

Tom and Gerd in their Bugatti Atlantic Elektron,
winning a first at Pebble Beach circa 1984

Gerd and I had Bugattis, Mercedes, Alfa Romeos, Bentleys, a Hispano-Suisa, a Squire, a Duesenberg, and many others. All (excepting the Hispano) were supercharged, and all were built between the two world wars. In 1984 I published a book about some of the cars in the collection, *Classic Supercharged Sports Cars*. Gerd and I enjoyed them immensely, and every year we participated in one or more car rallies in America or Europe.

By far the greatest of these were the AGM rallies (*Amis des Grandes Marques*—friends of the great marques) arranged for a small group of collectors by Michel Seydoux, one of the heirs to the Schlumberger fortune. Every participant was a keen collector and enthusiastic driver. The rallies were always in France over a five-day period, but rather than just driving around, Michel arranged ingenious events. Typically, a test of navigation was involved. But what a test! Each morning the participants, usually husband and wife, were issued a set of directions for the day, together with a bunch of sealed envelopes. Off we would go, on a staggered start. When we encountered an intersection on the back roads (invariably) selected, the directions might say something like: "Turn to follow the path of Charlemagne." The rally was an ingenious puzzle—the envelopes contained real directions to the next checkpoint, and the winner for the day was determined by which couple had opened the fewest, and arrived at the finish in the shortest time.

All of us were competitive, and the stresses called for in navigation were a severe test of married bliss. I remember one day when Gerd and I wound up following a recently married couple, and saw the frustrated bride furiously toss the maps, guidebooks, and instructions to the four winds out of the top of their roadster! Another time, Gerd and I were driving our very rare 1933 Triumph Dolomite (a Donald Healy knock-off of the 8-C Alfa Romero; he got sued by Alfa—hence the car's rarity) when we became seriously lost. The clouds were hovering low, and soon the heavens opened and the rain bucketed down into our open car in streaming torrents. We were totally soaked by the side of the road attempting to find a route from our nearly dissolving road map. I wondered how much fun Gerd was having. Then she started to laugh. The idiocy of our situation struck her, and she just couldn't stop laughing, hopeless laughter, the kind where you can't even speak—it wasn't long before I joined in. What silly fools we were, and what fun we had!

If I picked one single crowning event from these AGM rallies, it would be the day when Michel hired three hot air balloons, in three colors, to take off from the grounds of one of his estates. We assembled in our cars, organized into three groups by color of the balloons, to chase. By rising to different heights on this blustery day, surprisingly, the balloons scurried away in different directions, and

off we went. This is tricky driving, for the balloons don't follow any
road route, and one must study the map on the fly to stay ahead of
their course. Gerd was good at this. The things would descend and
I would run across the field to try to be first to obtain the chit from
the balloon pilot, but typically just before I reached the wicker bas-
ket, he would turn the heat back on and rise to carry on to a new
landing place. It was enormous fun, and our Bugatti roadster, originally built for Sir Malcolm Campbell, the former world speed
champion, was a perfect steed. (Some years later for a rally I organized in California for Bugatti Club members, I tried the same stunt.
The balloon rose straight up, hovered at a thousand feet, and after
about an hour, descended to within ten yards of its starting point.
Michel Seydoux was better at this.)

Collecting became all-consuming. There were only six Bugatti
Royals ever made and the then-famous giant collection assembled
by the late Bill Harrah, in Sparks, Nevada, had two of them; the four
others were all in museums. If I was ever going to own one of these
"holy grails," I would have to buy the whole Harrah collection, of
well over one thousand cars. I heard that Holiday Inn, who had acquired the Harrah casinos and hotels, also owned the collection and
might be interested in selling. I put a group of collector friends together, and I negotiated a purchase with Holiday Inn's management
in Memphis: ten million cash, another ten million in cash from a
bank loan secured by the collection, and a note from the seller for
the balance—a total of thirty million dollars. A couple of weeks before we were to sign, the governor of Nevada got into the act. He let
it be known that he considered the collection to be a vital part of
Nevada, responsible for attracting thousands of tourists, and he
would frown upon it being sold (his frown might possibly include
cancelling the companies' gambling licenses, my friends in Memphis feared). The deal was aborted, but to keep me calm they agreed
to sell me a Squire sports car—one of only seven made—so there
was a slightly happy ending. Holiday Inn agreed that the collection
did indeed attract thousands, but those visitors didn't gamble. After
the governor left office, they sold the mass of cars through a series of

auctions and other private sales (but not the Royals—which were donated to charity). By my rough estimate the auction proceeds greatly exceeded a quarter of a billion dollars: a ten-to-one return to my little group, had our offer been accepted.

I was a fanatic about restoring my cars to their original specifications, and the fame of my collection grew. I set up my own car restoration shop run by Phil Reilly, Ivan Zaremba, and gifted machinist Ross Cummings. These guys, all my friends, love cars and they are expert at restoring engines and rebuilding bodies. They did everything but the painting and they are still going strong, working now for other collectors.

I built the collection slowly, and though I paid, in many cases, record prices, the cars were skyrocketing in value. (If one is a collector, the reputation of overpaying assures you of seeing everything—this works equally well for venture opportunities.) In 1984 Gerd and I won best of show at the renowned Pebble Beach Concourse with our Mercedes 540K Special Roadster. I scoured the world looking for the finest examples and in the process I encountered a few of the dodgier types who, seemingly, infest all hobby businesses preying on the passion, if not the good judgment, of the dilettante participants.

There was a famous collector/restorer named Oscar Schmidt, an American who, apparently, had to flee his homeland to operate in France. It has been said that if Oscar had nine Bugattis, why not cannibalize them and make ten—after all, each would still be ninety percent authentic. Schmidt sold most of his automobile inventory to a restorer in Wisconsin—let's call him Steve Johnson—whom I was employing to restore a Type 55 Bugatti, a car so cute you wanted to hug it like a puppy. Most of the parts on this car were authentic, at least all had been made originally at the factory in Mosheim, France (now owned by Volkswagen, where the new thousand-horsepower Bugatti model Veyron is manufactured today).

While visiting Steve one day he showed me the remaining bits of an ultra, ultra-rare Buccialli TAV 12. The Buccialli brothers were, ultimately, more showmen than car builders, but every year their offering for the Paris car show, from the late twenties to the Second World War, was sensational. Their only claim to technical fame was for the (alleged) invention of the front-wheel drive (the TAV — *traction avont*) but always their cars were incredibly beautiful — literal showstoppers. The car in Steve's barn was the remains of the most famous of all, the Paris show star of 1932, with a twelve-cylinder Voisin engine (in itself this motor was a marvel; incorporating twenty-four sliding sleeve valves for virtually silent running) with a stunning body by the most famous of the Parisian custom builders: Saoutchik.

The pile of parts on the ground wasn't encouraging. The rare engine and the rarer front wheel drive (a massive and possibly impractical thing) were evident, together with the huge wheels, rising nearly to the waist. It was these wheels, as high as the top of the engine hood, which gave the car in photographs its fabulous good looks. Parts of the body were there and a lot of other stuff, but the car's chassis was missing. In car collecting it's the chassis which is most important for authenticity; it is considered the backbone, and though easy to make, without the original any serious restoration would be foolish financially. Steve told me that he had tracked down the original chassis in Europe and that it was on its way over in a container. After it arrived and Steve confirmed that the engine and other running parts fit perfectly — it was undoubtedly the one from the show car — I decided to proceed and to re-create the other less important missing pieces. I realized that this was going to be a hugely expensive undertaking, but the truly extraordinary beauty and rarity of the car made the goal worthwhile. Steve delivered my Type 55, and got started on the Buccialli. The project dragged on. And on.

As was my practice, I kept in touch by phone and I found ways to visit Steve in upper Wisconsin. It was during one of these visits, when he left me alone to run some errands, that a youth barely out of high school, accompanied me outside the barn when I went for a cigarette. After some shy talk from him about nothing much in particular, he said: "You know, I made the chassis for the TAV 12."

What?! The chassis looked very old, in serious need of restoration. It was flaked with rust and had the unmistakable patina
of age.

"When I finished we buried it for six months. I thought you
ought to know."

As soon as Steve returned I confronted him, and he didn't deny
the fake. I called the sheriff, we seized the parts, and I had Phil Reilly
send a truck back to collect everything. I never proceeded against
Steve for the deception; after all, I should have known better, and
didn't feel the need for further public embarrassment. Amazingly,
even accompanied by a letter from me pointing out that the chassis
was a fake, I sold the parts to another collector. Over a million was
spent restoring the car, and it was so beautiful when completed that
I almost wished that I had done the project as planned. More amazingly, the car was later auctioned by a very prominent house, claiming it to have been in my (now very famous) collection. With the
benefit of a lawyer, I sent them a letter pointing out that the chassis
was fake, and insisting that they acknowledge this via an insert in the
catalogue. To my knowledge they never complied, though perhaps
they informed the buyer. It took extreme willpower to not bid on
that wonderful flawed dream myself.

As the eighties drew to a close the Japanese, in particular, seemed
to be buying with abandon. This was a time when a square foot of
real estate in Tokyo was selling for zillions, and when the famous
van Gogh, *Sunflowers*, was bought by a Japanese businessman for
forty million dollars, a record sum. Classic cars were fetching obscene prices in Tokyo, ten to one hundred times what I had paid,
and I had the best ones of all.

During a business trip to Japan in 1987, I got a very uncomfortable feeling about the stability of their economy. I remember the
chairman of Nomura Securities assuring me that a price-to-earnings
ratio of sixty-five for the Tokyo Stock Index (at the time the Dow-
Jones PE ratio was about ten) was "as stable as Mount Fuji." (Hell,
the damn thing is a volcano!) As I was flying home I thought to
myself, "If I am right, they'll stop buying cars—the market will
collapse."

Though I had never acquired a car as an investment, I was not oblivious to the fact that my cars had become worth a fortune. It's one thing to take one of these classics on a happy spin when it's worth some tens of thousands, but pretty foolish to do so when it's worth, maybe, millions. I decided to sell the lot. Charles Howard, my London car broker friend, feared that I might single-handedly destroy the market. But we set about to do it. I personally dealt with Ralph Lauren, who was interested in my best gem, a rare (one of three) Bugatti Atlantic Elektron coupes (*Elektron* was the French name for the metal alloy used in the riveted body panels). This car was considered by a number of experts to be the most beautiful automobile ever created. Ralph and his wife, Ricky, flew from New York to San Francisco in his G-4 jet just to look at the stunning Bugatti.

It was August, and one of the hottest days of the year. Ralph was dressed impeccably, as one might expect, in jacket and tie, and we took off from my warehouse/machine shop and showroom down the freeway, with me behind the wheel babbling on about the splendors of the car, hoping that I could keep his mind off the extreme discomfort we were experiencing. The coupe was incredibly hot! Unfortunately, the highly stylized art deco windows couldn't be opened more than a crack, and heat was pouring in from the engine compartment. Plus the noise from the motor was nearly deafening and the visibility from the tiny rear window virtually nonexistent. By the time we returned, it was if we had been in a very hot sauna fully clothed! I couldn't wait to get out of the damn thing, and I assumed that Ralph would never buy it. But as he closed the door, he smiled at me and said, "Great car!" I knew that the hook was set. As he left after signing a check, I asked what a G-4 cost, and he said that I could easily buy one for the price of the Elektron. Ralph still loves the car, won best of show at Pebble Beach, and sometimes features it in his advertising. All my cars were sold in under a month, each at a world-record price for the marque. Charles said that I had proven that the values were rock (Fuji) solid.

I was about seven months early in my prediction of the collapse of the Japanese economy. As I had suspected, Japanese classic-car buyers dumped them on the market, and the entire phenomenon of cars as an investment tanked and has yet to recover fully. I doubt that it ever will. Now Charles says that only Henry Ford made more money in cars than I did . . . maybe.

Well, break's over. Let's get back to work,

and to the story of founding Kleiner & Perkins.

Chapter Six

A New Partnership, and a New Approach,
Change the Venture Landscape

Late in the fall of 1972 two totally displaced Californians could be found wandering the Midwest trying to raise capital: Eugene Kleiner, urbane, Viennese-accented, and aristocratic looking, and Tom Perkins, tall, lean, and impatient. Things weren't going all that well. We were driving north from Milwaukee, where we had struck out, failing to raise a penny from a big insurance company there. We were now on our way to Stevens Point, where we would try again. I always drove on these journeys, because being a passenger with Gene was just too nerve-wracking for me; he tended to drift off the road while conversing. As we talked in our rented car, we reviewed our pitch and the events that had taken us into this Wisconsin wilderness.

University Labs had, for me, been about as complete a success as one could imagine. From the initial idea through the development, the financing, and the ultimate liquidity, all had gone as planned. Of course I had help from many others, but it had been my baby, so to speak, and I had, most importantly, played the role of venture capitalist from start to finish. So it seemed reasonable for me to plan a career to do it over and over again. I had in mind more of a hands-on approach than was the mode at the time.

In the early seventies there was venture capital to be found, but the numbers were small both in the dollars and in the number of people involved. The total pool of true venture capital at the time—that is, capital available to be invested in high-tech start-ups—has been estimated to have been much less than one hundred million dollars throughout the United States, and all the practitioners could easily be assembled into one moderately sized room. The aforementioned Draper Gaither and Anderson group had dissolved, and General Doriot's American Research and Development wasn't doing much in start-ups, nor was it active on the West Coast. Instead, a handful of individuals with varying amounts of capital were placing bets. Two groups were most prominent: Sutter Hill, representing a Canadian corporation, and Davis and Rock, representing a number of limited partners. Additionally, John Bryan and Bill Edwards and Franklin "Pitch" Johnson were writing checks from their personal accounts. New York "old money" was also evident, principally the Rockefellers, the Whitneys, and the Bessemer group. But all these investors could more properly be called financiers than "operators" of the kind I had in mind. In my view, they spent most of their time in up-front analysis, rather than in after-the-fact management of the developing venture. To denigrate the approach, perhaps unfairly, it was more like a Las Vegas place-your-bets-and-take-your-chances experience than controlling the game itself, which is what I had in mind.

I thought that ventures could be managed like development projects within a corporation; the example of Packard and Hewlett, who were both marvelous entrepreneurs and superb managers, was at the forefront of my mind. In such projects, first the technical risk is reduced and then the other resources are added to build the business. The idea that the whole venture should be born complete, Venus-like, did not seem necessary, or even desirable, to me. But to become a player I needed more capital than I alone could provide. I knew Peter Crisp, a prominent figure in managing the Rockefeller family investments from the famous Room 5600, a whole floor in the Rockefeller Center in New York. Peter was impressed with my plans, and he "circled" one million dollars from the Rockefeller University's endowment (which he managed) for my fund, assuming that I could pull the remainder together. This was a good start, but I needed help for the bulk of the fund. I contacted an acquaintance and San Francisco investment banker, Sandy Robertson, to give me a boost. Sandy said that he had another friend, Eugene Kleiner, who "is just like you and who is trying to do the same thing—you guys have to meet each other."

Gene admitted to me later that he was just as reluctant to meet me as I had been to meet him. Our breakfast at Ricky's Hyatt House on El Camino in Palo Alto was arranged simply as a courtesy to Sandy, and neither of us expected the meeting to last more than thirty minutes. In appearance and temperament we couldn't have been less similar. I have been characterized as being able to radiate tension by just walking into a room; this is among the kinder things said about my personality. Gene, on the other hand, was soothing and calm, portly but elegant in demeanor with a cultivated manner of speech. I often thought his would be the tone Sigmund Freud would have used with a patient on the couch.

He had a fascinating background. Born and raised in Vienna,

Eugene Kleiner circa 1974

he, his parents, and his sister had fled Hitler's occupation of Austria shortly before the outbreak of World War II. They all made it, but Gene, separated from the others, had to follow a long route through Portugal and South America, and it was nearly two years before the family was united safely again in Brooklyn, New York. Gene joined the U.S. Army and served with distinction, returning to attend Brooklyn Polytechnic on the GI Bill at the war's end. He found employment at Bell Telephone Laboratories (at that time the world's preeminent research organization), where he encountered William Shockley, co-inventor of the transistor. When Shockley Semiconductor was founded in Palo Alto, Gene joined the start-up, along with the other scientists and engineers who all became very famous when they left as a group to found the pioneering Fairchild Semiconductor Company. That was the organization from which, eventually, the entire Silicon Valley can be said to have evolved. While at Fairchild, Gene Kleiner ran every department at one time or another, save research. With all the instincts of an entrepreneur, he then founded Edex Corporation, a venture in the teaching machine business, which he sold to Raytheon for a profit in the millions. Along the way, he became one of the founding investors in Intel, and a limited partner of Davis and Rock.

After Gene and I shared backgrounds over breakfast, we discussed our ideas for venture capital. To our surprise, we discovered that we were thinking along identical lines. The breakfast carried on through lunch and then to meetings at our respective homes. At the end of two days we decided that we complemented each other and that we should team up. With Gene's assistance I wrote a prospectus for Kleiner & Perkins. In rereading it now, some three decades later, I am amazed at how clearly we foresaw our future and how closely we followed our formula. Our emphasis was on management of ventures, and we had a chapter called "Making It Happen," detailing the differences between our approach and our competitors'. Another innovation was our "Investor's Bill of Rights."

Both of us had participated in various partnerships in oil, real estate, and cattle breeding, and all with the same miserable results. The best example was a call I once received from the general partner of a feed lot tax shelter who said, "Tom, your cows died." Under our bill no profits, ever, could accrue to us, the general partners, until the investor's capital had been returned in full. Further, all profits would be returned to the investors as they were achieved and not be reinvested in new opportunities. Thus the partnership would automatically run out of cash and would have to be renewed with a new partnership if the business was to continue. In this way the investors could see an end, and not be locked in for the indefinite future, and good money would not be invested after bad. To emphasize that aspect, we put a specific limit (eight years) on the life of the pool, so that it had to be wound up.

Additionally, and this was both unique and very important, Gene and I were to be specifically proscribed from putting partnership money into anything in which we, personally, had an investment, or an inside track. This corrected the practice, which we thought unethical, of putting investors into stocks for dollars per share that had already been purchased for pennies per share by the managing partners (this abuse was not uncommon at the time). Beyond this, we would invest in the partnership as limited partners, thereby putting us on exactly the same basis as all the investors. We would not, thus, cherry-pick for ourselves among any of the prospective ventures. And finally, we would not invest in anything whatsoever that was within the remit of the partnership. In other words, we could not use the partnership as a sort of lighthouse to attract ventures that we then might take for ourselves. Probably today this all sounds obvious and routine, but at the time it was not, and I think it has been the enormous success of Kleiner & Perkins and the follow-on partnerships that forced these standards upon the whole current multibillion-dollar high-tech venture industry. But our model still is not universal. Today I stand in awe at the way the managing partners of some of the huge buyout funds reward themselves: fees for raising the fund, fees for managing the fund, fees for doing the deals within the fund, and profit participation from individual investments whether or not overall profits are achieved. In one of these giant funds *your* cows can still die.

As I had a million dollars circled from the Rockefellers, so Gene had circled four times this amount from Henry Hillman, the Pittsburgh billionaire. Our first step, then, was to get our two "circlers" to agree on combining our two putative funds into a single larger one. We had decided to raise ten million dollars, and if the Rockefellers and Henry Hillman agreed to our plan, we would be halfway home. Peter Crisp agreed for the Rockefellers over the phone, but Henry wanted to meet me in person.

Henry is among the richest and, by careful design, least-known powerful individuals in America. He made his billions the traditional way: he inherited millions from his father (the last of the true breed of Pittsburgh "robber barons"—coal, canals, shipping, and smokestack industries) and then multiplied the fortune many, many times. I first met him in his Pittsburgh tower, the Grant Building, which he sold to the Japanese at the top of the market and then repurchased, years later, at the bottom. He took pride in the fact that the Hillman companies were invested in virtually everything in the U.S. industrial index—missing only high-tech venture industries. He owned, I recall, a large percentage of all the 747 jets in the world, leased to numerous airlines, and some of the largest real-estate investments in America. Tracts of downtown Boston belonged to Henry. But venture capital was a void in his portfolio. He loved technology, and he was fascinated when I showed him on my HP 35 pocket calculator how to calculate the compounding of capital at ten percent per annum. He had never seen Bill Hewlett's invention, but he certainly understood the potential of venture capital. He accepted our plan to combine forces, and he offered to provide fifty percent of the eventual total capital. I asked, "Why fifty percent, Henry?" His answer: "So that my phone calls will be returned."

With fifty percent of our potential fund in the bag, Gene and I were optimistic for the balance. With a hunting list provided by Sandy Robertson we started our fund-raising tour, and we started to strike out almost immediately. None of the contacts in Manhattan were impressed. The fact that we both had been managers of big operations, and that we both had been successful entrepreneurs, didn't impress; we weren't financiers, and that's what mattered to them. Gene's friends, the cofounders of Intel, Bob Noyce and Gordon Moore, invested a couple hundred thousand dollars (after extracting a promise from us that we would hold our salaries to no more than fifty percent of their previous levels), but even these big names weren't big enough to pull in other investors. We gave our pitch to about a dozen prospects on the East Coast with no luck, until we tried again in the Midwest. The Anderson family of Rockford, Illinois, clients of Sandy, agreed to sign up for a modest amount. (The Andersons have been in all subsequent K & P and KPC & B partnerships, our longest-term limited partners. Their charitable donations from the proceeds from these partnerships are of significant importance in their community.) We had had no luck in Milwaukee, and now we were on our way to Stevens Point to visit Sentry Insurance.

We were well received at Sentry and were nearly startled when the chief financial officer said, "Okay, sign us up." They liked the idea of a couple of Valley "techies" visiting them in Stevens Point; it may have been a first. On the strength of their endorsement I asked our host if he would call his counterpart at another insurance company in the nearby town of Wausau. My dad had worked his whole career for Wausau Insurance (Employers Mutual Insurance of Wausau), and I had spent a few years in the town as a grade-school kid. That place has probably the coldest winters on the planet; I remember that our postman froze to death one morning while he paused to rest along his route. (That was, of course, long before Al Gore became alarmed about global warming.) So after only a couple of hours' notice, Gene and I essentially made an unannounced call on the company when we arrived in town. Their CFO was polite, and when I offered that I had grown up on Ruder Street (how I remembered that street name I'll never know), he beamed with pride that a local boy had actually returned; perhaps another first. Incredibly, we made that sale too! So in a brief Midwest swing, we had brought our fund up to over the seven million mark.

However, that was the last of the easy money. Trips to Los Angeles and repeat visits to New York yielded only modest additional commitments. We were stuck at eight million total, and we realized that our goal of ten million was unobtainable, at least in a reasonable time frame. And we started to worry that some of our circled investors might slip away if we didn't close. That's when Gene said, "When the money is available—take it." I kidded him ever after that he had expostulated Kleiner's First Law; there were more to come. His most profound, I always thought, was "The more difficult the decision, the less it matters what you choose." Think about it.

So, short of our goal at the end of 1972, we drew down the eight million and established Kleiner & Perkins. It seems incredible to point out that this pool of capital, tiny by today's standards, was the largest fund in the entire world devoted to high-tech venture capital. The local comments were all negative, along the lines of: "It's too much. How can they possibly invest that much?" The great irony is that the locals were entirely correct!

We set up our office on Sand Hill Road in Menlo Park (now famous as the Wall Street of venture capital), and we hired two additional partners, both of whom had worked for me at HP: Jack Loustaunou, a financial guru, and a marketing whiz, Jimmy Treybig (who had been in charge of HP's computer peripherals). And then . . . nothing happened.

The telephone didn't ring, entrepreneurs didn't troop to our door, in spite of our efforts to promote ourselves. Gene and I spoke to every group a notch above the Boy Scouts that showed the slightest interest in hearing from us. We contacted numerous professors at the University of California and Stanford, and we wrote articles for the local papers. Still, no proposals flowed to our fund. We did begin to receive business plans through the mail, however, which we dutifully read—except those written in crayon (we knew that those were from inmates in mental institutions, and that the staff didn't trust the writers with anything sharper). I confess, right now, that K & P and KPC & B has never financed any plan that arrived through the mail. If the entrepreneur can't figure out some personal approach, it's just too hopeless to consider. But we read them anyway.

This was a tough time for Gene and me. We both had financial interests outside of the partnership—for Gene it was Intel, and for me it was Spectra Physics, the firm that had acquired my laser company. I was on the Spectra board and I think I nearly drove Herb Dwight, the company CEO, nuts with my "help." There was one board meeting when he became so frustrated with my interference that he climbed up on the boardroom table and walked up and down on it as he argued against my criticisms. I have forgotten the specifics, but I'll never forget the demonstration—somehow we remained friends.

K & P needed ventures! When you have a fund, there is pressure to invest; it is embarrassing to report the lack of progress each quarter to the limited partners. We began to haunt our competitors. Thankfully, Bill Draper of Sutter Hill let us participate in one of their investments with Qume, a printer company. It proved to be a good investment, and one on which we made a respectable return. But three start-ups we did thereafter were embarrassing disasters. The first was a semiconductor start-up in which we investors saw our money drain away like water poured onto desert sands by the inexperienced management.

The second, Tread-Two, had a longer life, but it too failed. A young entrepreneur had the idea of resoling expensive tennis shoes with new bottoms. The venture began to succeed, and thousands of boxes of shoes arrived, each containing a ten-dollar bill to pay for the new sole—so the business was in effect self-financing. But when he decided to come out with his own brand of shoe he was up against Nike and Adidas, and the inventory requirements and advertising took an enormous infusion of cash that we couldn't raise. We wouldn't commit it ourselves, so it too failed.

The third sounds the most ridiculous, and it was the idea that Jimmy and I talked Gene into having K & P back. It was called Snow-Job—admittedly a most dubious name, but that's what it was really called. We met an inventor who had figured out how to convert a motorcycle into a snowmobile. It really worked. I had a ball with the prototype in the snow fields up in the foothills of the Sierras for a whole day. It was much faster and more maneuverable than a conventional snowmobile, and it could be converted from one to the other in a few minutes. We put the money in, but before we had

Hell's Angels and their biker girlfriends on their hogs tearing up the pristine fields of snow, the government, in response to one of the country's fuel crises, outlawed the sale of gasoline for sports vehicles. That ban was later lifted, but at the critical moment we couldn't get dealers to stock our Snow-Jobs, so that venture crashed too.

If K & P hadn't been on the threshold of becoming arguably the most successful investment vehicle in the history of man, I wouldn't admit to all this stupidity. But after these failures, Gene and I changed our strategy. We decided to create our own start-ups.

■ ■ ■

Jimmy Treybig played a huge role in the transformation of K & P. We hired him because of his general marketing skills and not specifically for his computer background, but his computer savvy was excellent. He had the germ of an idea that he and I began to kick around. The idea was to design a computer that could not fail, to be used in mission-critical applications, of which there are many throughout industry. Both HP and IBM offered such systems, but they were simply lash-ups of conventional computers. They were very expensive, slow, and not really fail-safe in the fullest sense. Jimmy thought that an entirely new approach might be possible, one in which multiple computers all worked together, with no redundancy. Instead they would self-check each other, so that if one failed the others would take over. Since, often, computers don't simply fail, but rather "go crazy" and try to erase data, or write infinite streams of ones or zeros, the sane computers in the system would vote, and isolate the "mad" processor from further participation. The idea was extremely ambitious technically; it had never been previously attempted. But Jimmy and I agreed that if it could be invented, a large market could be found.

Our afternoons became dominated by this idea. Jimmy and I made diagrams of how the logic might work, and we couldn't prove to ourselves that it couldn't be done, so we took the step of hiring consultants, true experts, to see if it could be done. Mike Green was a software expert from HP and Jim Katzman was his hardware coun-

Jimmy Treybig shortly after
founding Tandem Computers

terpart. These guys, together with Bill Davidow, who had a PhD in computer science, started to work on the ideas Jimmy and I had sketched. The most difficult problem in clusters of interacting computers is that of "contention," that is, how to handle the problem of access when two processors request the communication circuits at precisely the same instant. This problem was solved, for the first time in computer systems, by our little group. But the real innovation was in the software operating system. I'll spare you the technicalities, save to say that it was packet-message-based, expandable to huge numbers of systems, and so hardware-independent that it survives to this day having been reimplemented through numerous generations of processor hardware. That system, which we called the "nonstop kernel," is one of the great breakthroughs in computer technology, and it led to a multibillion-dollar success.

We decided, after much debate, to call the nascent venture Tandem Computers—my vote for Datadyne lost out. We had fun naming things; names of my choice that did prevail included my Lasertron and, later, Computed Sonography for the company Acuson. After we persuaded Gene of the virtue of our ideas it was time to proceed. There was never any doubt as to who would become the CEO: Jimmy was the only name on the list, and Jack, our financial guy, decided to become the CFO. I signed on as chairman, with the job of raising the money.

I showed our business plan, which I had mostly written myself, to all the local potential investors with no luck. A trip with Jimmy back east fared no better. But the more we struck out, the more convinced we became that we were on the right track. The investors' rejection was based solely on general worries over the companies in the field: IBM, DEC, and HP. They had little understanding of the technical breakthrough we had achieved and how difficult it would be for those competitors to duplicate our effort and circumvent our patents already in application. These were financiers, after all, who maybe were clever with money but who had no feeling for or confidence in technology, the kind of investors who relied upon hired experts to tell them what to think.

Gene and I decided to finance the whole company, staking a very significant portion of our fund on the idea. Probably it was a courageous decision, but at the time we thought it to be a sure bet. In fact, every time I have written a check, I have felt utterly confident of winning. Then when I lose, it somehow gets buried in a different part of my brain, and doesn't get in the way of the next check. Gene and I were both on the Tandem board, with me as chairman; it was similar to University Labs, except that I could work on Tandem full-time, when needed. At the last instant before closing the contract, "Pitch" Johnson, a prominent Palo Alto private player, invested a token amount from his own pocket. The money wasn't enough to make much difference, but his endorsement of the idea was gratifying, and his investment had the great advantage of involving his associate, Brook Byers, into our mix. Brook would, in due course, play a major role in our future.

Tandem Computers is well known in the Valley and today, after its acquisition (first by Compaq and then by HP through the Compaq acquisition) it continues to occupy the top of the pyramid of HP's computer offerings. Tandem dominates the market for large fault-tolerant applications, with eighty percent of the world's stock exchanges, most of the credit networks, automated gas pump credit card systems, and so forth. You most likely depend upon some Tandem system somewhere every day in your routine activities; when you use your credit card, make a long distance call, buy or sell a stock, and so on. I am not going to take you through the history of the company, however. Rather I will simply point out that it fully validated the K & P approach of hands-on management of ventures, which became our trademark. I, as chairman, participated in every major step in its history, even writing the prospectus for its initial public offering and guiding its road show. That IPO was a big success when it came out in 1977; it put K & P on the map—and it put me off investment bankers for the remainder of my business career.

The term *investment banker* is marvelously misleading. Even the greatest firms on Wall Street have little to do with investments, and even less to do with banking, in the marketing of an IPO. The term *fee-charging middlemen* is clearly less attractive, but it's much closer to an accurate description of their actual function. The Securities and Exchange Commission (SEC) requires a road show, staged by the bankers, for the client enterprise wishing to raise capital from the public. This is part of the due diligence necessary to disclose the risks of the offering to the investing public. The bankers use the tour to build a book of orders for the prospective issue, so that the offering is effectively sold, and frequently oversold by a factor of two or three, in advance. The syndicate of bankers typically dissolves immediately on the first trade and the bankers almost never have to actually purchase (underwrite) the issue, and thereby take any risk, whatsoever, in the transaction.

The cynicism of these investment professionals is profound— shocking, really. The Tandem IPO had two firms heading the syndication, a New York outfit and a San Francisco bunch. (Both firms are now, deservedly in my opinion, long defunct.) In the fall of 1977, around Thanksgiving, I was at the biggest of the New York lunches for investors. Before I stood up to speak, the senior partner of the New York banking firm said to me, "Just look at them! They are all turkeys! Tom, you only need to stand up and say *gobble, gobble, gobble!*" At the San Francisco end, we discovered a rash of short sales, unusual for an IPO. Shorting is selling something you don't (yet) own. When you buy a stock, all you can lose is what you paid, assuming that it tanks and winds up with zero value. But when you sell what you don't own, by shorting, you have to cover eventually by buying the shares that you must deliver. There is a Wall Street limerick about this: "He who sells what isn't his'n, either delivers or goes to prison." If you bet wrong and the stock goes up and not down, you will have to pay more than what you received when you shorted—so there might be no limit to what you could lose. Shorting is dangerous and is rarely encountered in the clients of an investment banker managing or comanaging an IPO. I thought our banker should have discouraged the practice, as it can have a negative effect on the new company's stock price. Fortunately in Tandem's case, the shorters lost big-time as the price rose quickly in trading and the rise was then enchanced as the shorters scrambled to buy shares to cover their obligation to deliver.

Indeed, investors who bought shares on the IPO and held on eventually made twenty to one on their investment.

After decades of dealing with investment bankers, I find them to be exceptionally short-term-oriented; their focus is entirely on the transaction of that instant and their specific fee for that transaction. As my partner Frank Caufield says, "They have all the self-restraint of lobotomized sharks."

You may well ask: "If you are so disgusted with investment bankers why do you continue to deal with them?" You have a good question there. It's because they are the SEC-licensed gatekeepers to accessing the public market for capital; they are a necessary evil. Maybe, somehow, eventually through the Internet there will be a way around the bankers—powerful Google tried this in a hybrid IPO offering with both bankers and the Net; in my opinion with a very unfortunate result for the company because of, I think, the behind-the-scenes machinations of the bankers. At the end of the world, after the sharks have long gone, the investment bankers will out-survive the cockroaches. There is only one major exception: Bill Hambrecht, a San Francisco investment banker of uncompromised lifelong virtue . . . but, alas, he is a hopeless liberal Democrat!

Gradually Sand Hill Road began to accumulate other venture capitalists. Stanford University was proving to be a magnet for entrepreneurs and Kleiner & Perkins was proving that serious money could be made in venture capital; our success did not go unheralded. But Gene and I were uncomfortable in their company. We didn't want them to see who we were taking to lunch; we didn't want to be considered part of the flock. Eagles don't flock, was our joke. We moved our office to a tower top in San Francisco's Embarcadero Center and were there from the mid-seventies to the mid-eighties. Eventually we had so many Valley employees that we relocated back to Menlo Park, where we remain headquartered today, with our San Francisco office only a satellite. In our first year in the city we undertook our next significant venture, and we were also nearly wiped out financially—I'll deal with that near-catastrophe first.

Perhaps taking Kleiner's First Law too literally, Gene and I drew down the investor's full eight million dollars at the outset, rather than calling it down over time as the need for more cash arose, which was the practice we instituted in all subsequent partnerships. So we had cash in millions earning only the very low rates available from government bonds. We wanted to take no risk with this capital base; our ventures provided ample risk for the invested capital once committed. However, we heard about a prominent arbitrageur who was achieving excellent returns on playing bond spreads in the public market. When done properly every spread is hedged, so that the only risk possible is the loss of interest on the specific contract. (If this isn't clear to you, don't worry. We didn't exactly understand it either.) We checked the man's references, and he was praised to the sky by his clients, so we committed one million dollars to his management. The initial results were most encouraging: a return in the vicinity of thirty percent per annum! Since these arbitrage contracts were complex, I asked Gerry Myers, the gal who replaced Jack as our financial officer, to check them carefully, to be sure that for every short, or sell, there was a matching long, or buy, so that all the bets were hedged. The worst error would be to be "naked," or unhedged, and thus exposed to the unlimited risk (as explained in talking about the banker and the Tandem offering) of being on the wrong side of a short transaction. The contracts were complicated, typically requiring multiple transactions for a single hedge; very esoteric stuff. After some months, late one Friday afternoon, Gerry came into my office in tears. She said, "Tom, I just can't figure all this out. I can't make any of the recent stuff balance." I gathered the numerous trading slips and stuffed them into my briefcase, and I said in the most condescending way that I would do the balancing over the weekend and explain it all to her on Monday.

By Sunday night I was in a state of the purest panic! The contracts weren't even remotely hedged: our guru had put Gene and me into a naked, totally exposed short position of tens of millions of dollars! In trading these sorts of options it is possible to leverage one's capital hugely. It's an extreme case of trading on the margin. In our instance the arbitrageur had ignored his promise never to leave us uncovered and I found that we were vastly short. These kinds of transactions depend upon their profit by exploiting the tiniest of changes in interest rates between the two sides of a hedged spread. But with our being naked to the tune of countless millions (that we didn't have), a swing in interest rates could wipe us out—totally! Gene and I were personally at risk as the general partners; we could be destroyed in a few minutes in tomorrow's bond market. I called Gene at home and we agreed to meet our arbitrageur with our lawyer first thing in the morning.

Bruce Mann, our top-flight attorney, cautioned me to be silent as he explained the breach in procedure to the bond jockey in the latter's office. Maybe the guy was a crook, maybe he was a genius, but for sure as Bruce patiently explained, he was wrong. As our lawyer calmly developed his arguments on our behalf, I found myself trembling. I found that another person, actually a raging vicious beast, was inhabiting my body. Suddenly, I sprang up and nearly leapt across the table—later Gene told me that I was definitely frothing at the mouth—and I threatened the arbitrageur with horrible, terrible physical mayhem if he didn't immediately make full restitution! Bruce and Gene forcibly dragged me out of the place. They were still scolding me back in our offices when a messenger arrived with a check for the full amount. Apparently I had convinced the guy that I would, quite literally, kill him! We cashed the check. Nothing was lost. He went bust in a huge wipe-out some months later. And, to you Kleiner & Perkins partners of that period who are reading this for the first time, I apologize—it has taken me over thirty years to confess to this episode.

■   ■   ■

To replace Jimmy Treybig, in 1975 we hired Bob Swanson, a fledgling venture capitalist working in San Francisco for Citicorp Ventures. He was, coincidentally, the roommate of Brook Byers, whom we were getting to know through his involvement with Tandem. Bob enabled us to use the Tandem formula again, of spinning out a venture directly from the partnership. In Bob's case the venture was Genentech, one of the most successful companies ever created, and by any measure the highlight of my venture career.

Gene and Bob were both on the board of the early failed semiconductor company, and Gene believed that you could get a better handle on an investor's character in adversity than when things were going well. He thought that Bob's tenacity would be an asset, and when Bob became restless at Citicorp we offered him a partner's role with K & P. He was from MIT with a degree in organic chemistry and a master's from the Sloan School in business, both of which he obtained in just four years—smart guy! We had made an investment in a start-up in Berkeley named Cetus, founded by two medical doctors, Drs. Ronald Cape and Peter Farley. Their plan was to develop a new generation of instruments for use in biological laboratories. Labs hadn't changed much since the days of Louis Pasteur, and we thought that cell counters, and the automation of such other routine measurements, might be promising. However, in our opinion they were very slow in getting off the mark. It has often been said

Bob Swanson shortly after
founding Genentech

that a sense of urgency is the key ingredient required for a successful entrepreneur, and we were worried that Cetus didn't have enough of that ingredient. So we put Bob on the case as the partner in charge of the investment.

Bob would never be accused of lacking a sense of urgency. He spent much time at Cetus trying to spur the company into something that could lead to success. He became fascinated by biotech, at that time not highly developed beyond the era of antibiotics. With the hope of inspiring the two founding entrepreneurs, Bob arranged a brainstorming lunch with them and Professor Donald Glaser (winner of the Nobel Prize in physics in 1960), who was actually a minor founding shareholder in the company, and who was well under way in his second career in biophysics at Cal. Bob invited me to come along.

Glaser was amazing—a veritable fountain of ideas—none of which seemed to make much impression upon the two founders. During the discussion, the professor mentioned the pioneering work being done at the University of California Medical School by Herb Boyer, and that at Stanford being done by Stan Cohen, in the area of cutting and splicing strands of DNA (now commonly called gene splicing). Almost in passing, he said that it might be possible to use this new technology to create useful artificial genes (this is now commonly called recombinant genetic engineering). The idea, frankly, went over my head, and apparently it meant nothing to the Cetus founders either. But Bob caught its importance immediately, and he spent the next several weeks reading up on the technology and simultaneously urging Drs. Cape and Farley to take the possibility seriously. I caught some of his enthusiasm, and I called the two doctors, offering to loan Bob full-time to the company to help them, maybe, develop a potential business in the new science. They weren't interested. I'll not dwell further on Cetus, or my opinion of the company, except to say that after many years Cetus fell upon the technique of polymerase chain reaction (PCR) that won a Nobel Prize for their chemist, Kary Mullis, and led to their acquisition in 1991 by Chiron Corp. Eventually every pig finds its truffle.

Meanwhile, Bob had caught on fire. He had become fascinated with the idea of creating genes and developing whole new products from the technology. Imagine, he would say: we might be able to mass-produce anything, anything, that has DNA and that exists in nature—after we have done that we can move on to producing anything that doesn't exist in nature but that should exist! This could change the world! In medicine it could make antibiotics look like a small step! We could make rubber! We could make silk! It's the most important thing in our lifetime!

He pestered Professor Boyer on the phone, trying to get a meeting. Finally Herb agreed to five minutes on a late Friday afternoon. That meeting was possibly one of the most significant meetings of minds since that between Bill Hewlett and David Packard. Since we are still probably on the ground floor of what Genentech created, maybe it was even more important.

The five minutes lasted many hours, and spilled from Herb's lab into a nearby bar where a number of beers were consumed. Herb was not against the possibility of using the DNA cutting and splicing technology for commercial purposes; he just thought it too early. He and Professor Cohen held the basic patents (assigned to their respective universities and called the "restriction enzyme patents"). Boyer simply believed that the technology was too primitive to be commercialized. He thought perhaps another ten years of basic work at the university level would be required. Bob, however, kept repeating the questions: "Why will it take so long? What if you could bypass the whole cycle of writing proposals for government grants? What if you had all the money you needed up front? Would it then really take so long?" The more Bob pressed, the more Herb began to rethink. Maybe it really could be done faster. Over the weekend they continued to explore the idea of establishing a business right away. Within a week or so, Bob had drawn up a business plan that he put upon my desk, enthusiastically expounding on the idea and on why I should back the venture.

Twice before I had mastered new technologies, in lasers and in computers, so the technical aspect didn't daunt me too much. I figured that I could learn it. But it was immediately clear that this idea was verging upon pure research. Venture capitalists shouldn't *knowingly* fund pure research, everyone knew that; that's a ticket for losing millions—in pure research, by definition, there may be no payback—if the payback were guaranteed it wouldn't be research. And Bob was proposing, literally, to create a new form of life. In other words the idea was to assemble a desired gene, and somehow trick a bacterial cell into hosting it. This microbial Frankenstein would then have synthetic DNA possibly enabling it to produce a new substance entirely alien and unnecessary to its normal existence. Forgetting Darwin, would *God* permit us to create such a strange and unnatural new form of life?

Further, the plan called for an investment of nearly two million dollars. Space would be acquired, equipment purchased, scientists hired, and after all that, the experiment attempted — what if it didn't work? I didn't reject the idea out of hand. Instead, I asked to meet Dr. Boyer to hear his ideas directly. Bob quickly arranged the meeting, and for the first time Herb came up to our penthouse office in the Embarcadero Center to meet me. He was obviously brilliant. (What surprised me most, though, was his charm. That encounter was the beginning of a friendship continuing to this day.) Rather than get into an explanation of the scientific details, which I knew would quickly be over my head, all my questions were oriented along the lines of, what (specific) equipment will you need? How long will it take to the first step? How will you test to see if you have the expected results, and (again) what equipment will be required for the tests? Herb had all the answers. He had thought through each step in detail and could identify all the critical checkpoints. While he couldn't guarantee the result of the experiment, he clearly knew how to undertake the experiment in a very specific way. I was impressed.

The next morning I sat down with Bob for the most serious discussion of his career. I pointed out that even if K & P put up half the money I didn't think I would be able to find other risk investors — the project was just too far into pure research — and even if we could find the full amount of venture capital, the risk would be so high that the investors would own virtually all of the company. Bob and Herb's share would be nominal. I agreed, totally, that the potential payout could be enormous. I didn't need market research to persuade me that true human insulin, for example, would make obsolete the expensive-to-extract and allergenic pig and cow insulin then in use. There are millions of diabetics around the world; decades ago the discovery that porcine and bovine insulin could work in humans was a breakthrough, but the side effects from long-term use of this nonhuman substance frequently lead to severe complications (including death). True human insulin, really truly identical human insulin made abundantly, even if by a nonhuman cellular host, would be an astonishingly valuable thing. The list of potential products would range far beyond pharmaceuticals, as well, into the worlds of agriculture and industry: plants that would be naturally pest resistant and growth hormone for cows to multiply milk production are just examples from the tip of the potential iceberg.

I reviewed with Bob my experience with University Laboratories, how I had stretched a tiny amount of cash into a successful venture by subcontracting the work, so to speak. I asked him to think about how the experiment maybe could be split among existing laboratories. Once it succeeded, we could pour in the money. That way Bob and Herb would wind up owning far more of the company than if we tried the all-cash-up-front approach, because all the follow-on financing would be done at much higher (and thus less dilutive) prices. Bob disappeared for a couple of days after this meeting—I think he contacted some other potential investors and got turned down flat—and, for sure, he and Herb rethought the plan along the new lines that I was suggesting.

Bob came back with a radically different approach. He proposed to subcontract part of the experiment to the City of Hope Medical Research Foundation in Duarte, in Southern California, which was one of the two groups in the United States with the technology to build synthetic genes via organic chemistry (the other group was at MIT). The other half, the splicing of the created gene into a bacterial plasmid, would be done through a contract with Herb's lab at the UC Medical School in San Francisco. Further, to reduce costs, only a very short gene, that for the human hormone somatostatin, would be attempted. The experiment would be a proof of principle, to see if God would go along with our manipulations to create Frankenstein-like bacteria. If the experiment worked, we would shoot for the much longer gene for human insulin. I agreed with this approach, which reminded me of that taken for University Laboratories. And I agreed immediately to invest one hundred thousand dollars to get started.

Genentech was thus incorporated. It consisted in the beginning of only Bob, in his office, and his checkbook. He and I committed ourselves full-time to negotiating the research contracts with the two institutions and obtaining licenses to use the basic patents held by Cal and Stanford.

We visited the researchers in Duarte, and coordinated with them the steps needed, laboriously, to build the gene amino acid by amino acid using pure organic chemical techniques; the tricks to extract genes from nature lay far in the future. After some months the gene was ready, and it was transferred to Herb's lab at UC for implantation into a willing bacterial host. (I exaggerate. The bacteria may not have been at all happy, but a consent form was not required.) In due course Herb had a bacterial broth continuously producing somatostatin. This was a breakthrough in research of the very highest magnitude, albeit one with no immediate commercial importance. Bob and I agreed to underwrite the development for the gene for human insulin, and we pursued the same approach. In due course, Herb produced that hormone as well.

Now we were ready to tell the world! The announcement of the synthetic production of true human insulin by the hitherto-unknown science of genetic engineering was a headline-grabbing event of immense importance. Genentech had filed for fundamental patents in all directions, and Bob, Herb, and I, who constituted the entire board of directors, were sitting atop a venture that would rocket into history as, in percentage return, the most successful venture capital investment of all time. For an investment of only two hundred and fifty thousand dollars, K & P owned a third of the company—Bob and Herb owned the rest.

■   ■   ■

During this period in the life of K & P I was spending between one and two days per week on Tandem and Genentech. I was chairman of both companies, and it was my specific responsibility to see that neither ran out of money. This wasn't much effort for Tandem, which had good profits and a strong cash flow, but it was a continuing challenge for Genentech. During the fifteen years or so that I was responsible for Genentech, I raised around three billion dollars for the company. The first of the big financing steps was the public issue. The board was divided on the decision. I was strongly in favor; Bob was strongly against, knowing full well how much extra work it would require, Herb was the swing vote, but he ducked the decision by telling us both, "I will vote with the majority of my friends." In other words, work it out between yourselves, guys. The decision simmered for some days, but when I suggested to Bob that Cetus might be the first biotech company to go public if it wasn't us, he quickly came around to my viewpoint. Bill Hambrecht handled the offering. The issue was hugely oversubscribed, and the price shot from the low teens to nearly ninety dollars per share in the first hour of trading, which created more headlines for the company. If you bought shares at the offering price, held them, and reinvested as necessary, adjusting for all the splits, one dollar of the IPO would today be worth around three hundred and fifty in your pocket.

Keeping Genentech in cash took some financial inventions. Long before Enron's Lay, Skilling, and Fastow thought of off-balance sheet partnerships to convert losses into profits, Fred Middleton, the CFO, and I invented the idea, and we used it to finance Food and Drug Administration clinical trials. The difference was that we licensed these partnerships with the SEC, and they were fully approved; also, they proved to be lucrative for the investors. Further we invented cheap Junior Common Stock to use for options for our rapidly expanding employee base. Again the idea was fully SEC approved. However, over time both these ideas were so abused by competitors that the SEC shut them down, "grandfathering" those plans of Genentech's until their programmed expatriation dates. I was busy on the financial side, building the board by bringing my mentor Dave Packard on, for example. Dave was a marvelous director, who took a great interest in the company. As his hearing deteriorated with advancing age, he would mount the microphone of his hearing aid on a short stick he carried around with him, and thrust it in the face of whomever was speaking—he never missed a thing. The story around HP was that when asked: "Dave, have you learned a lot about DNA at Genentech?" he answered: "I haven't learned a damn thing about DNA, but I've sure learned a lot about financing."

Bob created an internal culture of profound significance. He was able to recruit many of the world's outstanding scientists from academia by giving them full rights to publish, provided only that they had first disclosed their discoveries to the patent department, and he developed a research department second to none. The academic papers published by Genentech today rival in number and quality those of the two most respected universities, Harvard and MIT.

By the late seventies, it was clear that thanks primarily to Tandem and Genentech, Kleiner & Perkins was the front-running venture partnership in America. It was time to bring aboard more partners and to restructure the fund accordingly. But those doubters at the beginning who said that we would never be able to invest eight million dollars were right. When we decided to put our new fund together, we still had about four million in cash, which, as promised in our Bill of Rights, we returned to our (very happy) limited partners.

Although this account is not a history of the Valley, or even a history of Kleiner & Perkins, and the following partnerships, I would like to give you a feeling for life within a venture capital group. And so, the next chapter probes that aspect.

One doesn't have to be an intellectual like Henry Adams to learn important lessons; even an operator like me pays attention when threatened with murder by an addicted CEO.

Chapter Seven

Coaching a Winning Team

Simon d'la Gare arrived early for the large cocktail party for the executives and their wives at lovely Carmel Valley's Quail Lodge, and he mingled readily with the crowd. A short, mustachioed Frenchman who was one of the key economic oil ministers for President Valéry Giscard d'Estaing, he was the after-dinner speaker for this gathering of KPC & B portfolio company executives. It was an important meeting for us, the first time we had pulled these CEOs and CFOs together, and the partners were anxious that everything should go smoothly. It soon became apparent that Simon was a potential catastrophe. He was arrogant and rude. He didn't get jokes, and he halted conversations so that the jokes could be explained to him, and he seemed, always, to not be amused after the explanation. During dinner he sent his plate back after only a few bites, and he refused to drink the quite excellent California wine on offer. By the time he rose to speak, the audience was thoroughly predisposed not to like him—and this was compounded by his ridicule of my accent in pronouncing *Giscard d'Estaing* during my introduction.

Simon then proceeded to give an incredibly boring opening, involving a long-winded review of oil production data. The audience was lapsing into a suffering state of despair as he gradually turned his remarks to America and then to Silicon Valley. However, his rudeness became more explicit as he piled scorn upon the Valley. While he gained momentum in his abuse, the guys in the audience began to display their suppressed anger. By the time he was excoriating specific KPC & B companies by name, they were ready to rise from their seats and rush the podium. My partners were red with embarrassment and giving me the deadliest of looks—how *could* I have picked this bastard to be speaking to us? With exquisite timing, Simon played the audience to the point of violent revolt when, with a born performer's finesse, he ripped the mustache from his face, the toupee from his bald head, and switched from heavily accented French to rich Brooklynese, beginning a night-club comedy routine. He brought down the house and guaranteed the success of our conference. I was the only person in the place who had known that he was an impersonator—I had hired him.

The conference was the first of its kind in venture capital, part of our effort to distinguish ourselves from the not-so-slowly gathering pack of competitors. It was an effort to build our team outside of the partnership, to convert our CEOs and CFOs into a network

Left to right—
Byers, Caufield, Perkins, and Kleiner

to assist each other, and to create a "sales force" to promote our interests.

Money is, I think, the least differentiated of all commodities. With water, you've got Calistoga, Perrier, and San Pellegrino, all noticeably different. With sugar there's the cane and beet variety; some can tell the difference. But with money it's all the same. So, as a venture capitalist in the business of selling money, it's commonplace to say that one must add value to differentiate oneself, and that's quite true. Gene and I had evolved a different approach to the business by essentially financing our own start-ups. While our competitors seemed happy to wait for fully fleshed-out business plans, and full teams, to walk through their doors, we were incubating our own new ventures, then building the teams to suit the needs. We had found a way to harness our impatience. I have never been good at just waiting. But to keep it going we had to add other partners who could replace Jimmy and Bob, and create more of our kind of ventures. Brook Byers knew all about Genentech from his friend Bob Swanson, and Gene and I had gotten to know Brook through his help to Tandem. Brook was the assistant to Pitch Johnson, the Palo Alto venture capitalist who was on the Tandem board. Brook wanted to join K & P, and we wanted that to happen, but I have always hesitated in hiring anyone from a competitor. In a future moment the competitor can become an ally, and hard feelings can last for a very long time. I sat down with Pitch and discussed Brook's situation frankly. We were prepared to make him a partner, with a piece of the action—Pitch, investing only his own money, was not able to make a similar offer. Pitch did the generous thing and released Brook to join us, and Pitch and I remain friends to this day.

Frank Caufield, the son of a prominent general, was managing the venture portfolio of Paul Cook, the founder of Raychem. We had been interacting with him in various ventures and respected his judgment enormously. We were lucky that his contract with Paul was winding up and he was able to join us as well—and so Kleiner Perkins Caufield & Byers was born. To accommodate these partners, we established a new fund capitalized at fifteen million dollars, with Henry Hillman taking his requisite fifty percent. This was the first of a long series of KPC & B funds, which, gradually over thirty years, rose to capitalizations of hundreds of millions of dollars each. By adjusting the ownership of the general partners' share of these funds we were able, later, to bring aboard such superstar partners as John Doerr, Jim Lally, Vinod Khosla, Floyd Kvamme, Joe Lacob, Kevin Compton, Doug MacKenzie, and Ray Lane. Since we always distributed and never reinvested profits (according to our Investor's Bill of Rights) we were, therefore, constantly running out of new money to invest. New partnerships were required for new money, and via new partnerships we could recarve the general partner's ownership slice of the pie each time going forward, both to reward high achievers, and to bring aboard new talent. (Gene became less active after the first two partnerships and he gradually retired from KPC & B to spend more time on his personal investments. He continued to be a close friend and was active in the Valley until his death in 2003 in his eightieth year. He was a true pioneer—*Time* carried his obituary.)

■   ■   ■

Our grow-from-within formula continued with a number of ventures. Most notable in this second partnership was Brook Byers's Hybritech, a pioneering biotechnology company in the field of monoclonal antibodies. The science was developed at Cambridge University, and with poor commercial instincts, given away via a scientific paper published with no patent protection. The technology enables the production of "single-clone," that is, ultra-pure antibodies. These antibodies are useful in clinical tests detecting, for example, the onset of prostate cancer, lupus, and heart attacks. The pioneering Hybritech (PSA) test for prostate cancer has saved hundreds of thousands of lives. Similarly these monoclonals can detect a drug user's substance abuse, and they are useful as carriers of "silver bullets" targeting attack on other specific forms of cancer. Brook continued the Tandem and Genentech tradition of K & P by being a partner/president of the company, but he eventually decided to return to the partnership and to replace himself as the CEO. Hybritech was a huge success (ultimately acquired by Lilly), and the experience led to Brook becoming America's most prominent and successful venture capitalist in the biotech field.

This is a behind-the-scenes look into the management and functioning of the KPC & B partnerships, rather than the story of the companies financed. But something must be said about the contribution of the ventures themselves, because so many of these companies have revolutionized their fields, and many affect our daily lives. The aforementioned Tandem is behind the scenes in probably eighty percent of our financial transactions; and Genentech offers treatments for heart attack and cancer affecting many families around the world; Home Health Care of America (now Caremark) pioneered the home health field; LSI Logic was first to develop custom logic arrays found in a host of electronic products; Acuson invented the ultimate in ultrasound imaging devices, found in virtually every hospital and large medical practice; Compaq Computers created the first portable computer and went on to become the world's leader in market share; Netscape made browsing the Internet possible; Sun Microsystems became the backbone for the World Wide Web; Amazon pioneered online retail marketing; and Google revolutionized search and advertising with the goal to bring all the world's information to everyone. Suffice to say that these new businesses have created some three hundred billion dollars in market value; have created a revenue stream for the companies of close to one hundred billion dollars; have created over a quarter of a million new jobs; and have compounded the investors' capital at rates of return—for a period spanning three decades—that are possibly the highest in history. Along the way we have financed or founded some four hundred other companies, many of which show great promise.

There is a tale behind each of these ventures, but the underlying story is the fact that entrepreneur after entrepreneur has come to KPC & B for assistance because of our reputation for offering more than just the money. Our passion for winning has become infectious. We have invested in serial entrepreneurs. For example, Netscape founder Dr. Jim Clark brought us his following two start-ups, which we also financed (even while in speeches he was calling us "vulture capitalists"—but we must have been doing something right for him!).

We were a highly motivated team with creative skills. My role was to be the coach, rather more than the captain, although I continued to sponsor specific opportunities along with the others.

Our partners' meetings were at the core of our operations. In the earlier partnerships, I was the senior and managing partner—responsible for raising the money, dealing with the investors, and overseeing everything—but I think I succeeded in creating an atmosphere where no one was boss, and I looked forward to our meetings. They were both exciting and fun. A characteristic of all the KPC & B general partners is a passion for winning and doing something interesting in the process. We rarely departed from the high-tech sector, and on the few occasions when we did stray from that specialty, we usually got our heads handed to us. Each partner had equal voice in the decisions; if someone's objections couldn't be eventually overcome, then the investment wouldn't be made. That applied to me as well, and I truly welcomed challenges. In a business as full as risk as ours, egos couldn't be permitted to prevail.

The whole process was fun; we teased and kidded each other constantly. Once Frank and I had a new nameplate for our door made that said only Kleiner Perkins and Caufield—we wondered how long it would take Brook to notice the joke. Only about ten nanoseconds, as it turned out. In the early days John Doerr exhibited his trademark excitement and limitless skill. He worked exhaustively subscribing to thousands and thousands of dollars' worth of technical publications, all of which he dutifully read. He has an electric intensity and is the best salesman for an idea I have ever encountered. This is a skill without compare. Frank's humor was always evident; whenever John or I would argue Frank to a standstill on some point, he would usually blow me away by saying something like, "Oh, that's just vintage Perkins!"

Our decision process worked like this. One of the principals in an existing venture would hear about a new opportunity, typically having been approached by the entrepreneur for advice on where to look for venture capital. That executive then would refer the entrepreneur to the KPC & B partner with whom he normally interacted. The partner would quickly arrange a meeting and review the idea. If it didn't appeal, that would be the end of the process. But if the idea and the entrepreneur were both attractive, the KPC & B partner would become the start-up's "champion," working with the entrepreneur to prepare a presentation to all the partners. Those presentations were very intense for the entrepreneur, with questions and comments fired from all directions. I recall one such pitch being made in our San Francisco office, atop one of the towers of the Embarcadero Center, when a mild earthquake struck. As the building swayed, we all hung on to the table with worried looks, but the entrepreneur just kept on going—he was so busy answering our objections that he hadn't noticed the quake. In spite of that dedication, we didn't write the check.

I have been asked numerous times, "How do you write a successful business plan?" I typically answer, "I can't tell you how to write one, I can only tell you how we read one. We start at the back, and if the numbers are big, we look at the front to see what kind of business it is. It's pretty sophisticated." Frequently the entrepreneur hadn't a fully developed business plan, and that was fine with us, as we would then work with him to develop the ideas, thereby tightening the idea to the partnership. Similarly, if the complete team wasn't in place, that was also fine, as we could fill in the gaps ourselves until we got the venture off the ground, and then we could help to recruit a very strong team. That, for example, was the case with Compaq Computers. John Doerr acted as the marketing strategist until we got the company well launched, and then he was able to recruit the marketing vice president of IBM for PC's, Sparky Sparks.

Once we made the commitment, the champion would usually continue to be in charge of the venture. For successful investments, this could be a very long involvement, frequently continuing after an IPO. I used to joke to the entrepreneurs: "You can't get rid of us by going public!" But when a company got into trouble, the problem became the responsibility of the entire partnership. Time during each partners' meeting was devoted to companies in what we called the ICU—the intensive care unit. We all then worked on the problem, and as in the hospital setting, the "patient" either improved and returned to normal life, or we might have to pull the plug on the life support system. That is, cut off the flow of money.

The fact that I was senior partner in no way made me immune to this ICU process for my companies. One of my companies was in the satellite earth station business. In order to facilitate its growth the management had acquired, for ten million dollars, a channel on a satellite to be launched in twenty-four months. We carried the investment on the company's books as a primary asset. The problem was that by the time the satellite was ready to fly, so many other birds had been launched that our channel was only worth a small fraction of what we had paid. The auditors would soon force us to write down the asset, which would wipe out the company. This dilemma had been much discussed around the table during ICU sessions. I was balking at taking the hit when one Sunday night Larry Sonsini, the prominent Silicon Valley attorney, called me at home to say, "Tom, did you hear the news? They launched the satellite from the shuttle, and it disappeared into outer space! How did you do that?" It was fully insured by Lloyds of London—we didn't lose a penny. There is little doubt that luck plays a role in the VC business.

■   ■   ■

And, of course, sometimes luck runs the wrong way. Prior to the KPC & B partnerships, I had been on the board of a very successful company, run by a PhD—let's call him Tony. I left his board, and he subsequently retired. A few years later, he returned to the Bay Area with the idea for a new company—let's call it ChemTech. Tony, who was short in stature but long on personality and who looked a little like Tom Cruise, was a winner from my past and I really liked his new idea. Soon I had persuaded my partners to make the investment. But I broke one of my own rules in this process. I didn't check Tony's references. Since I knew him so well it never occurred to me to question his upbeat account of what he had been doing since we had worked together previously.

We were well into the building of ChemTech; we had facilities, staff, and cash into the start-up of a few million, when Tony began to act in an increasingly odd way. Though brilliant, his explanations of things didn't quite make sense. He always left me wondering if it was just my stupidity preventing me from understanding. One morning he called me, asking for a meeting. As I was pretty busy I tried to talk to him about whatever it was over the phone, but he told me that his phone was being tapped. He drove up to my San Francisco office the next day and told me that he had been followed all the way. He rambled on about how his office was bugged, and how his vice presidents were conspiring against him. While articulate and calm, almost nothing he said made sense beyond this extreme paranoia. That evening, at a dinner party attended by my personal physician, I asked my doctor what would account for sudden paranoia in an otherwise normal healthy person. His answer—"Cocaine, and lots of it"—rocked me.

Only then did I check to see what Tony had been up to in the years since we had worked together. It was a horror story. He had wrecked his family life and had cost other investors a fortune in a failed enterprise, all because of his massive drug use. I confronted Tony immediately, but he denied using. I told him that he had to take a medical exam, on a confidential basis with the result known only by me, from my doctor. He did so, and the report was awful: Tony's cocaine use had destroyed his nasal passages.

And so began one of the most bizarre episodes in my VC career. Tony promised me that he would quit cold turkey. I insisted upon random urine tests, which he fought as an invasion of privacy (of course, they were). We ended up agreeing to pseudo-random tests, and he passed a couple (maybe using another person's urine?) and then he flunked massively. I promoted another executive to replace him. Tony then demanded that he be given a medical leave and that we pay for drug rehab. We did that, but he dropped out, and the company started to flounder. I discovered that he had embezzled a great deal of money. His habit was costing more than a thousand dollars a day. Apparently, free-basing is expensive.

One morning he called and, on short notice, showed up in my

office. Having been forewarned, I'd slipped a small tape recorder into the pocket of my jacket. He was raving, but the essence of it was that he was in huge debt to "the Italian guys in black suits." He intended that I assume he meant the Mafia. If I didn't fork over two hundred and fifty thousand dollars in five days, they would kill me! I threw him out and immediately called the police. They dismissed his threat as the ravings of a cokehead, but my partners insisted that I employ a bodyguard for the next few weeks. The company failed, and Tony disappeared from my life. Fortunately, not all bad ventures end so notably.

More fortunately, most of our ventures were golden, and we worked hard to achieve liquidity for our investors. After getting a company started and through the first phase of growth, the heavy lifting was by no means over. Somehow, the level of problems seems to keep pace with the growth of a company. It's a bit like the adage "Little kids, little problems; big kids, big problems." The struggle of personalities at the top of a company would astound an independent observer.

Hybritech, of which I was a director, was one of our most successful investments, eventually accruing close to a billion dollars of profit to the partnership. Brook was the first CEO, developing the business within the partnership. Then Ted Greene, an executive with a good record, approached us to fund a virtually identical idea in monoclonals. We were able to persuade him to abandon that, and to become the CEO of our start-up instead (Brook continued as chairman). The company skyrocketed—the PSA test was the first big hit—and any rivalry between Brook and Ted was healthy. But when the company had grown to require a president as well as Ted as CEO, we hired an executive to fill the job, and that mix became increasingly unstable. I found myself frequently called upon to keep everyone on course, if not entirely happy. Somehow I had developed a knack at working with highly motivated and very emotional entrepreneurs. In the VC role, one must always put one's own personality in the background—the entrepreneurs must be the stars, not the financiers. What seemed to work best was for me to attempt to express, as accurately as possible, the emotional content of each of the party's feelings in the presence of all the disputants. If I could get this right, then I could work toward a solution to the particular problem of the moment as an "honest broker." I sometimes had to do this during board meetings—sort of online psychotherapy.

Typically, the entrepreneurs will say at the beginning something along the lines of: "If I am not the right person to carry this company all the way to huge success, I'll be the first to recognize it, and I will step aside right away." Of course, they don't mean a word of it. Easing the founding entrepreneur out of his position at the helm is, I think, the most difficult of tasks—fortunately, the problem is reasonably rare. And I have been happily surprised by executives who seem to have no limit. Sam Maslak, the founder of ultrasound imaging firm Acuson, one of our big hits, was such a person. Sam, in his career before the company was founded, had never had anyone report to him; not one. Yet his instincts in management were superb. I learned a lot from him.

Jimmy Treybig and Bob Swanson, the two K & P partners who each founded such brilliant companies, exited the businesses in very different ways. By the time Tandem was a billion-dollar company in annual revenue, Jimmy had become totally identified with it and it with him. But the industry had to consolidate, and Jimmy just couldn't happily give up the helm. It became my duty to replace him in order for the company to merge into Compaq. I don't think Tandem would have survived without this merger, but it was a sad end to our personal relationship.

Bob, on the other hand, wanted to step down as CEO. The pace of the company was just so intense that he felt his personal life wouldn't be worth living unless he could find a way to be with his family more, and to enjoy the fruits of his huge fortune in Genentech shares. I, on the other hand, tried to keep him at the grindstone. He was brilliant. We finally agreed to hire Kirk Robb, an experienced executive from Abbott Laboratories, to become president. Bob remained as CEO, and I continued as chairman. This was the beginning of a years-long, successful but extremely rocky relationship between Bob and Kirk. It was hard for Bob to surrender the necessary responsibilities to Kirk to operate on a day-to-day basis. And Kirk, who always acknowledged Bob's founding role, wanted to run the whole show. Probably I, too, complicated the division of responsibilities, but I was essential to keep the two of them both in the harness. Looking back, I believe that I averaged a least a day each month in private meetings with them both to keep the lid on the potential explosion. Such matters as whose signature should go first in the annual report became matters of crisis. When I finally stepped down and retired from the board, Kirk was out within ninety days. Afterward the only thing Bob, Kirk, and the other board members agreed upon was that had I stayed on, the final explosion wouldn't have occurred.

After a number of years, I began to wonder if there could be another way to do venture capital, a way that would let us stick only to the choices of technologies and the management of the early risk, leaving the everyday details to others. We began to explore this idea, which in essence would make us wholesalers of VC, working with other firms that we respected around the country as our partners. We called the idea the New Industries Fund. We sought out Morgan Stanley, the premier New York investment bankers, to help us raise the capital, targeted at five hundred million dollars, which at the time would have been a record sum.

I flew back to Pittsburgh to sell the idea to Henry Hillman. He was not very enthusiastic and would commit to only a modest amount, but other investors in New York were wild about the idea. An essential component of the fund was to reduce our "carry" (that is, the portion of the profits we general partners would retain) from our normal twenty percent, which was the industry norm, to just ten percent for the new larger fund. (I am discussing the share of profit between the limited and the general partners. Of course, in a typical investment there might well be other venture investors in addition to the ownership of the entrepreneurs and the employees. Each investment had, typically, a different mix of these stakeholders.) Morgan Stanley was confident that the fund could be raised in a couple of months. A day before we made the final commitment to Morgan Stanley to proceed, Henry called me. He had been thinking, and he made a counterproposal. If we would just stick to the business as we had been doing it, and if we would give up this new, maybe grandiose, idea and not raise a fund larger than one hundred and fifty million, he would subscribe his usual fifty percent. Here was the clincher—he would be happy if we increased our carry from twenty percent to thirty percent! When I presented his proposal to the other partners, they agreed with me that it was persuasive. We tanked the new fund and proceeded as Henry wished. When other limited partners raised questions about our record-breaking new carry, we could truly say that it was our own keystone investing partner's idea.

All the foregoing will, I hope, give you a feeling for the KPC & B process. That process was in place, exactly, for perhaps the most famous of our investments: Google. Andy Bechtolsheim, one of the cofounders of Sun, a KPC & B–backed venture, learned about the search engine technology Sergey Brin and Larry Page were developing at Stanford University. When running on the Stanford network their searches were thousands, sometimes millions, of times faster than the conventional technology. In fact, the Brin/Page approach was so popular that the Stanford network became overloaded with the Google traffic—it was time for Google to move off campus and move on. Andy, together with a couple of others, put up the seed capital; the funding was less than a million dollars. This was an example of a brilliant technology, somewhat in search of a business plan. Andy brought the nascent company to his friend John Doerr, as so many other investments have come to us from executives in our network. Over the next many months John helped founders Brin and Page to develop a team—he went on the board and also recruited Eric Schmidt, an executive well known to KPC & B—to help run the place, and the strategy for selling advertising spotted to searches was developed. Together with our friends (and sometimes competitors) at Sequoia, twenty million was invested for about twenty-four percent on the company. We took half of that investment. To date it's our most successful home run.

■   ■   ■

In my novel *Zillionaire* the hero, Steven Hudson, takes great pride in seeing his name over his firm's door, and I certainly feel the same way. Probably superstar venture capitalists John Doerr, Ray Lane, and the others should now have their names there with Brook's, and the originals should be dropped, as Eugene is now deceased and Frank and I have emeritus status. The younger guys haven't wanted to do this as the KPC & B brand is so strong, they believe that the name shouldn't be changed. It's flattering to me, but if we do change names one day, I'll continue to trust that the partnership will carry on as before with the same kind of thinking, ethics, and (hopefully) results as when I was running the place, so many, many years before. My contribution is not to one particular venture or another but I think, rather, to the way we do things. Maybe someday that will be called the "Perkins way."

■   ■   ■

At about four minutes after five in the afternoon of October 17, 1989, I was driving across the Golden Gate Bridge on my way home when the Loma Prieta earthquake struck. Not surprisingly, I had never been on the bridge during a quake, and at first I thought that the violent action might have been normal. No one could continue to drive, as the roadway was moving too wildly; with the bucking and the swaying it was impossible to steer. Ever the engineer, I wondered to myself how many degrees of freedom the bridge could show—it was shaking, snaking, swinging, and twisting. About the time I thought the quake was due to end, it really became increasingly frightening—it was the longest fifteen seconds of my life. I made it across, but the ensuing chaos of burning buildings in San Francisco and downed freeways around the bay made it unlikely that I would be able to fly to New York on the following day for an extremely important meeting. Dave Packard and I were to be traveling together in a fellow Genentech director's G-4 from San Jose at eight the next morning. We were to discuss a pending offer to merge the company into Hoffmann–La Roche. I believed the long-term survival of the company depended upon this meeting.

I tried to call Dave at his home to see if he would be going, and I couldn't get through. All the phones were down. But I knew Dave

Packard. If he had an obligation, he would meet it. So I left my house at four the next morning, figuring it might take me hours to get to San Jose through the broken freeways. Actually, there was no traffic and little damage on my route; I made the trip in no time. Sure enough, Dave arrived on the dot, and off we went. Once in the air I asked Dave if there had been much damage at HP. He didn't know, since his phone wasn't working. Similarly, he didn't know if the superb aquarium he had built in Monterey was still standing. I was amazed. This incredible man had put Genentech's affairs before his own and was flying back to a board meeting that in the grand scheme of things wasn't *that* important. I had the pilot radio for the next couple of hours until we found that both HP and the aquarium were fine. Of course, Dave was happy to hear the news.

We arrived on schedule and were sitting together on a couple of bar stools having a drink before the other directors showed up. By then Dave and I had a decades-long relationship. I was no longer the kid who got his computer business going; rather I was chairman of the genetic engineering company that was shaking up the world — Genentech seemed to be constantly in the headlines: a blockbuster treatment for a heart attack and the production of human growth hormone to cure dwarfism in children were recent examples that Dave was familiar with from his seat on Genentech's board. I also was famous as a venture capitalist. Still, I always considered him my superior in every way, and I was grateful that he had never dominated the Genentech board in the slightest. He understood my chairman's role and never preempted it.

At that time Dave was experiencing troubles at HP. The company was losing momentum, and Dave had returned from retirement to run the place. It was common knowledge that the then-president, John Young, and Dave had fallen out, and that Dave was actively looking for a replacement. Before we had finished our drinks, there was a pause in our conversation about HP and its problems. Dave turned his bar stool toward me, and with a wistful smile said: "Tom, how did I ever let you get away from HP?"

I was taken aback and very flattered. This was the most significant compliment of my life.

Let's now take a break from the world of venture capital and business, and look into another world, that of the arts. What could be more soothing and satisfying than the ballet, for example?

Chapter Eight

If You Are Interested in Bare-knuckle Infighting,
Join a Civic Arts Group!

I arrived late for the meeting, and the only seat available was next to the very harried chairman. Both Gerd and I were on the board of the San Francisco Ballet, because we had given them a lot of money over the years, and most recently we had underwritten the completion of the new ballet school building, near the opera house. There was discussion about naming it the Perkins Ballet Building, but as it faced the Davies Symphony Hall across the street, I turned the honor down, maybe still worried about that long-ago dinner with the *grande dame* and the machine oil under my fingernails.

Gerd loved the ballet and often went to the board meetings, but I never did. It was only in recent weeks, when the organization had been on the front page of the *San Francisco Chronicle* almost every day, that I started to pay attention. The ballet was at war! The full-time president and general manager, Richard LeBlond, along with rich matrons and the other society figures who made up the board, wanted to fire the director, Michael Smuin. He was developing a national reputation as a gifted choreographer but it was thought by many influential directors that he was degrading the classical roots of the troupe, the oldest ballet company in America. He permitted the ballerinas to rehearse in their sneakers, not in their pointe shoes! He had staged a recent program that was danced to Beatles music! He had a motorcycle on the opera house stage! This wasn't ballet, it was cabaret!

The problem was, the audience loved it, and season-ticket buyers got to vote on who would be on the board. There was a good chance that a new slate of directors would be voted into office at next week's annual meeting. The matrons were at risk, and the *Chronicle*, in particular Herb Caen's beloved column, was ridiculing them on a daily basis: who says pointe shoes matter (they hurt) and what's wrong with a motorcycle now and then? The matrons, some of whom had danced themselves in earlier years, believed that if the organization didn't recover its classical heritage, it would so deteriorate that the fickle, fad-addicted pop culture audience would eventually abandon the troupe and the ballet would be in another financial crisis as dangerous as the recent one that nearly had wrecked the company. Ticket sales didn't remotely support the cost of the ballet, so the financial support of the existing board was crucial. If they got voted out, who would pay? Compounding the problem, the board was split among itself. Newer, younger directors (who didn't write very big checks) were solidly on Michael Smuin's side.

As I arrived too late to sit quietly in the background in the new building's meeting hall, the only place for me was in the seat next to the chairman, Neil Harlan. He was in trouble. Directors were shouting at each other. I never had seen feelings run so high during any board meeting in business. As I was soon to discover, in the nonprofit sector, the passions are the highest, possibly because the stakes are the lowest. I found myself making quiet suggestions to Neil, a man I hadn't met before, on how to regain control of the meeting. Gradually he did so, and after much venting of spleens, from all points of view, but without resolution of any kind, he was able to adjourn the meeting until the next day. It was hoped some sort of decision could be made about Smuin's fate then. As I started to leave, Neil said, "But you are coming to the executive committee meeting now, aren't you?" I told him that I wasn't on the committee, but he pleaded with me to attend, so I did.

To say that I knew nothing about ballet and its administration is to overstate my qualifications. The only reason that I was welcomed at the much smaller meeting that soon began was that I had absolutely no opinion on the Smuin affair. As the saying goes, I didn't have a dog in the fight.

As in the full board previously, this smaller group soon renewed their heated arguments. Finally I asked a question. "What is a ballet director supposed to do? An orchestra conductor doesn't write the symphonies, does he? Aren't we confusing choreography with direction? If Smuin's ballets suck, but he is a great director, well then, we can just ask him to stage other people's ballets. But if he is a lousy director, we have a problem: he'll never choreograph us into excellence because the dancers won't have the skills." My question seemed pretty simple to me, but apparently it struck a chord. Next thing I knew, my "analysis" was to be presented at the next day's renewed meeting. I should have thanked everyone, and never returned. But I agreed to present my ideas the next day.

It is said that Cicero's wife wept at the power of his oratory—with Gerd it was a different matter. When I made my point the next day to the full board about the distinction between direction and choreography, which was, I suppose, designed to coldcock Smuin, or at least relegate him to the choreography bench so that we could move on with a new director, Gerd wasn't buying it. But the other directors were. Looking around the table, I knew that my view would prevail. When the vote was called on my motion to hire a new director, I had the majority, but there was a shocked silence in the room when, in turn, Gerd voted against me. I wasn't the slightest bit fazed; I was familiar with her strong opinions, and found them just examples of a personality "comfortable in her own skin," as the French say. But this was the first dispute aired in front of others.

I returned to the office, not thinking ballet thoughts, and when I got home that evening I was amazed to find Gerd packing her suitcases. She was in tears. I asked, "What's up? Are you going someplace?" She replied that she thought that since she voted against me in a public forum, she would have to leave Dodge, at least until I cooled off. She said that's what would have happened in Norway. I said, "*Elskling*, it's about the *ballet*, it's not about us . . . besides, I won." I ducked the wash bag she flung at me, but I wasn't smart enough to duck the next round in my arts war.

Flattery is the most dangerous seductress; you always fall for her, and you always get screwed. When a few days later Neil called me just minutes before he had to chair the annual meeting, which I was too busy to attend, he said, "Tom, I am desperate. They are going to vote out the board and the only hope is to present you as the savior. Only you have the skill—only you have the dispassionate interest of the ballet at heart; they all love you—you built the building. I need, I really need, to propose you as the chair of the search committee to hire a new director. Tom, I apologize to you, but I honestly can't give you a chance to think about this, you simply have to say yes. Put your name behind your money—the ballet depends upon you! Say yes!"

So I said yes.

The attendees at the annual meeting duly voted me into the job. On the front page of the next day's *Chronicle*, I read that my new assignment was, to say the least, controversial. The husband of a lady director whom I thought to be an effete albeit well-known ballet connoisseur announced that my being appointed head of the ballet (hardly what I thought had happened) was "as absurd as me being appointed head of Apple Computer." In the office, the phone was ringing off the hook with calls from reporters, leading me to have an "oh-shit moment" when what I had agreed to do finally sank in.

Smuin (recently prematurely deceased) seemed to me to take the press and the PR initiative in as commanding and aggressive a way as General Patton charging through France; there was nothing effete about this guy. In fact, one of the most persistent rumors around the board and the town was that few gay dancers could make the cut. That may or may not have been true, but maybe that's why the New York critics said, essentially, that our guys couldn't dance their way out of a wet paper bag (though some were adept at making ballerinas pregnant). Some members of the ballet administration, on the other hand, were commonly rumored to balance the gay equation, and it was known to the board that the office and the stage detested each other. What was I doing in this picture?

But I had gotten myself into the fray; the best way out was just to do the job. As I sat there thinking, Richard LeBlond called to compliment me on the move to replace Smuin, going on and on about what a good thing that was. When I asked him who I should try to hire as a replacement, he blithely said, "Oh, all the good directors have contracts with other companies for years into the future." Great.

The new season was going to start in about four months, and we were soon to be *sans-directeur*. Maybe I could talk Smuin into hanging on to see us through this rough patch? I called him: virtually the first words out of his mouth were "I'll never trust that mothef—ing LeBlond again." At least that's what I remember him saying, though I may have cleaned up his language a bit.

There were just four months to identify and hire a ballet director. Those four months quickly became the single most challenging period of my career. I did a number of things immediately. First, I recognized that the criticism of me taking on an assignment for which I clearly had no credentials was valid. I needed help on the artistic side. I remembered seeing the world-famous dancer, the late, truly great Erik Bruhn, perform in New York; I knew that he was ill (he succumbed to HIV/AIDS a couple of years later) and had retired from the stage and was director of the Royal Canadian Ballet. I tracked him down. He already had heard about our mess in San Francisco, and before I'd barely started on a pitch about him maybe taking on our job, he killed the idea. He said that Smuin had destroyed the company artistically, that he was happy in Canada and "lots of luck."

That's sort of what I had expected him to say, so I spun the conversation in a different direction. After explaining that I hardly knew the difference between a pointe shoe and a combat boot, and that I was just a businessman trying to preserve our ballet, he warmed to my offer to become my artistic consultant. He agreed to help me, agreed that I could announce his participation, and agreed to fly down to meet me and make an on-the-spot assessment of our situation. He proved to be of huge value as the weeks went by, but it was his comment at the end of our phone conversation that proved most essential: "You know, there is only one person in the world who can take over your director's job. You have got to hire Helgi Tomasson, of City Ballet. But move fast, because he's going to take over the Royal Danish Ballet very soon." I put that in my to-follow-up-right-away mental file.

Helgi Tomasson—
star of the New York City Ballet

But first I assembled a search committee of board members. It was clear that unilateralism on my part would never be tolerated by the ballet or audience communities. I went out of my way to pick a couple of pro-Smuin directors to participate. I persuaded all whom I contacted to join the committee; it was comprised of a retired investment banker, L. J. Tenenbaum, who had been a major ballet fundraiser over the years; Lucy Jewett (she and husband Fritz were huge

financial supporters); a former dancer then on the board; the director of the San Francisco Conservatory of Music; and a couple of
others I thought would be helpful.

As soon as we had our first meeting, the leaks to the press about
everything we were doing commenced. I never knew who was doing
the leaking (where were the HP spooks? I sure could have used
them) and I dearly wished it to stop, but I had to proceed with those
I had chosen. The first leak, and virtually all the leaks were on the
front pages, about my retaining Erik, was actually helpful, but none
of the others were.

Then I made a couple of moves in the direction of placating
other constituents. I contacted the dance critics of the *Chronicle*
and the *Examiner* and asked them to participate, informally, in the
process as "consultants, for the community." Maybe this was blatant
flattery, but at least for one of them it seemed to work, and soon the
Examiner became more friendly to the idea of upgrading our ballet
performances. The *Chronicle*, on the other hand, never wavered in
its infatuation with the Smuin style. It took a major reportorial scandal (which I'll get to later) to change the editorial slant of this powerful paper. I came to dread opening it in the morning, and particularly
reading the witty but wounding spears launched by beloved "Mr.
San Francisco," Herb Caen, so beloved that a street has been named
after him. He was a great buddy of my "absurd as me being appointed
to run Apple Computer" critic who, epicene enough for San Francisco, was equipped with a trademark acid and highly quotable wit.
Herb was a faithful scribe.

These guys didn't cut me much slack, and everything Michael
Smuin cared to say—and it was plenty—seemed to get printed. An
avalanche of bad press brings results. Soon an amorphous group was
formed calling itself "The Committee for the Ballet." They vowed a
proxy war to unseat the board and restore Michael to the throne.
Then there were the dancers themselves. Michael let it be known to
many that if he were to be replaced, the new director would fire
them all. I tried to counter this by having the dancers elect a representative to meet with me and my committee. They did, but the
poor girl they chose was, in my opinion, so intimidated by Michael

that she was too nervous to say more than a word or two at meetings. Smuin then conducted an opinion survey among the dancers, which, amazingly, found them nearly unanimous in their support for him; many said that they would quit if a change were to be made. Of course, this survey was in the *Chronicle*.

But, pressing on, Erik flew down to San Francisco to brainstorm names of possible directors with L. J. Tenenbaum, me, and a couple of others from my committee. I figured that we needed at least five reasonable names from which to recruit. I knew from business boards that unless a committee is given a choice, it is almost impossible to advance a single name forward. At the end of our meeting we did have a viable list. It included a handful of famous names among about twenty in total. The most prominent was Natalia Makarova, a world-famous ballerina who might be ready to become a director, we were told. But some inquiries I made among the cognoscenti warned that unless San Francisco was prepared for another quake of 1906 Richter magnitude, we shouldn't touch her with a three-meter pole. During his visit Erik spent some time with Michael and the dancers. They were eager to impress this famous figure from the world ballet stage. His opinion to me afterward: "Provincial and mediocre. Hire Helgi."

I already had telephoned Helgi in New York. He was noncommittal and said that he had a contract in hand from the Danes, which he only had to sign to make final, but he was willing to talk to us before inking their deal. We decided immediately to fly Helgi out for an interview. I made the arrangements, and we agreed to meet the following day commencing at ten in the morning.

When I met him at his hotel, I found him with his wife, Marlene, and it was immediately clear that she would be part of any arrangement we might make. Helgi was considered by everyone to be, at least, the number-two male dancer in the world, second only to Baryshnikov, unless you considered the dance-off in Moscow where the latter won gold to Helgi's silver, to have been fixed by local judges biased toward the local boy, in which case Helgi was number one—that was my view. He had had an astonishing career, which recently included the choreographing of critically acclaimed new ballets.

He was an athletic man in his late thirties, old for a male dancer, very good-looking and self-confident without the slightest trace of arrogance. When we sat down for breakfast, he told me that he and Marlene already had taken breakfast with my committee, and they had been surprised to learn that my group wasn't interested in him.

What the hell?

I soon discovered that someone on my committee had leaked his arrival, hotel, and time of meeting to the hostile Committee for the Ballet group, and that they had pretended to represent me, and had preempted my meeting that morning. They had the balls to say that Smuin would be retained, and if by some chance, Helgi *did* wind up as director, the audience would boycott all future performances!

The bastards thus forced me to begin my meeting with Helgi by having to explain all the woes that we were experiencing, the mess with Michael, the divisions on the board, the troubles with the dancers, and having it all on the front page of the *Chronicle* day after day. My foes had made an extremely clever move—how could anyone be remotely interested in diving into this morass?

Helgi listened patiently, and surprised me by calmly saying that he still wanted to meet with me and my search committee as planned, and looked forward to meeting with some of the dancers, as planned. And at that instant I got my first look into the extraordinary strength of this guy.

He had become a superstar in the world of dance, from his origins in Iceland. Helgi's youth, spent in this remote, barren place populated mostly by fishermen's families, made the background of the kid in the wonderful film *Billy Elliot* look positively nurturing. If there was ever an example of pure talent overcoming nearly unbelievable obstacles to achieve greatness, it was Helgi Tomasson. He was not to be put off by squabbles of our kind, but he told me up front that he was "very much inclined" to accept the Danish offer. Still, he would listen to us seriously.

From the low point of that breakfast, things improved. My committee was quite impressed with Helgi. They were already predisposed to his candidacy because of his years working with the famous George Balanchine, the late director of the New York City Ballet, who was essentially the founder of modern ballet. It also quickly became apparent that Marlene, a noted former dancer, would be extremely helpful should he join us. They had two small sons, but she made it clear that she wanted to be part of the program too.

He spent a couple of hours with the dancers, watching them rehearse. He was very frank in telling them that many were not up to an acceptable standard, but that many had "potential" and by the way, if he took over, the girls would rehearse in pointe shoes. Surprisingly, this honest assessment was well received. I began to understand that the dancers themselves wanted to be pushed professionally.

My key ally on the committee, L. J., was also hugely impressed, and he wanted to make Helgi an offer immediately. But I knew that it was too early; the board would never accept a candidate unless we had run more names through the mill. Still, I agreed that Helgi had the class and backbone that we needed. So that night when I had him and Marlene to my home for dinner—they had to meet Gerd—I told him that if he would trust me and not sign with our Danish competitor, and let me interview a few lesser candidates to flesh out the process, I was pretty certain we would make him a very good offer.

Then I gambled and guessed out loud that Denmark might not be a bed of roses for him. He was fluent in Danish—that wasn't my thrust; rather I suspected that in that socialist paradise all might not be well in the arts. I was on target. Helgi seemed worried about the politically correct rules for the ballet in Copenhagen: the dancer's union severely restricted hours of rehearsal; the age of retirement for dancers was somewhat indeterminate, and fat ballerinas were permitted to wedge themselves into their sylph costumes and sweat their way through performances. He had been negotiating these problems for almost a year, but he wasn't sure that his artistic vision, as he called it, would prevail. We, on the other hand, were trying to pull ourselves up by our toe-shoe straps, so to speak, and the artistic vision would be totally his. I sensed that this was our strong suit. He left my house agreeing to give me a few weeks to try to make him a persuasive proposal.

But what to do about both my committee and the damned opposition? Anything that my search committee decided to do would be immediately leaked to the press. The only solution was not to make decisions at all. I notified them that we would just proceed with all candidates in the running, including even Smuin himself. We would vote on a choice at the last conceivable minute, and so there simply would be no news to leak. Period. Of course, even this non-news leaked, giving some hope to the Smuin partisans.

As to the opposition, I decided to play the Herb Caen card. I knew Herb pretty well, for we floated in the same waters in San Francisco society (not very deep waters, really) and I had given him amusing tidbits a number of times for his hungry daily column. So, I invited him to lunch at the stuffy Pacific Union Club, atop Nob Hill, with the promise of a really juicy item. Over lunch I tipped the outrageous news about the opposition's duping Helgi, pretending to represent me, and their threats to boycott the ballet if we hired anyone but Michael. Herb could hardly contain his delight at the story and he rushed back to his famous typewriter to deliver a blast in the next day's column. He accurately captured my anger at the foul play, and was very sympathetic to what I was trying to do. That column pretty much permanently destroyed the opposition's credibility.

Things were now moving fast, and I was working extremely long days, as things were humming at Kleiner & Perkins beyond my preoccupation with the ballet. Helgi had been in San Francisco a couple of additional times. During one visit we went to a performance of one of Michael's ballets, and after a particularly athletic toss of a petite ballerina from one of our husky males (a *ballerino*, to use the proper term) to another of our dancing brutes, I asked Helgi what was the proper terminology for this sort of *pas de trois* in ballet speak. His answer: "Crap."

To keep momentum, in quick order we flew in and interviewed several additional candidates. I was very taken with Patricia Neary, director of the Zurich Ballet; she would maybe be a good backup candidate if negotiations fell through with Helgi. In the middle of all this Helgi called inviting me to see "an important performance" in a few days at New York's Lincoln Center. I was a little slow to accept, and after a pause he told me why it was an important night for him. Though as yet a total secret, it was to be the last-ever performance of his career.

L. J. and I flew back together for the event, a quick twenty-four-hour trip. We were suited up in tuxedos in the midst of a glittering New York crowd for the performance of Stravinsky's *Le Baiser de la Fee*, awaiting Helgi in the role he had made his own as a young performer under Balanchine's direction. At New York City Ballet it was one of the most popular ballets in the repertoire. As the audience settled in their seats and the lights dimmed, an announcement was made that tonight would be Mr. Tomasson's final public appearance. As this news sank in a hush came over the theater; this was stunning. The curtain rose, and when Helgi appeared, looking strong and young, there was a long swell of applause. He danced magnificently. The role is very demanding, and his performance was simply electrifying. When the curtain rose for curtain calls at the conclusion, this audience stood as one and gave him a standing ovation that with not the least exaggeration lasted well over five minutes. Many were crying, and L. J. and I realized we had been privileged to witness one of the truly great events in performance history.

Backstage with Helgi, we asked him, "Why now?"

"I want to leave at the top" was his simple answer. L. J. and I were more than ever determined to hire him for San Francisco.

But it was not to be simple. I was stunned the next day when Patricia Neary called me from Europe to thank me for giving her the director's job.

What? What was she talking about?

It turned out that our very own Dr. Richard E. LeBlond, Jr., had called her telling her that the board would not hire Helgi (whom he didn't like—Helgi was too strong to be manipulated) and that the job was hers! He wasn't even on the search committee. I had the not-so-easy task of gently disabusing her of this false proposition, while at the same time trying to keep her alive as a candidate. She was totally innocent of any part in this appalling dysfunction of process, and I felt sorry for her. I had a sit-down with LeBlond the next day that I am sure he never forgot. I told him that if there were even the slightest further interference, he would be fired. Full stop.

When L. J. and I reported on Helgi's triumph in New York to the search committee, I felt certain that the group would endorse him as our choice. But I still couldn't let them vote—the leaker was undoubtedly sitting at that table and I couldn't give him, or her, further meat to throw to the press. Now all I had to do was close the deal with Helgi. And also, hopefully, to come up with some sort of détente with Smuin. If we couldn't reach an understanding with him, what were we going to stage in the season soon to be upon us? It was pretty much impossible to perform much that he didn't already have in the works; he had to direct that stuff. I refused to let myself think about the chance of all the dancers going on strike.

I continued to negotiate with Tomasson. He wanted to take our job. He liked the idea of running the oldest company in America and returning it to the excellence it once enjoyed. He was confident he could handle our environment of dysfunction. I thought to myself, well, maybe. Money was a problem. Our base pay was okay, but he had a family to move, and he and Marlene had visited some houses with a Realtor in San Francisco during their last visit and they had encountered the normal sticker shock at our insane real estate values. This was a phenomenon I was long familiar with; why everyone wants to live here is a puzzle that I'll think about, if I ever make the idiotic choice to move away. Without going into details, I was fortunate to be in a position to be able to offer Helgi a "signing bonus" (as for any sports star) from my own pocket, without needing anyone's knowledge or approval. He and I had a handshake agreement, subject only to the blessing of the board.

The board's contract with Michael was not complicated. If we hired a new director, Michael would have an agreement guaranteeing that he would be employed and fully in charge of any of his own

ballets that the company might choose to perform. Being the cabaret impresario that I believed him to be, I thought that there might
be many of them planned for the coming season.

So, the day of the big board meeting arrived, and Helgi flew
back to be there. My artistic consultant, Erik Bruhn, flew down from
Canada officially to endorse Helgi. The morning of the board meeting, Erik, Helgi, and I met at the dreadfully ugly Jack Tar Hotel on
Van Ness Avenue. It was a meeting at which I nearly overdosed on
adrenaline from suppressed anxiety.

Helgi and I had already ordered our fried eggs when Erik arrived. He immediately said: "Helgi, you *must not* accept this job!"

"Why, Erik?"

"Because I have met Smuin—the idiots on the board have made
a deal with him. They are going to *pay* him to hang around next
year. He will do everything he can to see that you fail!"

I sat there, in silence with my pulse racing, as I pretended to be
interested only in getting egg yolk onto my toast. If Helgi bailed now,
what would I do? My artistic consultant was being an honest and
decent guy—the unfaithful prick!

"Oh, Erik, I think that I can handle Mr. Smuin," Helgi calmly
replied. His confidence and cool were of historic proportions.

Another crisis had passed.

I convened my search committee for one final time an hour
before the board meeting. Finally, I let them vote, and as I knew
they would, they unanimously nominated Helgi to be our recommendation to the board.

I made the presentation. As we walked into the meeting the full
press was on hand, flashbulbs popping. Maybe not typical everywhere, but what goes on in ballet is a big deal in San Francisco!

I had prepared a slide show. Since I'd figured that everyone who
saw my slides in advance would leak our conclusion, I had the names
of *all* our candidates in the slide tray. I removed the other names at
the last moment, leaving only Helgi's name in the projector.

I had been thinking about how to deal with his relative lack of
experience as an actual full-time director of a ballet. Indeed, to be

brutally honest, he had *no* such full-time experience with a big company. So, one of my slides was labeled: HELGI TOMASSON: THE EXPERIENCE OF EXCELLENCE! My comments accompanying this slide were thoughts along the lines that during his years with Balanchine, the acknowledged epitome of all things good in ballet, Helgi had fully experienced this master's excellence. After the board approved our recommendation by a comfortable margin, and Tomasson was officially our new director, a number of board members approached me to say that it was his excellent experience that had swung their votes.

But this was not the end of the storm. When he arrived, Helgi received an anonymous death threat, and we put the FBI on it. The investigation was not successful in finding the person or persons involved and, fortunately, nothing further of this nature occurred. During Helgi's tense first season, he and Smuin somehow managed to work together and the dancers didn't strike. Finally, Michael formed his own troupe. In the end the love for classical ballet prevailed and Helgi Tomasson, with steady help from Marlene, delivered that in spades, frequently to sold-out opera house audiences.

■ ■ ■

Now, twenty years later, critics say that the San Francisco Ballet, still under Helgi's direction, is among the top companies in the world. A few place it, with no qualification, at the very top. The company tours New York, Europe, and the other major venues to universal audience acclaim.

But the breakthrough in critical review came following a scandal over a program near the end of Tomasson's first year. He scheduled a well-publicized free summertime performance of selections from the winter's season in a public park called Stern Grove. The exact program was announced well in advance. After the event the ballet critic from the *Chronicle* excoriated everything. He was very specific in his contempt. There was just one problem: at the last moment Helgi cancelled the original plan. All was changed: different dancers; different ballet segments. The critic had written his "review" in advance. He had not attended the performance!

The critic confessed in the *Chronicle* owner's office just before he had a heart attack and collapsed on the carpet. When he recovered, he was fired.

Hey, man, ballet is not for sissies!

Probably you have been wondering when I would get around to exorcism. Let's talk about it here between these chapters.

Gerd, being a Norwegian, always wanted to have a foot in Europe, but not necessarily in Norway — too cold — too egalitarian. A place in the English countryside, where she could create acres of garden, would be the ideal location. We looked at properties on and off for quite a while until we found the perfect place — Plumpton Place, at the foot of the South Downs, fifty miles south of London. Through agents, I bought the historic manor house from its previous owner, Jimmy Page of the Led Zeppelin rock band. Their recording studio was still there in the upper gallery, and a rare collection of antique guitars had been left behind. The medieval place was a mess and needed, more or less, total restoration.

Now, I never have met Mr. Page, nor for that matter been able to listen to his music. I have no knowledge of his taste in recreational pharmaceuticals, if any, or for that matter any direct insight into whether or not he, or any of his entourage, ever indulged in anything stronger than the infrequent cough drop. However, the local gossip was that he had wild drug-oriented orgies, in the manor house's great room where Satanic masses, whatever those might be, were celebrated. Maybe these didn't really happen, but it is not disputed that a local youth was found dead floating in the moat one morning. None of this was disclosed in the sales

Gerd and Tom Perkins on their way
to Ascot from Plumpton Place circa 1985

brochure for the property, of course. The problem was that we couldn't get anyone to clean the house, because the ghost of the young man was said to be pretty evident and pretty hostile to the intrusion of squares like us.

Gerd had in tow Captain Wright, a cook, butler, and general factotum in our employ at the time for help during her visits to the house in preparation for its restoration. (I originally thought that he was a captain in the English army, but it turned out that he was a captain in the San Francisco Butler's union.) Captain Wright was deeply religious and he had made contact with the local vicar from the tiny twelfth-century church that was originally part of the estate. They agreed that an exorcism was the only solution, and when I arrived, it was already a done deal planned for the following Saturday. I said, "Gerd, they are just conning you into giving the church a new roof!" She resented my insensitivity to local religious belief and practice. Also, she was afraid of the ghost.

Saturday rolled around, and a Volkswagen pulled up containing the bishop of Lewes, Lord Peter, instead of Father Laughton, the vicar. He was a monk in sackcloth, and he carried a bishop's crook with its characteristic spiral in rusted iron. We walked together, Lord Peter, the Captain, Gerd, and I to the entrance of the empty house. It was a gloomy day with distant thunder echoing and the threat of rain in the offing. Lord Peter paused on the threshold, before the massive oak door, and said to me, "My son, you may be wondering why I am here instead of Father Laughton. It's because the forces of *evil* are so powerful when they are suddenly released that should there be an emergency, I felt that I should be here." A cold shiver ran down my spine.

For a first exorcism, on my part anyway, I didn't see how it could have gone any better. Lord Peter was liberal in dispensing holy water, but what impressed me the most were his words to the spirit of the teenage ghost—some years had passed since the boy's encounter with the moat, but then, ghosts don't age, do they? So talking to him as if he were still a kid seemed right. The words were kind, even loving, but also very clear: find peace, *but get out!* Lord Peter was particularly agitated when we entered the old Zeppelin recording studio. He said that he felt a strong presence there, and he gave the holy water an extra shake. Afterward, he offered me a warranty on the job: "If you experience any further manifestations, just give me a call." I was thinking that, probably, it was the cathedral that needed the roof, but I didn't dare mention it to Gerd. She proved to be correct, in that we had no trouble in getting staff after word of the exorcism got out.

A few months later I was in my San Francisco office when she called, "Damn it—I hate it when you are right!"

"What are you talking about?"

"Well, we got a letter. But it's not the roof they want the money for. It's for the foundation of the little church."

I knew that a deal is a deal. I sent them a check to exorcise the death-watch beetles that were the source of the churches' temporal troubles.

■   ■   ■

Okay, okay, you're right. That story didn't logically follow any of the preceding chapters. Sorry. Let's get back to the serious stuff on competition: Winning the great ocean race!

Chapter Nine

In Ocean Racing, Preparation and Teamwork
Make the Difference!

Danielle stood with me on the deck of *Mariette* on a cold May morning while we made our final preparations for the race from New York across the Atlantic to England. As we watched the eighteen-man crew scurry about, Bob, our cook, came back aboard with a very small paper bag in one hand. I asked him what he was up to, and he said, "Oh, I just bought a few last-minute things." Danielle asked me, "Tom, are you sure you have enough food onboard?" Maybe she was just worrying excessively, I thought, probably because we had run aground the day before while practicing in the harbor beyond the Statue of Liberty, and that had scared the bejesus out of her. I said, "Of course, we have enough food."

"But have you checked?"

"Danielle, I don't micromanage my people the way you do your people," I answered with some asperity. "They have been planning this race for months. Everything is fine." As things worked out, I was to eat those words, since there was soon precious little else to eat aboard. But, I am ahead of the story. Let me fill in the background.

The New York Yacht Club was sponsoring a major race to commemorate their Great Ocean Race of 1905 during which the famous schooner *Atlantic* broke the transoceanic record. Perhaps the most famous of all professional captains, Charlie Barr, was at the helm. During the race very heavy weather was encountered. When the owner asked Barr to heave to and wait out he storm, the later famously said: "No, sir. You hired me to win this race and that is exactly what I am going to do, sir. Please go below and stay there." The

Mariette *at the start*
of the Atlantic Challenge 1997

record still stood even after all those intervening years. I had decided to race my schooner *Mariette*. We had been cleaning up the silver first place trophies from regattas around Europe for years. But those regattas were day "around the buoy" contests. I had never entered a major ocean race before.

Mariette sailed into Bermuda in late April after crossing over from Gibraltar, and I was there to meet her. I had a nice house in Tucker's Town at the time, and I invited the passage crew of ten to dinner. Their captain, Karl, decided to stay aboard and not join them. The crew was very edgy and it didn't take drinks for them to pour out their frustration with Karl. They simply detested him. And after drinks, they announced to me that they all had decided to quit unless I fired him. Each had his own reason, it seemed, but there was universal agreement that we didn't have a chance of winning with him aboard. Several pointed to an event that had occurred on the passage.

There had been only very light winds for days so they had been motoring. Finally a gentle breeze had come up and they hoisted the sails. It was midday, warm, and all were in shorts and many were shirtless. But, according to the crew, when Karl came up from his

Chris Gartner, captain of
the Mariette, *at the helm*

cabin to stand noon watch, he was decked out in full foul-weather gear, including boots and a Nantucket s'wester waterproof hat. Also, he was wearing his storm safety harness, which he clipped to the binnacle. The crew thought him absurd, for there wasn't the slightest danger. . . . well, perhaps sunstroke. When your crew decides that you are an idiot, maybe it's short of mutiny but it's the first way station on the mutiny express.

The following day, Karl came by the house. I had decided that I had to fire him, but before I could get to that, he announced that he was quitting. He knew the score. However, he was keen to preserve the reputation of the yacht and he wanted me to promise that I would use the navigator/meteorologist whom he had hired for the race. He was confident that with this famous French sailor and weather expert we would win, hands down. I agreed, and promised to take Jacques along. I decided to make Chris Gartner captain. Chris was the engineer aboard, and had already worked for me for several years, having literally sailed around the world on my boats. He was great with people and I knew that the crew would welcome his command. He faced a big challenge, though, to get *Mariette* ready for the race, just a couple of weeks away. And the job was complicated by the promise I had made first to take *Mariette* to a fundraising event for the Herreshoff Museum in Bristol, Rhode Island.

Mariette, at 108 feet on deck, and 135 feet overall including the wooden bowsprit (her sparred length), was the largest operable yacht remaining of the famous steel schooners designed and built by the "Wizard of Bristol," the most famous naval architect in history, Nat Herreshoff. *Mariette* was launched in 1915, but was in magnificent condition, as good as new and stunningly beautiful to boot. Her walnut-paneled saloon, complete with fireplace, was a classic example of Edwardian understated elegance. She pulled in a big crowd while at the pier in front of the museum that is now part of the original construction yard, and the dinner was a huge success. Halsey Herreshoff, grandson of the Wizard, was my host. He had been an America's Cup tactician and had long-distance racing experience as well. Also, he had been mayor of Bristol and was a member of the

New York Yacht Club, as was I. Over dinner I proposed that he join us as one of the three "watch captains" we needed. I had decided that I would be the overall racing captain, and would float among the watches as required by the tactical conditions of the race. Halsey accepted with enthusiasm.

The racing fleet comprised about a dozen yachts, including several classics against which we would be racing, We were considered the favorite to win and everyone thought that we would probably break *Atlantic*'s old passage record of twelve days, four hours, and one minute from New York's Sandy Hook to the Lizard off England's port of Falmouth.

The days before the event were filled with planning, some practicing (that's when we ran aground—an inauspicious sign that, maybe, our cocky confidence was inappropriate), and social events including a black-tie dinner dance that Danielle and I attended. The only part of all this that was not perfect was a skippers' meeting where our use of the meteorologist, Jacques, was protested. None of the other yachts had such an onboard expert. They would rely, rather, on radioed weather information. I prevailed when I pointed out that there was no prohibition noted in the race instructions, and that I had hired the man already and paid for his trip. They said okay in the end but that gift to us turned out, I was shortly to discover, to be the proverbial poisoned chalice.

The morning of the start, we put the well-wishers, including Danielle, ashore. Counting me, there were nineteen of us aboard. As we motored out into the Hudson River, one of the last shouts from the dock was from my friend Bob Stone, the "Commodore of the Commodores" of the club: "Tom, remember that every inch you sail not on the rhumb line is a mistake!" He meant, I knew, sail to the finish line over the shortest route, and don't get distracted by weather-oriented strategy that takes you anywhere else. What sound advice. How stupid I was to ignore it!

We had a good start in strong wind, between a big tug serving as the committee boat and a buoy about where the starting line would have been in 1905. Hundreds of spectators were aboard members' motor yachts. We had too much sail up, making for a great show, but rendering the yacht a little hard to handle. I, of course, was at the helm wearing my NYYC white cap, brimming with confidence.

We settled into our routine of three watches: four hours on and eight off, with the most recent "off" watch to stand by in case extra hands were needed on deck. We were all guys, no women, and a social psychologist would immediately point out that the presence of a woman in a group of males helps to prevent violence. That student of group dynamics would also have decried the composition of the watches. With me, Bob the cook, and Jacques the navigator not assigned to any watch, and with our first mate nursing a broken arm in a cast and not able to take direct part in a watch either, the crew divided evenly into three sets of five guys each, and the watches split up pretty evenly between Americans, Brits, and French sailors. I should have split up the nationalities, but I was oblivious to the latent jingoism that a combination of sleep and food deprivation might bring to the surface.

Now, I must present Jacques in his full character. He was a champion solo sailor and it soon became evident why—at least the solo part. Normal crew mates wouldn't be able to stand him. He was absolutely poisonous in his contempt of anything or any thought not French. He couldn't abide any of the crew save the "French watch," youths whom he quickly came to dominate. Also he was fanatic in his demands that the yacht sail in directions which only he could choose. We were to "sail the millibars."

At his insistence I had purchased a very expensive electronic barometer sensitive to one millibar (one thousandth of an atmosphere). Jacques was in frequent contact with a colleague at the Paris weather bureau for the big picture of the wind patterns. On board we were to sail a course along pressure ridges which, if done properly, would optimize our performance and presumably lead to victory. He ignored me, mostly by pretending not to understand English. I was pretty sure that he called me a "dilettante owner" to the French watch. He was determined to run everything, and he ignored Halsey and Chris as well as me.

The trouble was that "sailing the millibars" didn't necessarily mean sailing in the direction of the finish line. I had the exhortation from the commodore in mind: always sail the rhumb line. Halsey quickly clashed with Jacques over the millibar strategy. Halsey pointed out that it would only work for yachts able to sail much faster than we could, boats like the catamarans and trimarans, on which Jacques had won his races. These lightweight fliers could keep up with the moving weather fronts, but we couldn't—not with our one hundred eighty tons of weight, and old-fashioned rig, we couldn't. But for the first three days it seemed like Jacques might be right, because even though we were sailing greater distances than our competitors, he had positioned us in really strong winds.

We were all tracking each other's positions via information provided from a position transponder that, for safety reasons, each yacht was required to carry aboard. Graham, the mate with the broken arm, was keeping the plots on a large chart on the salon table.

I had decided to overlap every watch change by standing the last thirty minutes of the retiring watch and the first thirty minutes of the fresh watch. That way I thought that I could "glue" all the watches together. While this plan required me to be on deck only six hours in twenty-four, I also was doing a great deal of the steering, particularly as the wind steadily increased, and I was getting only three hours of sleep between the watch changes. It was a foolish program for me personally, and soon I was exhausted. The coffee, which we all needed to keep going, disappeared, mysteriously, after the third day.

And we were in really strong wind. It rose from force four (sixteen knots) to force eight (forty knots) during the third day; we were running very fast before this wind. The waves became really big, around fifteen feet in height, and we started to surf down them. Every yacht has a theoretical hull speed, which is defined as 1.3 times the square root of the waterline length (Froude's Law); for *Mariette* the number is twelve and a half knots: in normal sailing that's about as fast as you can go. But we were consistently exceeding eighteen knots in the power of this wind, and at one point we touched twenty-two knots, as measured, quite accurately, by our GPS speedometer. The speed was enhanced, also, from a favorable eddy in the Gulf

Stream which we had sought and found. During the noon-to-noon run between the third and fourth days, we sailed 328 miles—a record for any twenty-four-hour run for any of the yachts, it turned out. This is not bad for a modern yacht; it's stupendous for a classic like *Mariette*. According to Graham's plots, we were not only in first place but also comfortably ahead of *Atlantic*'s record from 1905.

But, the race was beginning to take its toll on the crew. Unlike my boat *The Maltese Falcon* (I'll describe her later), where the sail handling is accomplished by just pushing buttons, on *Mariette* everything is intensely manual. Men had to climb up the ratlines between the shrouds one hundred feet above the deck to get to the topsails, which needed to be furled by hand and reset by hand as the varying wind strength required. Similarly, the jibs flying from the end of the bowsprit needed to be taken in, or reset, with changes in wind velocity.

These are tough and potentially dangerous jobs. Falling from the rigging was always a risk, even though every man had a safety harness. Death would have been instantaneous if the guy landed on deck, a little slower if he landed in the sea—it being nearly impossible to recover a lost sailor at these speeds and in these waves. Similarly, working the bowsprit was dangerous. If the yacht turned head to wind, to slow her, the bowsprit dipped into the waves, soaking the crew working there. If she didn't alter course, it was dryer, but at speeds of eighteen knots, if she *did* dip her bowsprit, the sailors would be swept away by the force of the water, saved, maybe, by their harnesses, if those didn't break. It is not without reason that schooner rigs like *Mariette*'s are called widow makers.

Nearly every watch, crewmen had to perform these tasks. They were expending enormous calories, and eating accordingly to replenish their energy. They were a macho bunch keen to win, but I was worried how we would get through to the finish. Also I was increasingly aware that I wouldn't be able to live with myself if one of these young men was seriously hurt, or worse. The unshaven and unwashed sailors had taken to sleeping in the saloon, because it was getting too difficult to stay in the bunks forward due to the extreme motion of the yacht in the waves. The tangle of exhausted bodies, dead to the world, scattered about this room began to resemble the scene from a badly planned cult suicide.

The next day we found ourselves in gusts of force ten winds in the fifty-knot range. The waves were truly enormous. The decks were continuously awash from waves "pooping" us over the stern, and there were only three of us with experience enough at he helm to keep the yacht from broaching: Halsey, Chris, and I. A broach — where the helmsman loses control and the boat turns broadside to be swept dangerously by the cascading waves — is a true nightmare. During some moments at the wheel, I lacked the strength to turn it against the force of the water rushing past the rudder and had to shout for help. Fortunately, *Mariette*'s long keel tended to minimize the broaching danger.

Chris and I realized that we had to put reefs in both the foresail and the mainsail. On a classic like this boat, it's an all-hands operation that takes about four hours. But we simply had to slow her before someone was badly hurt. As we were planning the maneuver, nature took the decision from our hands. The force of the wind in the foresail caused the bronze hanger (a fitting that holds the sail to the upper part of the mast at the height of the spreaders) to break and the sail came crashing down, breaking its gaff boom in the process. Relieved of the wind pressure, *Mariette* immediately became more controllable.

It took all hands over an hour to gather in the foresail and get the broken gaff off. It took another couple of hours to get a reef into the main sail. We were fortunate in getting this accomplished before it too broke, or was torn to shreds by the howling wind. Though I didn't know it at the time, this was the turning point of our race. The Goddess of Victory lost interest — we were probably looking too scruffy for her. But we soldiered on (if this term makes sense for sailors; *sailored on* doesn't sound right). We stuck the broken gaff down through the companionway stairway. It was too long to get inside completely, but the broken end was warm and cozy near the fireplace, out of the fray on deck. We took the wooden splints from our broken-leg repair kit and spliced them around the splintered gaff and bound it all together using the epoxy normally employed to make a cast for the broken bone. A young doctor from the American watch supervised the work. Twenty-four hours later we had the foresail back up, and in the lightening wind we also shook out the reef in the mainsail. Back in the game!

But, this was to be a strategic turn in the race. In the lighter wind, Halsey wanted to sail directly for the finish. Jacques was adamant that we follow the millibars on a course virtually perpendicular to the rhumb line, confident that this would carry us into a new wind that would power us to the finish, still about two thousand miles away. I talked to his guru in Paris who urged me to take Jacques's advice. It was a tough decision, but I decided that Jacques was the professional and that I should follow his plan. Halsey didn't buy it. It was soon discovered that as soon as Jacques and I were off deck, Halsey and his American watch would change course and steer straight for the finish. They did this continually. When this deception was discovered, Jacques became nearly hysterical in his anger. Let me correct that, he *did* become hysterically angry. In no time the entire yacht crew was swept up in this dispute, with the French watch entirely behind Jacques, and the American watch entirely behind Halsey, with the Brits divided between the two. Chris was stressed trying to keep peace, and I sort of let them battle it out, being uncharacteristically indecisive.

Exhaustion and a mysteriously dwindling amount of food were taking their toll on us all. We all were starting to look drawn and gaunt, with a weariness, rarely seen in youth, overlaying the faces of the crew. One night there was close to a fistfight over the division of hungrily coveted M&M's in a candy packet. Friendly sharing had vanished many watches before. So, in increasing exhaustion and in a sort of a low-blood-sugar torpor, we zigzagged our way along, two watches steering the Frenchman's millibar course and the Americans, defiantly, steering the rhumb line route.

After some days we did find the new wind. It was strong and in a direction dead against us—right on the nose—diabolically coming from the direction we had to sail. Jacques couldn't have been more wrong. It meant tacking up wind, our worst point of performance. Our competitors, all far to the south, had the backside of this wind, very favorably wafting them along to their finish. Jacques blamed it on Halsey, who blamed it back on the Frenchman. I blamed it on myself.

The problem was made clear when a crewman asked me for our expected time of arrival. With our only making good about two knots in the right direction, with the wind and the waves against us, and with still about a thousand miles to go, I thought to myself, "We'll never get there." But I just put him off with "I'll get back to you on that."

We had to change the plan. We had to sail in some other direction to find a more favorable wind. Jacques was insisting that we keep sailing north, in a direction still farther from the finish. Halsey and I decided that we should tack to the south but no one really knew what to do. The weatherman in Paris said, "You're fucked," but my French is pretty poor; he may have said "You're *really* fucked."

So we tacked south; I figured I would rather wind up in Spain than Greenland. Jacques literally became hysterical again, and I am not kidding. Fortunately, he was a tiny man, or I think in his rage he would have tried to deck me. I couldn't follow his tirade, but some of the French crew said that he was screaming that I should be relieved of command.

In my career in venture capital, which had by then, I thought, covered all the bases, I never had to shout: "CONFINE THAT MAN TO HIS QUARTERS!" But that's literally what I did say at that moment, and the American watch marched him below, past the threatening looks of the French watch, and put him in his cabin, where I posted a guard to keep him there.

So we sailed south in an increasingly violent wind. Jacques was communicating in French to the French that I was insane to sail the yacht into such strong winds that we would be unable to tack (I think that in his catamarans he may have been right about that—but not my *Mariette*) and so we all would die! A very worried Brit, who was sufficiently bilingual to understand the French terror tactics, came to me and asked, "Is it really too late for us to tack?" I looked at my watch and said, "We will tack without problem in exactly thirty minutes." We did it, and did it with no problem, helping me regain some crew confidence.

We sailored on (I can't resist using this term) and in no time, two days, we were becalmed.

We had been upon the waters of God's great ocean fifteen days by now. The food had been dwindling progressively, and we all had lost weight. Good for me, punishing for most of the guys who were pretty fit to begin with. Now, we had lost all the wind and we were floating in a breathless oily swell in the vicinity of a dead duck, whose carcass was rolling gently alongside.

Bob, the cook, came to me later that morning of day fifteen after a pretty thin breakfast of unflavored, unbuttered, unsweetened oatmeal with a side of oatmeal, rounded out by some extra oatmeal, all cooked in water, to say: "Tom, we are out of food."

"Ah, these emotional artists," I thought to myself, "always exaggerating!"

"Come. Let's look in the galley and see what we can find," I said.

Bob showed me a single, large, uncooked platter of lasagna. He said, "That's it. That's all that is left to eat."

"Oh, Bob, let's look around. Surely there are other things!" I looked. The cupboards were clean, not a can of anything in sight. The storage locker was empty. The freezer was void. There was absolutely nothing, not a bean, not a strand of spaghetti, not a tiny hoard of rice, of sugar, of wheat, of anything. But wait! I forgot to look under the floorboards. That's where I would find the reserve stores. I looked. Nothing. Had we had rats aboard they would have been goners; were we soon to follow?

"Bob, are you telling me that there is just this one platter of frozen lasagna for nineteen starving sailors aboard this boat?"

"Yes."

"How could this happen?"

"Well, the record is twelve days, four hours, and one minute—you must have been going slow. I figured you would break the record and we would have food to spare." How can you kill someone who had such great expectations for you, and whom you had so severely disappointed? Clearly it was all my fault.

I assembled the crew in the aft deck area and we had a group meeting. I explained our situation.

When should we eat the lasagna? "Now! Right now!" was their answer to my first question.

We have seventy-five miles to sail to the finish line, I said. That might take another day, I said. It would be nice to finish the race, I said.

This was a much tougher question. After much to-ing and fro-ing, it was voted that if the wind came up by eight the following morning, we would tighten our belts another notch and finish the race, even though we knew that because of our errors in navigation, we would be in dead last place, no matter what. If there was no wind at eight the next day, we would fire up our engines and motor to Falmouth, forfeiting all racing honor.

It was a painful night of hunger, and at eight the next morning, we hadn't sailed an inch. The dead duck was still our only companion on the empty flat sea. Only seventy-five miles to sail. Of course, there would soon be wind, maybe by noon, but a deal is a deal. I didn't even assemble the crew for another vote. I started the motors, and threw them into gear. Soon the dead duck was left far behind.

We reached Falmouth late that afternoon, and sure, the wind had come up. Too late. We pulled alongside the floating dock in midharbor, and Richard, my longterm shore-side chef, appeared in a motor launch with seventy-five hamburgers and seventy-five milk shakes. The crew plunged into an ecstasy of caloric intake, but I couldn't bear to stay aboard another ten seconds. Just before I departed, I offered my hand in friendship to Jacques. "Let bygones be bygones," I said. "Let's shake hands."

"*Non!*" And he turned on his heel and walked back into the midst of the French watch.

Ashore, my hunger pangs were adamant. Before driving away, I stopped in a little fish and chips shop on the quayside and ordered the traditional fare. It arrived shortly, soaked in rancid fish oil, revolting in smell and appearance. How could the English eat that stuff, I wondered. I couldn't do it. A lager saw me through.

And so ended my Great Ocean Race, with all its tough choices.

It affirmed once again how exquisite preparation and flawless teamwork, particularly the interpersonal relationships at the very top, are the fundamentals behind every success. Carly Fiorina says important, original things like this (carrying her trademark phrase: "I deeply believe . . .") in her book, *Tough Choices*. I wish she had written it before this race. I could have kept it mounted on the main mast in a little glass case with a hammer alongside; the sign would have said: "Break Glass in Case of Emergency."

It is simply too difficult for me to write directly about my relationship with my ex-wife. But I understand that readers of this book may be interested in knowing something about Danielle Steel and me. So, I present without edit or comment, in its entirety, an interview to be found in a recent issue of *Celebrity Wire*. I caution readers with the usual warning to be wary of trusting anything to be found in the popular press; one shouldn't believe a word.

Chapter Ten

CELEBRITY WIRE *1 April 2007*

INTERVIEW WITH TOM PERKINS
BY NATASHA STEINMETZ, SOCIETY EDITOR

C.W.: *So, Tom . . . What's Danielle Steel like?*

PERKINS: Well, Natasha, she is an incredible woman!

C.W.: *Of course, but can you give some insight into her personality?*

PERKINS: Sure. First of all you should say personalities. She has about ten of them. There is the world-famous writer. That's the creative, artistic personality that everyone knows. Then, behind the artist, is the shrewd businesswoman, who negotiates tough contracts for books, perfume, TV deals, and so forth. But the more basic Danielle is the loving mother. She is absolutely devoted to her children; they are very literally the most important part of her life. There were nine of them, including two stepsons, and not counting kids who have been informally adopted and live with her. There are a couple of those.

C.W.: *Goodness. I had no idea. So there are three Danielle personalities?*

PERKINS: Oh, Natasha, three are only a start! There's the glamour queen. You know that she has been voted the best dressed woman for years running, and she has a famous collection of jewelry to go with the dresses and furs. Seeing her step out of her Rolls at the opening of the opera is a photographer's treat!

But then there is the saint too. That's a far more important side of Danielle. She is profoundly religious and she does major, truly major, anonymous things to help the poor. I promised that I wouldn't "out" her in this interview, Natasha, but without getting specific in the details, I can tell you that she gives several million dollars away every year. And she is personally deeply involved, very deeply involved, in the work with those less fortunate who are the beneficiaries of all this money. I am talking about hundreds of hours of hard work. She works on this charity until she is so exhausted that her health is at risk. She has done this for years. One day the papers will discover what she has been up to for ever so long, but I promised her that I wouldn't tell.

Danielle and Tom aboard Mariette
off the coast of Ireland in 1997

C.W.: *That's fascinating and very generous, but does her charity work truly indicate a different personality?*

PERKINS: Well, I said, saint. At times the glamorous personality, and the mother, are entirely replaced by the religious woman who has, from time to time, entered serious discussions with the church about becoming a nun. A Carmelite nun. The kind that aren't permitted to speak.

C.W.: *But that's incompatible with the other personalities.*

PERKINS: You bet it is! Though a strong element, the mood usually doesn't last for more than a few days. I used to kid her out of it by saying that she should be more considerate, that the Catholic Church couldn't survive both the homosexual scandal and Danielle Steel in the same decade!

C.W.: *Fascinating! But let's get back to personality number one: Danielle the romance novelist. What can you say about that?*

PERKINS: Natasha, first of all, she would be very offended by your calling her a romance writer; that's the kind of writing *I* did with *Zillionaire!* She is a broadly based novelist, and a damned successful one. She will finish her one hundredth novel this year, and she has sold more books than any living writer—around six hundred million—and the records show that her books are second in sales only to Agatha Christie's, and Danielle is still writing, so she'll probably surpass Agatha eventually.

C.W.: *But Tom, be honest, aren't her books formulaic? Isn't there always a happy ending?*

PERKINS: Sure, there is always a happy ending. In fact the tag line for her new perfume is, *"Believe in happy endings."* But that's the only constant theme. Some of her plots are historical, and there is no consistent type of plot to the others, except the reader can expect a good cry or two, and yes, the happy ending. Her books cover the waterfront, wars, high society, the poor, and pretty much everything in between. It's amazing how she comes up with the plots. I think she has sunk the *Titanic* three times and the *Lusitania* at least twice!

C.W.: *I know that you have been a thinly disguised character in some of them. Have you ever gotten involved in helping her with the plots or the writing?*

PERKINS: Not the writing, but yes, a little with the plots. I started reading her manuscripts when we first met, about twelve years ago. She encouraged me to make suggestions, but I figured "don't fix what ain't broke." Still, when I noticed some mistake, like a love scene set on Long Island with the couple watching the sunset over the ocean, I would point it out ("The earth rotates in the other direction, Danielle"). However, gradually I got more involved. For example, in her book *Irresistible Forces* the plot timeline is based upon a public offering for a high-tech company. I provided that and it's really accurate, which gives more foundation to the plot, I think.

C.W.: *Did you ever change a plot?*

PERKINS: Only once. It was for her book *The Kiss* of a couple of years ago. The story is about a pretty French girl, unhappily married to a miserable banker in Paris. The girl has a platonic friendship with an American diplomat. The two accidentally meet in London, and of course, they fall in love. But before anything serious happens in the sex department, while riding in the back of a limo, they have a passionate kiss. Their driver is watching them and fails to notice a bus crossing in front. There is a crash, many are killed, and the couple wind up in intensive care together.

C.W.: *Gee, that sounds pretty gory!*

PERKINS: Oh that's nothing! In one of Danielle's books, at Christmas a terrorist blows up the children's department in a shopping mall store and kills Santa Claus. In *Irresistible Forces*, a plane crashes into a Manhattan skyscraper and hundreds are killed. The book was written long before 9/11.

Anyway, the couple nearly die. They have identical "light at the end of the tunnel" visions in which they find each other. The guy has a broken back and will be wheelchair-bound for the rest of his life.

C.W.: *OK, so what did you change?*

PERKINS: Well, as written, after many days have passed with both of them barely away from death's door, the girl crawls into bed with the man and they have great sex! Then, when he finds out that he will be paralyzed for life, he lies to her about how bad his injury actually is. He knows that she will stay by his side, and he is so honorable that he doesn't want her bound to a cripple. He returns to the States, and on phone calls he tells her that he is back to playing tennis. Eventually she sees him on TV in his wheelchair, understands how noble he has been, and flies to his side. And then there is the happy ending.

C.W.: *Well, it's pretty unrealistic. The sex in the intensive care unit is just not believable.*

PERKINS: Exactly! So that's the part I changed. In my version, she crawls into his bed in the ICU, and he can't get it up. Christ, he's got a broken back! So he thinks that he is impotent, and *that's* the reason that he rejects her. Eventually, of course, he recovers his sexual powers and I put the passionate sex at the end of the book.

C.W.: *So how did Danielle react?*

PERKINS: Oh, she was very reluctant to change anything. The book already had been approved by her publisher, and she said that her readers always expect some sex in the middle, and not at the end. But I was just adamant that she had to make the change. She finally did. Her publisher wrote back after reading the finished version, say-ing, "Only a writer of your courage and strength would *dare* to put an episode involving impotence at the center of a novel!" What a kick.

C.W.: *Is one of her books your favorite?*

PERKINS: Oh for sure, it's *The Klone and I*. I had a lot to do with that plot too.

I was going to New York for a board meeting, and Danielle didn't want me to leave. I said: "No problem, I've had Genentech clone me. He'll arrive tomorrow—you'll like him!"

I got a fax from her at my hotel later in the week: "Don't worry about hurrying back—the Klone arrived, and . . . well . . . he's pretty good. Oh, was it OK for me to let him use your Bugatti? He says the damage won't be too hard to repair."

And so began a running joke between us. The clone, which she always spelled with a K, because "he likes the idea of being Jewish; his first name is Isaac," became my alter ego. She was brilliant at flip-ping every personality trait of mine into the opposite for him—for example, he dressed in spandex and always bought flashy jewelry.

I was astonished when at Christmas she gave me a novelette, written just for me, with the title *The Klone and I*. I devoured it im-mediately and thought it very funny. The plot is clever; a lonely, re-cently divorced woman winds up falling in love with a serious guy and simultaneously with his wild alter ego. How she sorts out which to choose is pretty funny, and involves a little sexual innuendo of a very personal nature.

C.W.: *Oh, tell me!*

PERKINS: No way! You'll have to read the book and make your own guess. Full stop!

Anyway, I talked her into expanding the story into a full-length book and into sending it to her publisher. After a lot of back and forth, they decided to print it, but in a different size and with differ-

Author Danielle Steel, and Danielle Steel
posing as her clone, for the back cover
of her bestseller The Klone and I

ent colors on the cover. They wanted the readers to know that it was
not the usual Steel book. It got really good reviews (most of her
books don't get sent for review at all) and it sold very well, but to a
different audience.

   She actually got hate mail from her core readers. One letter that
I saw said: "Don't ever do this again! We buy your books to cry, not
to laugh!" So the businesspeople told her in no uncertain terms: no
more humor! It was too bad, really, because she has a huge talent for
comedy.

Danielle is, I think, underestimated in this country as a serious writer. The French, on the other hand, consider her to be the modern Balzac. A little while ago, they awarded her the Legion of Honor, their highest award.

C.W.: *So how does she actually do it? What process does she go through to write four books a year? Four good books; or even four not so good books, either way, that's a staggering amount of writing.*

PERKINS: It is. Danielle works most of the time, Natasha, and is thinking about her books all of the time. She'll say, for example, "I have been thinking about a Jewish nun during World War II." Next thing, she starts to write an outline of a book on that subject. She puts major effort into these outlines; they are very long, not just a few pages of ideas. Rather, they run to well over one hundred pages and include, really, the essence of the book. All the key conversations are there and all the key emotional events. She then sends the outline to her agent, Mort Janklow, one of the top literary agents, and to her editor at her publisher, Delacorte, for their opinions. Maybe she'll make a few changes based upon the feedback.

After that she sets the outline aside for about six months, letting it, I think, seep through her subconscious. In the interim she edits and proofs other books already in the pipeline.

After that six-month gestation, she blocks out time on her calendar to write the book. Usually she blocks out enough time to write two books. And, by "block out" I mean really block out. No breaks of any type, no phone calls, no social interactions, nothing is allowed that might divert her concentration. Food trays are left outside her closed door.

C.W.: *Does she dictate them?*

PERKINS: Oh no!
Danielle says that "Ollie" writes her books, and she sort of has a

magical belief that it's really so. Ollie is her decades-old Olympia typewriter, on whose wizardly keys she will soon finish the hundredth book, the milestone I mentioned before. Ollie is a mechanical brute. After twenty hours of nonstop typing, Danielle sometimes has to wrap her hands in ice, the machine is so demanding. And though computer literate, Danielle has the belief that, somehow, only Ollie can do the books. Needless to say, over the years Ollie has been rebuilt numerous times by an old man, a typewriter expert who flies out from New York and cannibalizes parts from the dozen Ollie duplicates stored in the basement vault.

So, after a final rereading of the outline, she tosses it aside and starts typing. Like Mozart, she says that she literally "hears" the book and she types as fast as she possibly can to get it down on paper while the voice is speaking. Danielle produces roughly one hundred finished book pages per day. Astonishingly, a four hundred and fifty page book—her average—is finished in four and a half days! If it takes five days she says that she is experiencing writer's block. Remember, though, she is really just fleshing out the outline, which is wonderfully complete. And then there will follow months of editing and rework until the book is really finished.

I have watched her at work. The pages fly from Ollie. She doesn't stop to reread what she has already written. The pages flow, steadily, one after the other without pause. Even after a few short hours of sleep—when she is writing she works roughly twenty hours per day—the flow resumes immediately.

C.W.: *Wow! That's amazing. I thought every writer labored over and over reworking what's already been written.*

PERKINS: Well, maybe most do, but not Danielle Steel. It's both the greatest strength, and maybe the core weakness in her books. Her publisher once told me, "Danielle writes emotion, no one does it better." And that's probably true. The emotion just surges and flows in her novels; all her readers feel it. I have seen her crying at Ollie's keyboard, as she herself is caught up in the pathos of the text. And even when I know the plot in advance, from having read the outline, she makes me cry every time! She'll catch me wiping my eyes, and with a grin she'll say: "Got you, didn't I."

But the speed makes it tough to avoid some repetition, and the speed makes her vulnerable to critics who crave subtlety and more inner clockwork to the characters' personalities. But the critics don't write books that have accrued over six hundred million in sales. She pays them no heed.

C.W.: *Tom, that's all interesting. But, I have to ask: you were husband number five, and the official marriage didn't last for much longer than a year. Whatever were you thinking?*

PERKINS: I resent the way you have put that, Natasha. You are implying that it was her fault that the marriage didn't work. If there was fault, it was on my part. And, we have been together off and on for over eight years.

C.W.: *Sorry . . . tell me about it, please.*

PERKINS: Well, Gerd and I had known Danielle socially and her husband John Traina, to whom she was married for seventeen years, around San Francisco and the Napa Valley. She and John, coincidentally, were married at a house in the valley foothills that Gerd and I subsequently acquired.

After Gerd's death, which happened around the same time she and John were starting to think of breaking up, Danielle and John attended a dinner party I gave for Patrick O'Brian. I was pleased to renew the acquaintance and after she and John separated we began to see each other. We enjoyed each other's company tremendously, and her sensitivity over Gerd, whose passing was nearly a mortal blow to me, was of great help. Danielle and I were good together but if fate hadn't intervened, the relationship would probably have remained only one of deep friendship.

One Saturday afternoon in September of 1997, I was serving as tactician aboard a friend's sailboat in a race on the bay and as soon as I got ashore, Kathy, my assistant, tracked me down. Nick, Danielle's nineteen-year-old son, had committed suicide early that morning, and Danielle needed my support. I rushed up to her house, the old Spreckels mansion, and found her traumatized nearly beyond human endurance by shock and grief.

Nick Traina was a remarkable young man, brilliant, charming, very handsome, and very talented. Girls, and women for that matter, were his whenever he wished. He was a poet of genius, and a rock musician with three CDs to his credit, a Las Vegas debut already accomplished, and his bands, Link 80 and Knowledge, had large followings in the teenage set. He was on his way to big-time stardom; he was already a star in his age group, and his recent concert tour had been a smash success.

C.W.: *He sounds like wonder boy. Whatever went wrong?*

Perkins: Wonder boy he was!

But he had suffered from lifelong bipolar disease, commonly called manic depression. He had attempted suicide before. The penultimate attempt had nearly succeeded, and I had spent time with him at his bedside in the locked hospital ward where he was recovering. He was very articulate. He told me, "When it's bad it's like having hornets inside your brain. You can't escape them." Nick liked me, because I was good to his mother. He loved Danielle with an intensity rare even between mother and son; everything was super intense with Nick. He told me one night in the hospital that he understood that if he killed himself, it would destroy her. He pledged to me that it would never happen. I believed him, and I think at that instant he really did mean it. But the very next day some of his friends smuggled poison into the locked ward "to help him out. What are friends for?" they later said. He started to take the stuff, but that time, the hospital attendants caught him in the process and saved him.

Finally, that September morning, after a day when everything seemed to be great for him—a good rehearsal with his new band; a good date with a new girl in whom he was interested; about twenty telephone calls to friends (it's now clear that they were good-bye calls) but no call to his mother, who would have sensed immediately that he was teetering on the brink of the decision between life and death, he injected himself with so much morphine that he died before he hit the floor.

C.W.: *God! That's awful. I just thought that he was a druggie who simply overdosed. I think that's what the papers said.*

PERKINS: The papers have always taken the greatest pleasure in trashing Danielle. She's such an easy target, so trashing her son came naturally, I suppose.

C.W.: *Tell me, please, how that day led to the marriage later.*

PERKINS: Danielle was so devastated that I didn't see how she could survive. She was hardly functioning and to this day she can't remember whole segments of that weekend. I think it's nature's way of protecting the mind from such a staggering blow. But there was much to be done, family to be told, funeral arrangements to be made, a casket chosen, all the mundane but dreadful duties that fall upon the survivor. I was with her most moments, helping her to get through it. The funeral was in Grace Cathedral, and it was literally standing room only. Hundreds of his rock fans attended. He still has a cult following with some of those fans. Danielle was walking through all this as in a dream. My heart went out to her. We bonded during those awful days.

Later, when we were alone again, she was so depressed that I became deeply worried. Her lethargy was totally uncharacteristic and I was frightened for her. I remember taking her by the hand into her tiny office, the place where all of the books are written, and sitting her down in front of Ollie. She just slumped in her chair. I put a fresh piece of paper in the machine, and said: "Danielle, write

Nick's story." I left her there, and after some minutes I heard Ollie's type begin to strike the paper. I think Ollie saved her life. The book, her only significant work of nonfiction, came to be called *His Bright Light: The Story of Nick Traina.*

She donated the proceeds, and it was an immense success, to a foundation in Nick's name for the benefit of sufferers of bipolar disorder including research for a cure. The book has had a major positive impact on removing the stigma of that form of mental illness upon families. The book remains popular and a lasting tribute to Nick. It's Danielle's greatest writing.

C.W.: *And the marriage?*

PERKINS: Later that year, in December after the divorce from John, I made a long-planned voyage to Antarctica aboard my yacht *Andromeda*. December is summertime down there and we were very lucky with the weather—it was even nice sailing around dreaded Cape Horn. The icebergs we saw and the scenery were spectacular. I had satellite telephone, and I was talking with Danielle every day. Christmas had been extremely hard for her without Nick. She was still very depressed. One evening I simply said, "Why don't we get married when I return?" It was surely the first time marriage has been proposed from a yacht surrounded by floating bergs to a woman thousands of miles away. She said that we would decide when I got back.

I think from the beginning Danielle suspected that it wouldn't work: for good reason. I had backed out of two previous tentative proposals, one of which we had announced to close friends. We both led hugely complicated lives. I traveled a lot both for business and pleasure and I had houses scattered around the world; she had a big career and numerous children with all the responsibilities that entailed. Also, I hadn't recovered completely from losing Gerd. She put her finger on that aspect once when she said, "If Gerd were to return, you'd choose her over me, wouldn't you?"

How do you answer that one?

But we persisted in talking about marriage, and via three-way discussions with a friendly psychiatrist we decided that everything would be fine.

I assumed we would have a simple ceremony, a few friends, some flowers, a string quartet quietly playing something soft and unrecognizable in the background. She had something of an extravaganza in mind, and of course, that's what happened. I kidded her that our marriage would be more grand than the wedding scene from Verdi's opera *Aida*. I said, "Danielle, we are going to have everything but the elephant!" On the day, she had a huge papier-mâché elephant delivered to stand in the courtyard.

In my (I am becoming a "Man of Steel") speech at the reception, I kidded that we should have downsized the wedding and joked that previously I had downsized, as many of our friends knew, by eliminating the bride herself!

The baby arrived on the weekend of our matrimony.

C.W.: *Baby! What baby? What are you talking about? You and Danielle didn't have a child together, did you?*

PERKINS: We were having dinner a few days before the wedding, just the two of us in her elegant dining room, when Martha, the "alpha nanny," entered (I call her the alpha nanny because at that time there were six nannies on the staff, and Martha was the boss nanny). She was excitedly whispering something in Danielle's ear, and I distinctly heard "baby coming" a couple of times. After Martha left the room I asked, "What baby is coming?" Danielle was very flustered, embarrassed, and finally told the story. During the Nick crisis, when Danielle had no extra scope to deal with additional problems, Martha had begged her for permission to adopt a baby. Danielle, thinking that adoptions take forever, acceded, never realizing that sometimes unwanted babies—who knows, maybe from distressed situations—can be obtained about as easily as overnight delivery via FedEx. Or so it seemed to me.

Now, you have to understand, as Danielle patiently explained it to me, that nannies are not "staff," nannies are "family." So the nannies live with you all the time, take all their meals, vacations, and so forth with the family. Martha had the bedroom across the hall from ours, and of course, that's where the baby was. The baby did a lot of crying in the early months, and I hadn't expected to be rediscovering that sound at my age (mid-sixties) when I moved in. The baby traveled with us, and even spent fourteen days on my yacht, to the astonishment of my visiting yachtsmen friends.

The baby and I shared one thing in common, though: it was hard to find a place for our stuff. The Spreckels mansion is, I think, the largest house west of the Mississippi—all fifty-five thousand square feet of it. Danielle found a closet, about the size of a phone booth, for me when I moved in. All the other closets were stuffed with the clothing and shoes, lots and lots of shoes, of Danielle and the four girls living at home.

Her son Maxx, then around nine, and I were the only guys in the place. Shortly after I moved in, Maxx opened the door to my bathroom while I was sitting on the toilet, and chucked in a cherry bomb. So, I knew that he thought I was OK.

C.W.: *So what was it like living in that mansion? Was it glamorous?*

PERKINS: Oh, very glamorous. The ballroom can hold a band, tables to seat around one hundred people, and still have plenty of space for dancing. Danielle gave lots of parties. Christmas was beautiful, with three huge trees in the ballroom, and big piles of gifts for everyone, nannies included, of course.

Danielle is hugely generous, overcoming, I think, the memories of a very unhappy childhood—she was an only child with abusive parents. Just read the first chapter of *The Long Road Home* for a sketch of a monster mother; the sequence where the mother smashes the favorite doll and strikes the child hard enough to cause permanent hearing damage is unforgettable. My guess is that feelings like that don't come from a vacuum.

So, glamorous, yes. But living there was pretty chaotic and a bit like trying to take a sip from a fire hydrant of emotion. We ate dinner together in a circular room of marble walls, floor, and ceiling. All of us at a huge round marble table. With all the kids, all the nannies, and almost always a few extra friends of the kids present, the group could range up to fifteen or more at each dinner. The baby, crying or not, was always there in a high chair. There also were four or five small dogs, the kind that yap constantly. Every time, and I mean every time, the butler opened the door to bring something to the table, all the dogs went nuts. The chaotic sounds bouncing around and around that marble room reverberate in my memory still.

Mother's Day was also an important time. The children would gather in the sitting room off our bedroom and give their mom gifts, love and kisses before breakfast. I was there with my big dog, a Rhodesian ridgeback named Tomba. Gerd's cat, Kitty-Cat, was relegated to the basement, because Danielle is deathly allergic to cats. There, her muscular Moroccan bodyguard stroked Kitty sitting in his chair, looking just like the villain from a James Bond movie. That Mother's Day morning one of the girls, I think it was Vanessa, came in with her tiny teacup dog, a Mexican hairless, following behind her. Tomba leaped up to greet the creature. Her dog shrieked in pure terror. Danielle fainted, but I caught her while simultaneously restraining Tomba. Danielle came to on the floor, with Tomba licking her face.

If this was glamour, we had plenty of it.

C.W.: *You have mentioned emotion a couple of times. Did you and Danielle have a really stormy time together? Is that what went wrong between you two?*

PERKINS: No, Natasha, that's not it at all. True, Danielle was into "relationship" talks. I think Gerd was very exceptional among women in disliking such talks. She had the basic insight: most women think that men can be improved; most men don't think that men can be changed, so it doesn't occur to them to try doing it to women. I recall one weekend with Danielle when the talk started Friday evening and was still going strong with fresh things from her to say on Sunday evening. I ended it that night by sleeping with Tomba in the basement.

But we were always calm. Danielle was an only child and she

had, I believe, a very, very lonely and unhappy childhood. Though born into wealth and privilege, with schooling and travel that make her totally fluent in five languages, she was, I think, starved emotionally. Her mother abandoned her while she was a little girl. So as a child she invented happy stories to tell to herself, obviously leading to her enormous success later as a novelist. I think her father cheated her out of a trust left for her by the grandparents. Anyway, before his death the millions in his charge were gone. Shortly before her mother's death, and Danielle supported her in a life of luxury in New York, that narcissistic woman took great pride in telling Danielle that she had never read a word from any of the books. I probably am not the first man to have detested his mother-in-law.

C.W.: *So Danielle was* not *emotional?*

PERKINS: I used to kid Danielle that "you invented perpetual emotion."

But that's not quite right. It's more like she has seen more than her fair share, and understands *everything* on an emotional level. Danielle is truly empathic; in pop culture she would be called an "empath." I have seen total strangers, like airport attendants, given a few minutes with her, pour out their innermost emotional secrets, all the tragedy and all the drama of their lives.

Don't get me wrong. Danielle is not a drama queen seeking drama in the lives of others or in her own life. Truly not at all. Rather, things happen in her life—serious, important things—that keep the emotional pot boiling. I'll just give you a flavor. Nick's primary caregiver was a woman named Julie who was very depressed by his suicide. After Nick's death Danielle took Julie into her life like a daughter. A year or so later, Julie moved away and also committed suicide using a shotgun in front of her three-year-old. More trauma for Danielle.

There have been very real, very serious death threats, and stalkers. Tourist buses blocking access to the house. Police investigations into plots and scams, and so on.

A radio station launched an attack on her (to build listenership) which wound up with a male prostitute having sex with a blow-up doll in front of her driveway. He was arrested, and the station taken to court.

Then there was the paper cut from one of Ollie's flying pages on her little finger which led to septicemia and the threat of amputation of the finger. I flew back from England to be with her, but she had recovered sufficiently to be still typing.

I sometimes teased her by asking what had she done in a previous life. Had she been, maybe, Lucrezia Borgia? What brings on this stream of bad karma, this stream of misfortune?

It continues to this day. Her staff of around twenty-five are very happy; she is wonderful to them, and I think that they love her. But there is the occasional bad apple who sues her, trying to get an unwarranted settlement. She always fights; on principle every suit is fought until thrown out by the court or there is a nominal settlement. One of the last was for gender discrimination, which is a real hoot because for years Danielle had a male assistant who sometimes showed up as "Jeanna" in full six feet four inches of drag, not counting the high heels. One of my yacht crew asked him once, "What do you call a man that dresses like that?" The answer: "Sir!"

C.W.: *Tom, that's all interesting, but you are ducking my question. What went wrong? Why did you divorce? When you reconciled, why didn't it last?*

PERKINS: Natasha, more went right than wrong. We are still the best of friends, and we see each other often and we e-mail each other a couple of times a week. We still play liars dice together—it's a game I taught her, and she is a total addict to it. She gives liars dice parties about once a month.

C.W.: *Still ducking!*

PERKINS: OK. Most of our friends didn't think our marriage would work: two lives too big to meld comfortably together; harder than merging GM with GE. That was the obvious problem.

But the inner problem is that I am too selfish and too self-absorbed to be the companion Danielle needs. Her disastrous childhood left her with the deepest, the most fundamental of her many personalities: that of the needy child. Underneath all the huge success, and all the glamour, and all the talent, is a frightened little girl whose hunger for acceptance and love can never be fully satisfied.

My heart still aches for that child.

C.W.: *And you won't say any more on that subject?*

PERKINS: No.

C.W.: OK *then, Tom, let me wind up with a personal question just about yourself. You have accomplished a lot. How would you like to be remembered: as the venture capitalist who helped start Silicon Valley, or as the yachtsman who created the breakthrough vessel,* The Maltese Falcon—*which man will history remember?*

PERKINS: Natasha, your question puzzles me. I expect to be remembered for winning the Nobel Prize in Literature. You know, for *Sex and the Single Zillionaire!*

We are going to be coming up on a chapter that is set in Holland. Before just jumping into that, I want to give you some idea why I was so intrigued with the potential Dutch breakthrough at the root of the tale. I am very fond of these people.

During the summer of my junior year at MIT, I had the chance to work at Philips N.V. in Eindhoven, Netherlands. The institute hosted a student-operated program to make all the arrangements, and I was active in the little group, thereby insuring that I and my friend Jim from the fraternity would get a shot at participating. I was intrigued by Philips because another school chum, Diek, an older married friend, was from Holland and his father was the managing director of the company at the time. Then, as now, Philips was a leader in technology and I was very excited by the prospect of getting a look into the company.

Neither Jim nor I had ever been out of the country, and the prospect of a long summer in Europe was very exciting. We took a ship from Montreal to Bremen that was packed with students, and of course that was a lot of fun. We were both amazed at the devastation of the German cities that was still evident in 1952 from Allied bombing during the war. When we pulled into Eindhoven on the train, the Philips buildings seemed to go on forever The company then had its original name: Philips *Gloeilampenfabrieken* — light-bulb works.

I was lucky—probably being a friend of the boss's son helped—to get a summer assignment in the NatLab (nature laboratory) where some pretty pure research was being done. The lab was the European equal to our famous Bell Labs in America. My boss was Professor Stumpers, a Dutch chess master, who was developing a new kind of radio telescope. It was a great job. The professor had me build an experimental linear amplifier. Of course, in 1952, there weren't transistors (and the group in the lab working on their development was the only group I was forbidden to visit) so this was done with vacuum tubes, which the Europeans always called "valves." We got it to work, but not for very long at a time, as it was unstable with changes in room temperature caused by the heat from all those tubes themselves. But, it was a great summer, living with a nice Dutch family, and cycling to work every day with literally tens of thousands of others on their bikes. Philips, Holland, and Europe made a hugely favorable impression on me, maybe explaining why I wound up married to a European and living in Europe for much of the time.

Anyway, when I got a call from a management recruiter in the mid-nineties, looking for an American "high-tech type" to join the Philips board of directors, I said yes immediately. He was stunned, having struck out with all the others he had contacted; few apparently were willing to make the trek to Eindhoven, that nether region of the Netherlands several times a year. But I felt a loyalty to the company from all those years ago, and I was also extremely curious as to how a board of a giant company in Europe worked. It wouldn't take me long to find out, and to bring my trademark (exasperating) impatience to that board's attention.

Big companies in Europe are organized much differently from ours in the U.S. Typically there is both an inside board, made up of company managers, and an outside or "supervisory board" made up of non-employee independent directors. I joined this latter board, which contained some very impressive individuals, the former CEOs of both Shell and Unilever, for example. The CEO of the company, a tall, silver-haired man named Cor Boonstra, had visited me in San Francisco before my first meeting to bring me up to speed on current problems and he asked for my help to solve them, including developing a better working relationship between the board and the company. He said that the directors seemed indifferent and remote, not very involved.

The boardroom in the Eindhoven headquarters was extremely impressive. The polished wooden table seated some twenty men: ten of the company managers and us ten "supervising" directors. Everyone had a microphone and a big book containing the presentations that were being given. The speaker (English is the official language of the company) stood at a podium in front of a giant screen upon which his data were projected. The setup couldn't possibly have been more formal or less conducive to interaction. I had been on the board of Corning Glass, which was similarly huge, but the directors got involved in the action. This was totally different: frozen, stiff, inflexible, and preordained were the words that came to mind.

About twenty minutes into the first presentation, I interrupted the speaker with a question. There was a shocked silence. The chairman of the board glowered at me and said: "This is your first meeting, so you don't understand. We hold all our questions until the end of the meeting."

"No," I said. "I want the question answered now; I think that there is a mistake in the assumptions behind the data."

The silence was deafening, and the chairman's glower began to verge upon a snarl, but finally the speaker broke the impasse and answered, pointing out along the way that perhaps my view of the assumption was really the correct one. I got the cold shoulder from the chairman for a few of the subsequent meetings but slowly, to his credit, when my interactive style of working with management gradually began to become the normal style of the other directors, he came around to my way. When I had to leave the board after only a couple of years because of increasing competitive overlap between Philips and Compaq (where I also served on the board), he thanked me publicly for my help in making the board more functional. At my last meeting we approved moving the headquarters to Amsterdam.

You just have to admire the Dutch. They have achieved a wonderful culture of hard work intermixed with the most liberal of social views. Amsterdam is a beautiful and cosmopolitan city. I have always loved to go there, and after one gets used to the occasional sight of an addict shooting up in a doorway, one comes to accept the approach, which seems no more damaging to society in general than our "war on drugs." That's the libertarian in me showing through.

On a recent visit I poked my head into a "coffee" shop in which hashish was openly being sold and openly being smoked, all quite legally. The place had a large refrigerator with a glass door displaying little baskets of "magic mushrooms." All the baskets were the same price, but the Dutch, true to their core values, were entirely honest on the printed labels on each shelf. The top shelf had these psychedelic "shrooms" labeled "for beginners;" the middle shelf said "for a good safe trip," but the bottom shelf said "only for the deeply experienced—don't even think about these if you aren't sure!"

My friends dragged me out before temptation took hold of my better judgment to test their truth in advertising.

So, with this plug under our belts for the land of tulips and technology, let's look at the best venture capital deal of my experience. It's also the worst.

Chapter Eleven

The Deal of a Lifetime Ends a Life

Roel Pieper called me one afternoon in the summer of 2000 at my home in England: "Tom what would you say if I told you that I have an inventor who can put two hours of video, including the sound, on a smartcard?"

"Roel, remind me of how much memory is on a smartcard—it's not much, is it?"

"Right, very little, only seventy five kilobytes."

"Well, two hours of video would take much more, megabytes, no gigabytes probably, so I would say it's impossible."

"It's possible. I have it working in my office. With this invention we can put every single motion picture ever made in history and all the sound tracks to go with all those movies on one big computer disc."

"Roel, that defies Shannon's theorem and I think maybe Fourier's and Green's too. It's impossible." If I could have thought of any other theories to throw in I would have done so. It seemed to be a loony idea.

"Can I come over and see you . . . tomorrow?"

"Sure," and so began a remarkable adventure into science, greed, ecstasy, and ultimately into death and frustration.

■　■　■

I picked Roel up at Gatwick Airport in my McLaren F-1 on which I had just taken delivery. It was street legal—maybe insane, but legal.

Roel Pieper,
noted Dutch business executive

The car, one of sixty built for the road, and one of about ten in England, would go two hundred forty-one miles per hour; perhaps not very practical in a country so crowded with cars that getting out of second gear was a notable experience. Roel is a very big guy, a former basketball star, and he had a little trouble squeezing into one of the two passenger seats, which straddle the driver's center position — it's a wild car. He began talking about the inventor's idea on the way to my house.

Roel and I had long experience working together. We first met while I was chairman of Tandem Computers; he had been hired to run one of the divisions. Though Dutch born and educated with a PhD in computer science, he had a long history in the American computer industry, having been instrumental in making the UNIX operating system a commercial success. When Jimmy Treybig, the founder of Tandem, stepped down (under pressure from the board) as CEO, Roel took over the job. He was instrumental in merging Compaq with Tandem and wound up as executive vice president of the combined companies.

Almost simultaneously with my leaving the Philips board, Roel, still in his early forties, was recruited away from Compaq to become senior vice president of the Dutch company. The betting was that he soon would become the CEO of Philips, so Roel's returning to Holland was like the homecoming of a conquering hero. He had become as famous in the Netherlands as Bill Gates had become in America, and his pronouncements were similarly followed in the press. However, Roel was not to be crowned the king of Philips. A dispute over the strategic direction of the company found Roel and the supervisory board stacked against the internal board and the CEO. When the latter refused to budge, Roel resigned, and the dispute was debated in print. Within a few months external events proved Roel's ideas correct, and he became even more prominent, a national figure. That's when he decided to go into the venture capital business and when I became one of his investor limited partners, and a member of his advisory committee. So, it was perfectly natural for him to be bringing me this, his new idea.

Over lunch he attempted to explain it to me. A Dutch inventor by the name of Jan Sloot, who had no academic credentials and who had been for most of his life a television repair technician, had come up with an astonishing new concept. He had been working on the idea for about fifteen years, and only now with the advent of the latest and most powerful of microprocessors was it practical. It was not a scheme for a new kind of data compression, Roel explained to me. The idea did not depend upon throwing away most of the data as in normal data compression. Rather, Sloot's invention generated images from look-up tables.

This was not at all clear to me. "I don't see how you can get a couple of hours of television onto a card with almost no memory. It just turns information theory on its head," I said.

"Sloot makes an end run around conventional information transmission," he said. "Think for a minute: if I want you to see an image of the *Mona Lisa*, I could scan a photograph and send the bits in a stream to you and you could reassemble them into the picture. That would take a lot of bits and a lot of time. Or, I could just tell you to look on page seventy-five of an art history book, and there you would find the image. The second method takes almost no bits and is very fast."

"So think of the system the system working this way," he continued. "On the transmitting end you have software that receives an image in real time and converts that image into a very limited string of bits for light and sound based upon instructions in a look-up table. The transmitting box sends those bits to the receiving end where those same bits are used to look up in the same table the light and sound needed to regenerate the original image."

"It sounds like black magic to me, Roel."

"Tom, it's better than black magic. It's truly revolutionary! Because the data rate is so low with this technology, television can go over normal wires. The picture telephone is a trivial first application. No more cable, no more fiber optics are needed! Whole libraries of video can be put in the consumer's pocket. Tom, I have come up with a name for this company: 'Fifth Force'—there are the four forces of nature and then there is us! We are the fifth force, the force of information!"

We discussed the invention in greater detail over the next couple of hours. Roel's own skepticism had been as great as my own initially, but he had put some of his staff on the project, including another PhD in computer science, and his team had become believers. The inventor, Jan Sloot, had revealed every step in the technology, save one key piece of knowledge—he was keeping the software program, the "compiler," the logic that did the actual conversions of image to look-up table indices—secret until he had a final offer from Roel. All the hardware was standard off-the-shelf electronic components available at a reasonable cost. The Fifth Force products could sweep the world. They had a written preliminary agreement on everything, but not a final commitment. Roel wanted my personal participation before taking that last step.

Although still very much the doubting Thomas, I agreed to fly over to Amsterdam the following week to have a look in person. I was suspicious of some kind of trick; maybe, a secret disc hidden somewhere, or maybe a concealed antenna. Before I promised to make the trip for a firsthand look, Roel agreed to my conditions of a demonstration in real time: we would record a television program which I would select at random and we would play back that exact program immediately. Roel said, "No problem."

Roel and Ricka Pieper live in a mansion near the seafront on the outskirts of Amsterdam; the property is vast by Dutch standards, making it like the King Ranch (the Texas farm bigger than Rhode Island) of the tiny Netherlands. I arrived and found Roel, his team, and the inventor, Sloot, a small wispy guy who looked vaguely like Adolf Hitler, together with his assistant, a largish young man, who turned out to be his son. Everyone and everything was ready for me, and with a minimum of chit-chat, I fell upon the two boxes set up on a table in Roel's office: the "recording" box and the "playback" box. They were open and ready for my examination, each about the size of a regular briefcase and each with a slot to receive a normal smart-card. I studied them very closely. The circuit boards were loaded with standard integrated circuits, nothing special at all, and there was nothing suspicious: no hidden disc, no secret antenna. Every-thing was very routine.

Mr. Sloot was not interested in any further delay. We turned on the TV and I selected a program on cooking that was airing at that time. He took a smartcard out of his pocket and inserted it into the recording box, and pushed a button to start the process. We sipped our coffee while the boring kitchen class droned on. After about twenty minutes I announced that sufficient time had gone by. If the recording was being made in the normal way, the card memory would have been swamped thousands of times over.

The inventor removed the card and stuck it into the playback box, pushing another button to start the action.

It was all there!

He could fast forward, he could backtrack. He could freeze the frame, he could speed up and slow down at will. The picture quality was almost equal to the original. In simple terms, the original was of

the standard European TV quality, and the playback was a little better than standard American TV quality (the U.S. standard has fewer
lines of information per screen), but Jan assured me that the playback quality would be equal to the original when he substituted the
very latest and faster microprocessors coming out soon.

I had witnessed the fifth force.

Roel and I excused ourselves. We needed to huddle over the
next steps to be taken. He had already invested well over a million
dollars in getting the technology far enough along for this demonstration and he would be investing more. My role was also to put in
near-term cash, and, more importantly, to assume some responsibility for raising the huge amounts that would be needed to carry
Fifth Force to global prominence. I had not the slightest doubt that
we were about to become the proprietors of a phenomenon which
would accrue billions of dollars of value to the share owners. One of
the biggest would be Jan Sloot. Roel and I made a handshake agreement between ourselves, and we returned to the others waiting in
his office, where Roel accepted the final contract with Jan Sloot.
Fifth Force was going to happen! We all would become rich beyond
the dreams of avarice. Ricka suggested that it was time for a little
celebration and shortly a chocolate cake appeared, together with a
big bottle of Champagne to wash it down.

We were all excited. My decision to help in the financing was
the golden moment for the group. I studied Jan Sloot. He was in a
state of . . . well . . . bliss. . . . That's the only word I can find to describe the expression on his face. He had labored in obscurity for
fifteen years, and at this moment all his dreams, all his plans and
fantasies were coming true. He was literally the happiest man I had
ever seen.

It was a nice moment, but the afternoon was drawing to a close
and I had one of Roel's staff drive me back to Schipol Airport for my
return to London. That night I couldn't sleep very well. The Fifth
Force opportunity had me in its grip. My mind was reeling with all
the opportunities the technology would open: whole movies on
small silicon chips; the picture telephone would be child's play (be-

cause video bandwidth was not needed); satellites would be able to broadcast individualized programs, so little of their channel capacity would be required; and so on, and so on. I planned to get Rupert Murdoch involved once we were a little further along. His NewsCorp, being a major owner of content, could be transformed by our new low-cost system of delivery; it could give them a huge jump on their competitors, making their satellites enormously more competitive. I was planning to have his company become one of our major funding sources. Then there was the whole new market for picture telephones to be developed. The telephone companies wouldn't have to modify their equipment in any way. Fifth Force would be a gold mine for them. How much should we license? How much should we manufacture ourselves? My thoughts excitedly ran on and on.

The next morning I waited until around eight o'clock my time, which would not be too early for me to call Roel; Holland was an hour ahead. I was very excited and wanted to discuss everything all over again with him. He picked up on virtually the first ring.

"Roel! I have been thinking. We should make some demonstration units for the telcos and I want to get Rupert up to speed as soon as possible, and—"

"Tom, he died . . ."

"—and after we have got him interested, we should bring other players into the picture; I am thinking Sony should be among the first, because—"

"After you left he died."

"What?"

"Jan Sloot died."

"What do you mean, he died?"

"Tom, not long after you left, he keeled over onto the floor. We tried CPR and then rushed him to the hospital, but he was already dead. He suffered a massive heart attack."

"Oh . . . Well . . . We are still doing the deal, right?"

"I think so. I have already talked to his widow and the son. We have a signed contract which binds Jan's family to the venture, but more important, they want to proceed as soon as possible."

"Roel, it's tragic what happened. Poor Jan. But we own all the technology now, so we can proceed. Right?"

"Right. We just have to find the compiler. It is on a floppy disk, I think. Jan always read it into the system somehow before every demo. Without the compiler the system doesn't work."

"It must be on the table in your office."

"No I have already looked. It isn't there."

"OK, Roel, sorry to hear this very sad news. Let me know when the disc shows up."

■   ■   ■

The disc didn't show up in the next few days. Jan's widow and his son helped with the search. The youngster wasn't really familiar with the technology, and couldn't offer any insight on how it might work.

After a week or so, Roel adopted a two-pronged approach. On the one hand he would try to reverse-engineer the technology, working backward from the patent disclosures already in hand. He put his team of experts, including the key PhD, on the task. On the other, he hired a firm of private detectives to help in the search for the essential disc.

Meanwhile, I was planning to proceed. Roel agreed to ship the hardware to my place in England where in a few weeks I would be hosting a weekend party that among many other guests would include both Roel and Rupert. I knew that we could find some spare minutes to show Murdoch the breakthrough. The equipment would be set up in my barn, and Roel's technicians would be there to make it work.

But, shortly before the event, I had a disturbing call from Roel. They wouldn't be able to stage a demo. Without the key compiler, the system wouldn't function. His engineers were stymied; they couldn't derive the compiler from all the other pieces of the technology in hand. Worse, the detectives had come up with nothing. The disc could not be found. Panels had been removed from the Sloot living room and the woodwork behind them had been searched. The rose garden in the back of the house had been dug up. Mrs. Sloot had provided a list of Jan's friends, and they all had been asked. No one could think of where else to look. The wife and the son were getting desperate, but Mr. Sloot's secret could not be found.

Over the following months I kept the pressure on Roel, but finally he said: "Look, Tom, I have sunk a big pile of my money into this thing; so far you haven't risked a dime." This was true. "I am going to pull the plug; I have got to get on with other things. If the compiler ever shows up, we can start again. But for now it's over."

The disc was never found.

The Fifth Force remains to be unleashed.

■   ■   ■

Looking back on this now, I am reminded of the Hemingway story "The Short Happy Life of Francis Macomber." It makes the point that a brief moment of ecstasy can outweigh a lifetime of dreary travail. I think that's exactly what happened to Jan Sloot. That afternoon, in Roel's office, with a glass of Champagne in his hand, he was experiencing a joy so profound, the prospect of a life so incredibly rich and rewarding, just his for the taking, that his life was entirely fulfilled. It was unnecessary to continue: leave at the top.

■   ■   ■

And so ended the "deal of a lifetime" for us all. There was bad karma to follow. My McLaren, which somehow I always associated with Roel and this venture, exploded one day not long afterward in a spectacular fire—I was lucky to escape unsinged. Worse was to follow for Roel. The Sloot story accrued a lot of publicity in Holland. This, compounded with his already well-known name, attracted a lunatic to the Pieper estate who, armed with a long knife, attacked both Roel and Ricka, putting them both into intensive care. The insane man "who wanted to kill the rich" was caught and locked up. Fortunately both Roel and Ricka totally recovered.

We don't talk about the Fifth Force anymore.

Sometimes I have undertaken something

because of curiosity about where it might lead and what I might learn. I wrote a novel for these reasons. I became a fireman from the same impulse. I'll tell you about the book; the fireman story is funny—let's do that first.

When we—Gerd, the kids and I—first moved up from the peninsula to Belvedere, just over the Golden Gate bridge, the first weekend we were there a house burned nearly to the ground. Some few weeks later there was another serious fire. I inquired with the neighbors and discovered that Belvedere didn't have a real fire department, only volunteers. I dropped by the firehouse the following Saturday afternoon out of curiosity and the (volunteer) chief told me that they really needed more men, and why didn't I sign on? So I did. I thought there was much to learn.

Over the next few years I became a trained part-time firefighter. As a kid I had always admired firemen; maybe that's why I did it. And it was fun. We got together every two weeks for an evening of training; learning all the equipment on the two fire engines; learning first aid and CPR; learning how to use a defibrillator; learning how to rescue a cat from a tree; and, most exciting, learning how to behave in an actual fire. About once a year all the volunteers in the county would gather at abandoned military base and a controlled fire would be started in one of the old barracks. Rubber tires also would be set aflame inside the building to add a murky black smoke to the experience. We would get suited up in our flame-resistant outfits, don our breathing apparatus, and crawl on elbows and knees into the burning building. It may be so obvious as not to require explanation, but the experience of being in heat of that intensity is incredible. One feels it as a physical pressure, seeming to press down with tons of force. We would extinguish the fire, crawl out for a breather, and then the fire would be reset and we would do it all over again.

The Belvedere volunteers were a social group, pretty tightly knit. Our annual beer-bust fund-raising party was the big event in the town for the year. The community was fond of and proud of us. The problem was that most of us weren't in Belvedere during the days, and sometimes there would be a fire and nobody, or too few, would show up to put it out. The fire could thus get pretty well established before the next town's firemen, who were full-time, arrived on the scene to do the job. I used to kid my fellow firemen that our motto should be: "We never lose a foundation." Maybe the highest per capita income town in America, Belvedere was nevertheless pretty skinflint. Our fire hydrants were of three different kinds and we had to sometimes grope the plug in the dark to guess which adapter was required before we could "make the hydrant," or get the water flowing; the city fathers were too cheap to spend the bucks to standardize. Also, our fire mains were old and rust filled. It was hard to get enough flow, so we normally had to pump the water using one of the engines, being careful not to suck the water out of every house in town in the process.

The highlight of my firefighting career came one New Year's Eve. Gerd and I had hosted a party during which some very serious drinking was accomplished. I fell into bed around three in the morning. It was one of those times when the bed was unstable. Whenever I closed my eyes the bed would start to rotate. It would stabilize if I opened them, only to start flipping end over end as I tried again to sleep. As I lay there in this alcoholic mess the bedside radio began to squawk about a fire. The voice said, "This is a working fire," in other words, not a false alarm. While Gerd slept, I staggered around my dressing room getting myself into my rubber suit, finding my fire hat and getting my heavy rubber boots on. It must have been comical to behold. I drove down the hill to the station. (Yes, I know that I shouldn't have been behind the wheel, but if a cop had stopped me I had the only perfect excuse: I really *was* going to a fire.)

But by the time I got there both engines had already left and no one was about. However, I could see smoke and flashing lights about a block away, so I drove directly to the site. The guys had everything almost ready and hoses were snaking across the lawn. A ladder had been set up against the house; flames could be seen behind an upper window. As I floundered into this scene, the chief spotted me and, I suppose, thinking that I had been there from the start, and that I was my usual sober self, he shouted to me: "Perkins! Up the ladder!" I drunkenly staggered up the ladder, with the bronze nozzle over my shoulder dragging the hose with me. At the top, I smashed the window using the nozzle, and, thank God, I remembered enough of my training to get my left arm through the window to hang on to the house before shouting: "Make the hydrant!" With the nozzle under my right arm the force of the flow would have thrown me fifty feet if I hadn't remembered to hold on. For the next several minutes I filled the house with water and put the fire out. There was water damage, but we saved the home, and with the adrenaline rush, I had nearly sobered enough to laugh at Gerd's "What have you been up to?" when I returned.

Normally I never attended Belvedere town hall meetings (these exercises in democracy tend too much to bring out the fascist in my nature), but when the next debate came up on whether or not to replace us volunteers with paid professionals, I showed up and made myself very unpopular with my fellow firefighters by coming down strongly in favor of a real fire department. It passed and our amateur days were over for good.

Some while later I was driving down Interstate 5 to Los Angeles when I got pulled over for speeding. The cop had finished writing the ticket when he spotted the little firefighter's decal I had on the side window of my latest Ferrari. "You a volunteer?" he asked. When I acknowledged that I was, he tore up the ticket—my first experience in life of "professional courtesy." Ever since my fireman's days I have had a profound respect for all of these men. I'll never forget the heroism of those firefighters on 9/11.

I had learned a lot as a volunteer. It was diverting for me and useful to others as well. Writing a novel was also diverting, but I fear that opinions differ on the book's value. They *really* differ!

Chapter Twelve

The Best Ever Argument
for Book Burning

Mr. Thomas J. Perkins
Embarcadero Center #4
San Francisco, CA 94111

Dear Mr. Perkins,

I have a fantastic idea! I am the executive producer of Acme Studios, and I want to make you the star of our new reality television show. I want you to meet and play with a dozen twenty-five-year-old stunningly beautiful girls, and at the end of our thirteen-week series you will marry the one you choose—she will become your bride on national television!

Clearly this is an outrageous idea—matching an older, single, wealthy man with young, sexy women—but it will be wonderful for the right man who adores women and who has a sense of adventure.

We will select the young ladies from an alluring array of models, actresses, athletes, and others based upon their appearance and personality. You will have the opportunity to know them in your home and at various glamorous locations, to see them competing for your love and attention. Of course, if at the last moment you don't or your chosen bride doesn't want to proceed, the wedding won't happen. But you must understand that marriage is the whole point of the show, and you should enter it in that spirit. This is not a frivolous proposal. We are authentic producers with a long track record, and this show has a very high probability of being aired. If you are the right man, with the right chemistry, please call me. I am offering you a life-enriching experience that will be impossible to dupli- cate.

Very truly yours,
Jessica James
Executive Producer

This letter arrived in my San Francisco office out of the blue in a FedEx envelope one morning. My first reaction was that it was a joke from a friend. But the name of the studio on the letterhead (not Acme) was known to me. The idea seemed so outrageous that I picked up the telephone and called Ms. James (not her real name), simply to see if the letter was genuine. She was indeed very real and she immediately went into a sales pitch as soon as she realized that I, one of her targets, was on the line. I didn't let her get beyond first base. The prospect of meeting a bunch of beautiful young women was attractive, of course, but the premise of marrying one of them was out of the question. I couldn't imagine the idea of marrying a girl younger than my daughter. So I thanked her for the attention, and asked her who else was a prospect—she wouldn't tell me, except to say that I might know one or two of them. It was a brief conversa- tion, and we never talked again.

But for a few days I carried the letter around in my pocket when I went out with friends to let them read it. All found it very funny. I put the letter aside and a week later I was about to chuck in into the trash, when the idea struck me that the idea of this reality show could make a very amusing semi-satirical novel.

Where do ideas come from? The human brain has been studied interminably but no one has the answer. The idea for the book came to my mind fully born, with the whole plot entirely clear. It would be about a man similar to me, who had been in the grip of depres- sion brought on by the death of his wife of many years, who is then returned to a happier life via the machinations of the insane TV show idea. There would be numerous false starts, humorous epi- sodes, disappointments, and then a happy ending. Danielle and I were divorced, but still friendly. I had been reading all her outlines, and all the drafts for her books for about seven years, and I thought this idea might make a good Danielle Steel novel. She had used some of my ideas in the past, so it was not unusual for me to think about giving her this one. I jotted down an outline, about twelve pages, one for each chapter, and faxed it to her.

She loved the idea, but after about a week she told me that the book had to be written by a man; she just wasn't comfortable with all the sex the plot dictated. Danielle's books are pretty discreet in this respect, almost chaste; it's not unusual for the reader to be left at the door of the bedroom, to rejoin the couple at breakfast the next morning. So my plot was not comfortable to her. She said, "You write it." I just dismissed the thought and put the outline away.

But if there is one thing about Danielle that stands out, it's persistence. She just kept after me. She said, "You know how to write, you always said that the reason you hadn't done a book was because you didn't have a good plot idea. Now you've got it. So if you don't get going, it's just because you're lazy!" This began to get to me. Every time I picked up a book to read, the thought occurred to me: if you've got time to read, you've got time to write. Finally, I decided that I had the time between Christmas and New Year's, and I asked Danielle if she would edit anything I came up with, and she said, "Of course." So I had to have a go. And, frankly, I wanted to have the experience. I had been so involved with her books for so long, I wondered if I could do it too. Was there an element of competition in this? Absolutely! And so, again, I jumped into a most interesting experience.

My house in England, thoroughly exorcised as it was, was a perfect place to write over the holidays. Outside, the weather was lousy, but inside was cozy and quiet. I don't write well enough to experience writer's block, so somewhere in the vicinity of three thousand words a day was not demanding. I found the process fascinating. Unlike Danielle, who writes an exhaustive outline before beginning, I wrote chapter by chapter with no thorough outline. Rather, I would jot down on a large piece of paper all the things that had to happen, the jokes, the conversations, the locations, but in no order. Then, I would take a short break, put the paper aside, and start to write. It's a miracle, which I don't understand, where those first words come from. Without question, at least in my case, those words come from the subconscious. On taking a break for the night, the next morning's work was ready, without conscious thinking. Always before in writing, everything was in the forefront of my mind, but in this much more creative process of getting the novel under way, an inner being was doing the work for me. Unlike Danielle, I read and reread what has been written, which helps me get a "seamlessness" which some of my readers have admired.

In about three weeks I had the thing finished and I sent it off to Danielle for her editing and criticism. She liked it very much, but as I was attempting to write a kind of romance, her home ground, after all, her negative comments in some areas were very important. In the story the heroine, Jessie, has a boyfriend who has to be disposed of in due course for the plot to wind up with her in the arms of the hero. In order to make this easy for me to do, I portrayed the boyfriend as a real jerk. Danielle pointed out that a serious heroine like mine simply wouldn't have such a loser in her life. She said that I had to make him credible and likeable, so that when the ultimate break-up came it would be a big deal for the reader. Advice like this from such an expert was too important to ignore. So I began the first rewrite.

Then I discovered an interesting thing. The characters assume a life of their own. If you start to change one, the interaction with all of the others needs to change too. And that's something that Danielle had pointed out to me previously. She said that for even the most minor characters it was important for the author to think through their entire life's background, where they were born and so forth, so that although none of the background would be ever mentioned, the character would be genuine on the page. I talked with her from time to time on the phone and she said, "I'll bet you aren't the slightest bit lonely now, are you?" Of course, she was correct. I had some fifty characters including all the minor ones inhabiting my thoughts constantly. I came to like them; I miss their problems now that the novel is published and they can never change.

After this pretty thorough rewrite, I thought I was ready to find a publisher. Without an agent an author can't get access to a publisher; there is just so much junk out there that the agent assumes the role of gatekeeper. Mort Janklow, Danielle's agent, was the best possible choice, I thought, and she agreed. She called him on the phone and extolled my book. He agreed to read it, and I sent it off by FedEx immediately. But by the time it arrived in his office, he had second thoughts. He returned the package unopened and called me to explain why: "I can't keep up with you and Danielle; now you two are friendly, but sometimes you're not. If you and she get out of phase, there is no way I can represent you if she isn't happy about it. And maybe your book is great, but she's the number one author in the world—she is where my interest lies. Sorry."

He gave me the names of a couple of other agents, Danielle had a few additional names and I called a couple of author friends to get suggestions from them as well. In all, I had around fifteen potential agents and I sent off copies. My name will open a lot of doors in the venture field, but it means nothing in publishing. Of the fifteen I contacted, about half of them never responded in any way and all but two of those remaining rejected my book with a form letter. However, two actually read the book and wanted to represent me. I was pretty lucky to have these good choices.

The agency representing Dan Brown, of *Da Vinci Code* fame, was very positive and I am sure would have done a fine job, but I thought that they were so swept up in the phenomenon of that mega-bestseller, with all the follow-up projects in the wings, that they might be too busy to help me very much. Also, they are in New York, and so were not readily available to me in San Francisco. The other potential agent, Fred Hill, was based in San Francisco. He and I had lunch. Before that meeting Danielle had cautioned me that Fred is of the old school, extremely demanding and famous for being very critical of any author's writing, so I shouldn't have my feelings hurt if he was rude.

Fred opened the conversation by saying that, in principal, he never read a new author's stuff within the first month, but he had glanced at my first page, took the book home, and finished it the same night. He really sunk the hook when he said that I wrote like Tom Wolfe, "maybe better!"

Not surprisingly, Fred and I struck a deal. But he said that my book was too short; another two or three chapters were needed to flesh it out, and that I didn't have the "arc" quite right. I hadn't heard this term before, which is, I suppose, familiar to every liberal arts graduate. It means the emotional progression of the plot building to a peak (or maybe a valley) which then leads to a satisfying and natural feeling to the inevitable conclusion. In my case Fred said my hero had to be betrayed about three quarters of the way along in the story. The main character needed to be disillusioned and then to recover his equilibrium before moving along to the denouement. I asked him how I should do that and he said: "I have no idea—you're the author!"

So, I undertook another rewrite. This was a big one. In order to add the extra chapters I had to invent some new characters. I am particularly proud of the son I created for the heroine, an autistic teenager with, I think, some depth. By making the boyfriend detest the kid and having the hero really like him, it made, I think, the bond between these two principals seem inevitable. I was even able to have this boy-genius mouth my own conjecture about quantum gravity in one short sentence. Months later I got a letter from a reader in Indiana expressing appreciation for this touch—he was probably the only one to pick up this reference to abstract physics in a sex novel.

I was starting to have mixed feelings about the project. The book was, after all, a soufflé, a thing hardly worth the effort I was putting into it. But, on the other hand, soufflés are nice—a good one complements the meat and potatoes of daily fare. Finally Fred was satisfied with my rewrite, and we decided to try to sell the book. He contacted a couple of publishers who were mildly interested, but we decided to try to interest Judith Regan, who ran a subsidiary of giant HarperCollins, as our primary target. Judith has a reputation for taking big risks and she has had a long series of hits. We thought my book might be offbeat enough to appeal to her. I was going to be in New York, so we sent her a copy and I set up a lunch date. (She is the publisher who recently tried to print the extremely controversial "nonconfession" of O. J. Simpson, as well as hosting a two-hour TV interview with him. But there was such a public uproar of indignation that her bosses blocked both the book and the broadcast at the last moment. Not long thereafter, she was fired.)

Judith is an extremely attractive woman, who coincidentally is a dead ringer for Jessie, the book's heroine. This was pure coincidence, since I had written the book long before our luncheon, but maybe the coincidence appealed to her, because she was enthusiastic about publishing the book. By the end of the meal we had an agreement but she threw me a curve ball when she asked me to change the subplot rather drastically.

As written, the hero has two kids in their twenties. They get involved in their father's adventures to a degree, but not in a big way in the original. Judith wanted the son to be a playboy competing with his dad for the series of young potential mates, and she wanted the daughter to have a more serious relationship with her lover than the one I had sketched. As she explained what she wanted, I had to admit that her ideas would improve the manuscript significantly, so I agreed to yet another rewrite. Also, she hated my original title *Lions Need Love Too* and insisted that the book be called *Sex and the Single Zillionaire.* I said okay to that too.

So, after the third rewrite, I had put more hours into my pulp fiction than probably Tolstoy had in *War and Peace*. But I was in no way near the finish because Judith then put *Zillionaire* through the editing cycle with two guys with lots of experience in this trade, John Paine, a consultant, and Doug Grad, her senior editor. It is amazing how something like my book got nitpicked. We had long e-mails over single words in my text. I expected it to be dumbed down, not that I was using a very high-powered vocabulary in the first place. I hung on in many cases, but yielded to every edit finally in the end. The last word to go was "prepotent" (meaning the primary, or most powerful—a favorite of my hero Patrick O'Brian). Doug pointed out that I am no Patrick O'Brian, so it went too.

Meanwhile Judith was thinking about how to promote my book. She decided to bring it out on Valentine's Day, and Rupert and

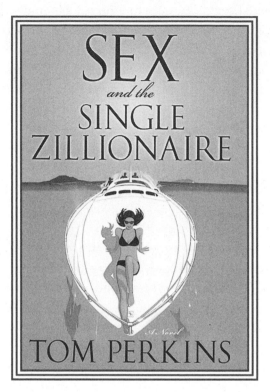

Cover of
Sex and the Single Zillionaire

Wendi Murdoch graciously offered to host a book party for me in New York, which proved in the event to be a great evening. But Judith's most original idea was to offer me as a prize. She struck a bargan with Kathryn Falk, the owner and publisher of *Romantic Times*, the monthly magazine for readers of romance, to promote a contest in which women would submit an essay on why they should have a date with me. Naturally, to win, one would have to buy and read the book to have some insight into my personality and to be able to write a convincing essay. When Judith sprung this brainstorm, my first reaction was one of horror, but I said sure, figuring that it probably would never happen. But it did happen, and I'll get to that story soon.

First, though, the book had to get printed. By the end of the editing process I had a master copy on my computer as perfectly written and as well edited as possible. From this master to the typeset galleys would be a simple process, I assumed. In this computer age it's quaint to have an industry as out-of-date as publishing. The type is set manually by an operator reading the text from the computer and inputting it into the machine that justifies the margins and "leads" the space between the lines. This could easily be done by a software program, but apparently, the industry has not made that investment. Instead my book was, I guess, typed into the machine by the chimp who has been trying to type *Hamlet* for ever so long.

The galleys arrived by Express Mail with only three days for me to read them and to make final approval. I couldn't believe the errors. Words were missing, the spelling was awful, and in places paragraphs were absent. The manuscript came with a deadline of only those seventy-two hours' turnaround and a "Dear Author" form letter telling me that any changes I needed to make had to fit within the original line length and line count per page. Changes that I made that exceeded these limits, which might require resetting more than the page in question, would be charged to my account! Anyway, by dint of three twenty-hour days I got it done, but I still spot errors in the printed book. Sorry for that; I have tried to catch them all in the paperback edition.

So, with the books coming off the printing press and on their way to the bookstores, Judith cranked up her publicity machine and I made a number of promotional appearances on TV, notably *Fox and Friends*, Maria Bartiromo's *Wall Street Journal Report*, and a long interview on the *Charlie Rose* show. But by far the best break came with a front-page *Wall Street Journal* article including a picture of me and Danielle. The reporter, Pui-Wing Tam, normally covered Silicon Valley and this story was a nice diversion for her. That big plug triggered some other good newspaper and magazine stories as well.

The book sold well, achieving fiftieth rank on Amazon for a day or two and coming within striking distance of the bestseller's list, but not making it. Each of Danielle's hardcovers sells more than a million copies. I was content to achieve three percent of that number; for a first-time novelist that was about ten times normal (and ten times the numbers for her first book). I gave one hundred percent of my royalties to Harvard.

During this period *Romantic Times* was promoting the contest to win a date with me. The original idea was for there to be a single winner. I, however, insisted that there be three winners. I didn't like the idea of maybe getting shot by a jealous husband or boyfriend; with three winners no one would take the whole thing too seriously, I thought.

Romantic Times was started more than twenty years ago to cater to the market for romance novels. These books are sometimes called "bodice rippers" (*"overcome by passion, he ripped the bodice from her lovely shoulders, exposing her marvelous breasts"*); you see them on drugstore shelves with a powerfully built, bare-chested stud holding a woman—she usually has long, streaming blond hair—in his powerful arms looking passionately into her blue eyes. For years the Italian superstar model Fabio was featured on these covers (he too has long, streaming blond hair). There is an enormous market for these books. Kathryn Falk realized that no one ever paid attention to them in the normal media, so she started her magazine to inform the readers. Her publication rapidly grew and thrived. Currently subscribers number over one hundred thousand from around the world.

Every year there is a "book lovers" convention hosted by the magazine, where more than two thousand romance novel addicts assemble for five days. Predominantly women, they are heavy readers; Kathryn's subscribers average one book per day. For this to be the average, some are reading two or more per day. There are a few hundred authors working in the genre, and many of them also attend to promote their latest books and to meet the fans. Though not a romance of the kind this market really likes—mine is too satirical to be taken seriously—nevertheless, about one hundred essays were submitted for the win a date contest. Judith's staff screened them all and picked three winners. The best one, I thought, was in the form of a multiple choice quiz, with funny questions and even funnier answers.

The convention was held in Daytona Beach and I was to fly in

Friday afternoon in time to attend the Fairy Ball. This turned out to be the day following my last fateful HP board meeting and I was in a poor mood for fairies. In the event, my plane was late, and by the time I arrived at the hotel, the party was on its last legs, or rather its last wings, judging by the drooping gossamer plumage attached to a number of ladies I found wandering around the lobby, some rather on the heavy side for fairy flight, I thought.

The next morning was the annual book fair. Judith had contributed one hundred free copies of *Zillionaire* to be given away, and by the time I arrived at my table, a couple dozen ladies were standing in line to get a signed copy. There were about a hundred such tables manned (rather I should say "womaned") by other authors who were selling their novels. The ladies attending the fair were heavy readers, in both senses of the word *heavy*; they carried shopping bags and were busy laying in a hoard of books to be consumed over the next few weeks. It was a long day at my table, but when I got the occasional break from selling my book—the free ones were gone in the first hour—I wandered around and talked to some of the other authors. They were typically women in their forties, looking more like librarians than bodice-ripper writers. They averaged about three books per year, year in and year out, and it seemed to provide them with a decent living. It turns out that there are cycles in romance novels. History is on the wane, but vampires are really hot now. I was assured that there is something very sexy about vampires. Some believed that space exploration would be the foundation for the next cycle. My book wasn't anywhere in this picture.

There were a few husbands accompanying the ladies doing the shopping, but it was mostly women filling the book fair hall, except that I noticed a young guy wandering around, looking very bored. He was dressed in skin-tight black jeans and T-shirt, showing off a torso like the men on the book covers, and that's what he turned out to be. He was the last winner of the "Mr. Romantic Times" contest, and indeed he was on the cover of a few of the books on sale. He stopped at my table and chatted for a while. His name was Andrei Claude, his English was perfect, but I detected a slight accent that I couldn't place. It turned out that he was from Malta, where I have a berth for my boat, and, in the usual small-world syndrome, was best of friends with one of my crew, also a native of that tiny place. Of course, he was clued in on the day's events and he was there to participate in the evening's contest to pick a new man for the following year. I then understood what Kathryn was talking about when she had explained that I was to make a little speech, meet my three winners, before the end of the "show," which I was expected to attend. The show was this year's male beauty pageant.

I got into a jacket and tie to look like a prize worth winning for my three essay writers. This was not without some trepidation as, judging from the ladies I had met during the day, these girls were likely to be on the generously proportioned side of the female anatomy scale. So, around six that evening about fifteen hundred of us "book lovers" assembled in the grand ballroom of the hotel, which had a stage already set up. There was a smooth master of ceremonies who introduced the evening with some finesse, the music swelled, and ten young men, all incredibly well built and wearing jockstraps only, charged onto the stage. Words fail to describe the screaming ecstasy of these women at the sight of these nearly naked guys. I was embarrassed; this seemed beyond decadent. What the hell had I gotten myself into? But the program had a clever script, and there followed a "talent" contest, in which a jury judged these Adonises for acting ability, modeling capability, and general personality. In spite of myself, I found it interesting. There were questions from the audience. One was, "What part of a woman's body do you find most attractive?" The guy who said, "Her heart, because when I have won that, I have won everything" proved to be the ultimate victor, the clever bastard.

While the judges' votes were being tallied, I was called onto the stage. Kathryn asked me to explain what I sought in the perfect woman, and who I hoped had won the contest for "me." I mumbled and stumbled through some sort of awkward answer, but thankfully after a little of this she called the essay winners onto the stage. I was astonished to see three very attractive ladies come from the audience. They were all truly good-looking, slim, well dressed, polished, and a very nice surprise. Maybe I had won the contest! The audience seemed pleased too.

And so began a great evening. After next year's stud was crowned by Andrei Claude, the retiring champion, the ladies and I repaired to the bar to sample my brand of martinis and to become acquainted. I was surprised at their quite different backgrounds. One was from San Francisco; she was in the export-import trade in Asian art. Another had a rich Brooklyn accent; she was in the personnel business living nearby in Florida. The third was a bond trader from New York—she had written the clever multiple choice essay which I found so charming. We all got along immediately, and interestingly, they got along well together. They had one thing in common: they loved my book. They were more familiar with it than I was, since I had all the unpublished versions in my head, so their view of what really happened was the most accurate. I was flattered beyond description. If writing a book could bring on this sort of adulation, I was hooked.

Our dinner was in a good restaurant atop a tower nearby, hosted by Kathryn and her husband. We all had plenty to drink and we played musical chairs, so that everyone got the chance to sit with me. It was great. During the dinner Kathryn gave me the secret to writing a successful romance novel; she had read a thousand of them so she knew of which she spoke: "The alpha male finally commits." That's all there is to it, she claimed. Since women are the buyers, the description of the man must be exhaustive: his body, his eyes, his hair and his teeth and smile must be exact; but the heroine should be very vague, so that it could be any woman reading the book, in her own fantasy. There, you have it. With this secret, you too can have a table at next year's convention and sign your books for adoring readers.

We wound up a very fine evening back at the hotel, my winners and I. This time the drinks were on me and we really enjoyed ourselves. I left the ladies to themselves, getting along famously together, and retired alone (sorry to disappoint anyone hoping for a real sex story in this account—the alpha male didn't commit!).

And so ended my adventures as a pulp novelist. It was a significant chapter in my education, and I am glad that I chose to jump in.

It ended except for the reviews. I got off pretty easily from the newspaper critics. Most of them found something nice to say, if less flattering than I would have hoped to hear. But the amateur "reviews" on Amazon were pretty amazing—no wonder Danielle never reads hers. Overall they were positive; the average was three and a half stars. But some were really brutal: "Stick to your day job, Tom;" "Doesn't this guy have an editor?" And the worst: "This is the best argument for book burning I have ever encountered." I still wonder what bothered him; too much sex or not enough?

It is an easy slide from my struggles as an author into a chapter about one of the greatest writers of the twentieth century. I was honored to have known this man.

Chapter Thirteen

The Man and the Myth

It was not until around 1990 that the writing of Patrick O'Brian came to my attention. An acquaintance, who is a professor of literature at Stanford, first brought up his name, claiming him to be the best living author in the English language. When I discovered that his genre was the square riggers of the British navy in the Nelson era, I was hooked. And thus began a correspondence, and ultimately a friendship with the man himself.

I read the entire works of O'Brian, and then I read them all again. I became steeped in the world that his genius created. The characters Jack Aubrey and Stephen Maturin seemed to capture all elements of the human condition. Every swirl of complexity, of action and of introspection, of rationality and passion was there. He had a rare insight into the nature of women too; his character Diana Villiers will live through the history of literature. The themes of man and God, plan and fate were explored. I came to believe that if one understood O'Brian, then maybe one had a shot at understanding nearly everything else. I was mesmerized by the brilliance of his genius. I honestly believed that O'Brian had so enriched my life that I was, truly, in his debt. How could it be repaid?

The idea came to me that since he was so experienced in every aspect of the sea, and was so obviously in love with it, I could give him a cruise aboard my boat without my interfering presence — just with his friends aboard — to repay my debt. A cruise on this big yacht would be, probably, a unique experience for him, I thought. So I wrote him offering just that. After a few weeks' delay in correspondence, his finely crafted reply accepting my invitation was received: "I accept your kind offer with, perhaps, obscene haste."

I also learned that he planned a book tour of America, including San Francisco, and that he would be there in just a few weeks. He accepted my quickly sent dinner invitation, and I looked forward to his lecture the evening before the dinner at my house.

Patrick O'Brian was a charmer. His lecture was a sell-out and he did not disappoint. The audience hung on his every word, and was charmed by his lightning-quick wit and rather acerbic manner. He was very much the "intellectual" entertaining the great American unwashed, in the grand tradition of so many Brits before him, except that O'Brian was Irish. He was about eighty, slight in appearance, rather frail—but very much "The Lion." I looked forward to the following night's dinner.

Author Patrick O'Brian
at the helm of Andromeda la Dea

He arrived with his equally intellectual wife, Mary—the grand-daughter of Count Tolstoy—together with a group of my friends interested in literature, which included Danielle and her husband, John. After dinner, and after my other friends left, he, Mary, and I sat around my glowing fireplace, and he and I undertook the serious obliteration of some very fine brandy.

It quickly became apparent that his reserve was hard to melt, even though we were progressing through the Cognac at a prodigious rate—we were each still calling ourselves "Mr. O'Brian and Mr. Perkins"—but more curious was his naïveté about things nautical. I was proposing an itinerary for his cruise aboard my forty-seven-meter ketch *Andromeda*, but he just didn't seem to understand the limitations of speed and space. He outlined an itinerary involving a dozen Mediterranean stops, over thousands of miles, which would have required months to complete—not the two weeks on offer. How could an old salt like O'Brian be so oblivious to the realities of the sea? But the final surprise was his sudden insistence for a non-negotiable condition to my gift: namely, that if I didn't agree to accompany his party, he wouldn't accept. Extremely flattered and pleased, of course, I acquiesced.

He lived in Collioure, a tiny village near the small fishing village of Port Vendres on France's Mediterranean coast, just north of the border with Spain, in the heart of Catalonia. I had a miserable time getting *Andromeda* to him from Italy. The Golfe du Lion, south of Marseilles, can have awful Mistral winds, caused by a high pressure over France and a lower pressure zone farther east. Although usually with clear sky, where those two counterrotating air currents converge, the winds can blow to sixty knots, sometimes even more. Myth has it that a Mistral blows for one day, five days, or eleven days. If this wind, which howls down the Rhône valley, blows for a longer time, allegedly one is permitted to kill one's mate without danger of prosecution—the wind is *that* debilitating. Anyway, this storm was of the one-day persuasion, but the waves grew to a sufficient size that we broke the yacht's inner forestay in the violent motion. However, we made it into the small harbor in Port Vendres and O'Brian was on the dock to greet us.

Mary invited me to lunch at their attractive but modest home where he showed me his winemaking equipment in the cellar; the grapes were grown on their property. Most interesting was his office where the walls were all lined, floor to ceiling, with the books he used for research. They were in several languages with topics of geography, medicine, botany, and history—but not one of them newer than around 1820; he was almost literally immersed in the period of his writing.

The next day his guests arrived: his agent, his publisher, and his first editor, now a close friend, by the name of Richard Ollard, the foremost authority on Pepys. O'Brian still seemed tense and unhappy with my negative attitude as I remained adamant that a three-thousand-mile circuit of the Mediterranean, and certainly a visit to Istanbul, was not in the cards for his fourteen days. But the weather was fine and soon we were sailing downwind to Minorca, with our enormous "ballooner" set at the bow.

He seemed ecstatically happy once under way, foaming through the crests, under the blue sky in the brisk but balmy breeze. The conditions were so perfect that I suggested that he take the wheel and steer the boat. Almost immediately he began to put us into a free-standing gybe—a very dangerous thing. I jumped to correct the course, and then he tried to do it again. It was immediately clear that he didn't have the slightest feeling for the yacht or for sailing. But how could this be? He had let it be known in an interview that as a sickly teenager he had left Ireland for a several months' long restorative voyage on a rich relative's schooner, upon which had acquired the sailor's skills to "hand and steer" a ship. This moment was my first inkling that O'Brian might be of a more complex alloy than pure Irish iron.

We sailed all night and I worried that he and Mary might not have sea legs. This was fortunately an unnecessary concern; they both were fine for the entire trip, as were their guests. The next morning we arrived off the city of Mahon, the scene of the first meeting between his two primary characters, Jack and Stephen. The entrance to the harbor is up through a long passage bounded by cliffs on either side and he requested that we sail, not motor, into the port just as the square-riggers from his books would have done. It was a tricky thing to do, but I pulled it off, to his huge satisfaction. We spent the afternoon looking at the town and I was impressed by his command of Catalan; he seemed as fluent as was his Dr. Maturin. Back aboard the yacht that evening, after testing my composition of a couple of martinis, he suggested for the first time that we call each other by our first names.

And so over the next few days Patrick and I began to develop our friendship. He was fascinating to listen to, and his debates with Richard Ollard were rich, each displaying an awesome knowledge of history, art, philosophy, and music. Patrick O'Brian was an intellectual giant; but his reluctance to discuss any aspect of his personal life was pronounced. This became very clear one night at dinner when he casually announced that he had destroyed all his diaries and letters so that "some postdoctoral American fool" wouldn't be able to write a biography. Ollard was shocked, calling that a crime against history. The discussion became very heated; only Mary, who remained silent, understood Patrick's motives.

Now, after his death, we know that he was born English, not Irish; that his real name was Russ, not O'Brian; that he was not university educated; and that he had abandoned a wife and two children after he met Mary during the Second World War. During this trip, we all simply adjusted to the fact that his history would not be revealed, and we learned not to ask.

The following day, while gracefully sailing under our huge spinnakerlike balooner at the bow, and following (as it turned out) an inaccurately marked Spanish chart, we attempted a passage between a small island and the coast, where we ran hard aground in shallow water. This was in the Mediterranean: one can't simply wait for a higher tide to carry one off. Starting the engines and going hard astern accomplished nothing. I blew out our centerboard trunk and fresh water tanks with compressed air to lighten the ship, over ten tons, and tried again: nothing. The Spanish Coast Guard came by and gave us a tow, but even with their and our engines at full power, we didn't budge. Finally I secured a hawser to a very sturdy rock at our stern, and with bar-tight tension from our anchor windlass, and with our bow-thruster waggling us from side to side, we inched backward off the bar, and at last we were free. Patrick keenly observed all these nautical operations, thinking, I believe, that we staged it all for his amusement. He had a great afternoon.

Every day around one thirty after lunch, Patrick retired to my office in his suite to write his book then in progress: *The Yellow Admiral*. He asked me if I thought Americans would understand the title. To one familiar with the terminology of eighteenth-century British Admiralty customs, one would immediately recognize this term to be that of designating an admiral on "standby," to be recalled to duty only in the most dire of straits. I said, "Patrick, I think Americas will think you mean a cowardly admiral." He thanked me profusely, and later published the book with exactly the original title. I think he intended the ambiguity. He asked me for the charts of France in the area of Brest, which figures prominently in that book focused upon the blockade of Brest. When later I read the book, it had an extra meaning for me: I could picture him poring over my charts in his cabin. He showed me his handwritten pages after each day's writing. Mary told me that this was very unusual. She said that he had never shared his work with anyone before publication; I was very flattered.

Our friendship slowly developed. One morning at breakfast he said, "Tom, I would like to ask you a question which will betray my utter ignorance of everything in this modern world. What is software?" My answer, "The piano is the hardware, the sheet music is the software," satisfied us both. We cruised with no further troubling events. Patrick was fascinated with the thousands of birds flocking and swooping around rugged Cape Formentor on the northern coast of Majorca—a scene straight from the wild poetry of Byron. He was an ornithologist at heart, like his character Stephen Maturin, whom Patrick resembled both mentally and physically.

The pressures of business required Patrick's guests and me to depart, regretfully, after ten days. He and Mary sailed uneventfully back to Port Vendres with the crew. The cruise was a great success and his highly informed understanding of the world of Nelson and the era of square-riggers made me ever more conscious of their glory.

We always talked a lot about the clippers, the ultimate sailing ships. In the following years Patrick and I continued our friendship, meeting two or three times a year.

One amusing evening occurred at his London club Brooks's, a famous place featured prominently in several of his books. Captain "Lucky" Jack Aubrey was a member. As always with Patrick, we began with martinis before moving on to the heavier stuff. After a tour of the club he conducted me into a small dining room off the very large one. He said, "You know they have begun to admit women into this place, but with any luck there won't be one in this room tonight."

During the course of an excellent dinner he inquired politely about Danielle, and asked how her books were selling; as usual, she had three bestsellers published that year. He had met Danielle at a party for him at Plumpton Place where she had given out place setting favors of silver miniature books, each engraved with the title of one of his novels. I said that her latest hardcover had sold somewhere between one million and one and a half million copies (my guess, incidentally, is that three million is the total number of books O'Brian sold during his lifetime) and that, so far, total book sales since volume one were pushing six hundred million. He paused and carefully set down his knife and fork before inquiring: "Dear boy, in England and in Ireland a million is ten hundred thousand. What number is a million in America?" I answered, "It's quite the same, Patrick."

He clasped his hands together, as in prayer and quietly said: "May the saints preserve us."

As the dinner progressed, a man and his woman companion occupied the other table in the little room. I have to admit that she had a very raucous sort of cackling laugh. Patrick began to seethe more with each of her outbursts. Finally in quite a loud voice, clearly intended for her to hear, he said: "Wouldn't you think that the Almighty, in his infinite wisdom, would have created a more attractive form of the female for the species?" She didn't notice.

After a number of brandies in the library Patrick decided to call it an evening. "Dear boy, would you be kind enough to help me find my car?" We were both on the street before it dawned on me that *he* was the one overnighting in his club. *I* was the one who had to sort out finding my vehicle and comprehending its principles of operation.

The most memorable, and I think among the last, occasions we met was at a dinner in the absolute heart of Nelson's and the British navy's sailing ship tradition, held in the Painted Room of the Greenwich Naval College. It was a black-tie affair attended by several hundred of his admirers, arranged to honor him. I'll not soon forget the scene with Patrick walking alone down through the rows of tables set in that magnificent hall to a prolonged standing ovation; it must have been the high point of his life. Danielle and I were honored to be seated next to the O'Brians at the head table. Patrick had specified the menu: authentic ship's fare from the early nineteenth century—hard tack, pea soup, boiled beef, fried parsnips, with a pudding of suet roly-poly, all accompanied with warm beer. A Frenchman was seated across from me during this ordeal. He gave me a number of bewildered looks. I knew what he was thinking: "How could these people have defeated us at Trafalgar . . . how *could* it have happened?"

I have gone on at such length about Nelson, O'Brian, square-riggers, and clipper ships, so that you may understand that this has been a lifelong interest; I came to believe, as did Patrick, that such ships were the epitome of all that was glorious about the sea.

The era of the greatest sailing ships, the clippers, was very brief, only a few decades beginning in the mid-nineteenth century. They were done in by the opening of the Suez Canal and the increasing efficiency of steam power emerging in a new era, but during their brief heyday these ships were the finest of man's creations on earth. Magnificently beautiful, fast (the term "clipper" arose from their ability to clip the times off passages between ports), and of the highest technology of their time, they fire the imagination still. Clippers were real fliers, much faster than their successors, the iron-hulled windjammers, a few of which survived in service until the Second World War and a very few of which remain in portside museums today. But, save for the wonderful *Cutty Sark*, all the other wooden-hulled clippers are gone.

If one had to pick a date representing the height of clipper ship glory it would be May of 1866 and the tea race from Shanghai to London. Over the preceding weeks several ships had loaded the fresh tea crop to race it to England; the first to arrive would obtain the top price for her owners. The fastest two clippers were the *Ariel* and the *Taeping*. Each captain and crew was keen to win. Incredibly, after racing for fifteen thousand miles, through the South China Sea, across the Indian Ocean, around the Cape of Good Hope, and up through the Atlantic, over ninety-nine days, frequently with each other in sight, the two marvelous fliers finished in a virtual tie—only eight minutes separated them at the Thames pilot station.

But the *Cutty Sark* was the iconic clipper, capable of running before the strong trade winds at speeds sometimes over twenty knots, and logging 363 nautical miles during one notable day. As a kid I studied her logbook, which had been preserved and annotated by sailing historian Basil Lubbock. I must have been a sailor in some previous incarnation, because I have always been drawn to these square-riggers. While in high school I became aware of Nelson and his battles. Later I consumed all of the Hornblower books.

Not long after the dinner in the Painted Hall, I encountered an old friend, Mikel Kraft, who is the owner of the Star Clipper sailing cruise ships. He has three of them operating in a very successful holiday business. Mikel had just commissioned the biggest one, the *Royal Clipper* of over four hundred feet in length, capable of carrying hundreds of guests. It had pulled into St. Tropez, and he had given me a complete tour during the afternoon. We had dinner aboard *Mariette* that night and at midnight his ship was scheduled to depart. Although the wind was little more than a breath, Mikel prevailed upon the captain to depart under sail; we followed her in my little classic tender. As the sails began to unfurl semiautomatically from her many yards, the *Clipper*, at first slowly, but then as certain and strong as a tide, pulled steadily away—soon at flank speed in our little diesel launch we couldn't keep up. She was incredibly beautiful sailing away into the moonlight.

The moment was an epiphany for me: there *could* be a modern square-rigged sailing vessel, albeit one requiring a significant sailing crew—Mikel had proven that. Maybe I might be able to create a clipper yacht, combining the sailing glory of the nineteenth century with the fully automated technology of the twenty-first century. I was inspired to try!

Chapter Fourteen

What If Orville and Wilbur Had Really Gone for Broke?

There were about eighty men on deck: electricians, plumbers and engineers of all kinds, including software programmers. The *Falcon* had passed her engine trials with flying colors, motoring at just under twenty knots, but this was the day of the sailing trials. The boat wasn't really finished, hence all the people. Anything might go wrong; all the experts were truly required. She was a vessel of a new kind, experimental and unproven. She had been in the water for the first time only a few days before in the preceding week—the skeptics so outnumbered the believers that I had stopped listening. Nearly six years of risk-taking engineering was on the line. I was exposed; if she performed, she would be world famous; if she failed, she would be even more famous, indeed infamous. The betting was against me.

The naval architects, the spar engineers, and all the others had agreed to a carefully controlled program of gradually escalating tests to prove the concepts on trial. The stakes were so high, nothing should be left to chance. The wind was a mild six knots as we motored away from the coast of Tuzla, Turkey, into the sea of Marmara. I pushed the control screen and, as I had designed, fifteen sails emerged from their housings in the masts and were automatically spread upon eighteen yards high above the deck. In a short space of time, a world record of sail area, some twenty-six thousand square feet, had been set automatically in just under seven minutes. For the first time in history, the vast sails of a square-rigger had been deployed quickly and with no intervention from a single crew member. The

The Maltese Falcon *sailing at eighteen knots*
off Viareggio, Italy, 2006

sail handling technology seemed to work. But would the yacht actually perform as expected?

The wind was soft, but in the distance I could see that there was a serious breeze making up. I turned the boat toward the wind. As the *Falcon* began to heel, I glanced to Gerry Dijkstra, the naval architect—in that glance and with just a nod between us, we discarded all the planned slow testing which had been so carefully outlined; we were going for it. We would put the new clipper yacht hard on the wind for the first time. He, a man famously of very few words, said: "In five minutes we'll know everything."

And after those minutes the results of five and a half years of work, and the investment of the national budget of a banana republic, were indeed in: the yacht was a stunning success—a stupendous breakthrough. I had gambled and I had won!

■   ■   ■

Gerd and I had a long history with the Italian yacht builders Perini Navi and with the owner of the company, Fabio Perini. He is a mechanical engineering genius whose paper converting machines dominate the industry—automated yachts were a diversification for him. In 1984 we became his second clients for our first Perini, the 42-meter (138-foot) ketch *Andromeda la Dea*. The boat was thus among the first to use his ideas for the automation of a yacht's sails. Thanks to Fabio's inventions, it became practical to own a big sailboat without the need for a big crew to tend to the sailing. I added a few touches of my own, principally a "fisherman staysail" to fill the gap between the main and mizzen masts. This sail became a standard feature on Perini yachts. In 1990 we commissioned our second boat from the yard, a 47-meter (154-foot) ketch, also named *Andromeda la Dea*. This yacht was a marvel, and she sailed over two hundred thousand miles under my ownership in a ten-year span. She sailed around the world, and visited all the continents, including Antarctica. In many ways this boat was the perfect yacht—fast, beautiful, and practical. In 2001 I didn't need another vessel; I owned *Mariette* and her support boat *Atlantide*, as well as *Andromeda*. So with this personal navy, I hardly needed another yacht. But I needed a project.

A dozen years ago Fabio had an order for a really enormous yacht, the largest private sailboat in the world at 88 meters (289 feet). The hull and superstructure were completed at the company's yard in Tuzla, Turkey, but then the customer got cold feet and the work stopped. The vessel just sat in the build hall waiting for another client. Fabio had discussed this boat with me several times, once even proposing that he and I coventure and race the vessel across the Atlantic and attempt to set a new record.

But I didn't care for the proposed sail plan, which was essentially an expansion of my fisherman staysail idea (I thought the plan would put the center of effort too high above the deck for good strong wind performance). Still, this hull had been in the back of my mind for years. Finally I asked Perini Navi to make a proposal for using the hull for a square-rig design, just to see if the idea might be feasible. The idea of a fast clipper was haunting me. I said not to spend much

money, because there wasn't a great chance that automating something so complex would be practical. They contacted three naval
architects, and after a few months said that there were some ideas
ready for me to look at.

I had not been back to Turkey since the years between college
and grad school, so when my daughter and I were on a visit to Istanbul, part of our trip was a stop in nearby Tuzla to look at the hull and
study the drawings from the three designers. In shifting things around
at the yard, one of the biggest in Europe, the hull had been tempo-
rarily put into the water. Thus my first look showed the yacht in her
element, and I thought her lines were very beautiful. The proportions were so good that her size seemed minimized—she looked
very sleek. Inside she was like Mammoth Cave, absolutely enormous. With nearly the length of a football field, and a fair fraction of
the width, with her four decks, she had plenty of space for accommodations!

This was one of those moments when a discussion was occur-
ring between my conscious and subconscious minds. My rational
self was saying: "This thing is too damned big—don't let your ego
get in the way of your better judgment!" The inner self was saying:
"Cool, man! Go for it."

Back in the office, Giancarlo, the Perini Navi general manager,
laid out the first architect's plans. I'll not share his name, because
they looked awful. The same was true for the second designer's effort. Each of them had added a long bowsprit, which looked silly on
this modern sleek hull. Then they had each put conventional yards
on all the masts. In other words, they had transferred a clipper ship
rig to a modern hull. Their ideas looked anachronistic, and there
were hundreds of lines (a sailor never uses the word "rope") running
down from the yards to the deck. It seemed to me to be a hopeless
solution to the problem; dozens of automatic winches would be required. I didn't see how any of this could ever be made to work.

But it was a different story with the proposal from Amsterdam-
based Gerard Dijkstra and Partners. Gerry was proposing something
clean-looking and completely new. The esthetics fit the hull perfectly: three masts with eighteen curved yards. The sails resembled

airfoils—airplane wings—mounted vertically. It looked fast and modern. But I didn't have the slightest idea of how it might work. Giancarlo called Gerry on the phone and I spoke to him within minutes of seeing his design.

He said that his drawing was based upon the "DynaRig," a technology developed at Hamburg University in the 1960s and paid for by the German government. That was a time of worry over Middle Eastern oil supply, and the government thought that maybe sails could power big cargo ships and thereby save fuel. Much wind tunnel work had been done, but the idea had never been tried full scale. The patents had expired, and Gerry thought the invention would be perfect for large sailing yachts. Dijkstra had an excellent reputation, and was the author of many beautiful big boat designs. I took this

The one-sixth-scale rig sailing aboard
a dinghy in an Amsterdam canal, 2002

idea very seriously. So I parted Tuzla telling Giancarlo: "Don't sell the hull to anyone else—I'll get back to you soon." This was a joke—no other buyer was even remotely in the offing—and I arranged to see Gerry and his partners the following week.

Their office is on a canal in the old part of town. Gerry has five or so principal partners, younger guys—all have degrees in naval architecture; and all but one are exceptionally tall. Indeed, the Dutch are among the very tallest races of people on the planet.

We dove into the DynaRig idea immediately. It comprises three masts, each with six curved yards, between which are stretched five sails, so there are fifteen sails in total. Thus a huge sail area can be split into a large number of smaller sails—just like on the old clippers. So when the wind grows too strong for safe operation, some sails are furled, starting at the top—again just like the clippers. But, unlike the clippers, the sails are stretched taut between the yards; they do not billow. This aspect together with the curvature of the yards, and the ability to rotate the masts, is unique to the idea.

The sails are rolled up in a vertical position inside the masts, and when set the whole system looks more like an ellipse than the sails of a conventional square-rigger. With the sails fixed to the yards, which in turn are fixed to the mast, by turning the whole rig toward or away from the wind, any point of sail can be achieved. Gerry said that in theory a DynaRig vessel can point (that is, sail close to the direction of the wind) as well as any conventional boat with a multiple mast design. The tremendous advantage of the idea is that the sails become highly efficient, being free of the wind turbulence surrounding the masts. This turbulence is the bane of all other sailing yachts. The wind tunnel data from the sixties indicated that a big DynaRigged yacht should be blisteringly fast. To top off these good aspects, it should be possible to make the system fully automatic—a push-button clipper yacht!

Probably the key reason that no one had ever taken up the idea has to do with metal fatigue. The original German design contemplated a rotating steel tripod of immense strength and no flexibility—but so inexpressively ugly that the idea would be unacceptable on any yacht. Gerry's design showed elegant free-standing masts but since the rigs must rotate and can have no stays for support, as with normal masts, they must be able to twist and flex with the motion of the vessel and the forces of the wind. Gerry estimated that in a big blow with all sails set, the top of the masts might move plus or minus eight feet or so.

Metal, all metal, simply wears out or "fatigues" from this sort of motion. You have experimented with this effect if you have ever bent a spoon until it breaks. The strongest material which is impervious to fatigue is carbon, in the form of carbon fiber (neglecting boron and a few other impractical composites). This is a relatively new and expensive substance, but it can flex and bend indefinitely. They said that it ought to work perfectly in this new kind of rig.

After a couple of hours' discussion, I summed up the project that they were proposing:

1) Use the DynaRig idea, never proven in practice.

2) Modify an already unproven design, the tripod, into a new, even less explored free-standing design.

3) Build everything in a new material, carbon fiber. Only the U.S. Air Force used the highest quality stuff in quantity in the famous stealth bomber, and each of the three masts on this boat would use more material than one of those planes.

4) Because it was military grade material and on export hold, we would have to find a source of carbon thread outside of America, and then find someone to weave it into cloth.

5) The whole experiment would be mounted on the largest yacht in the world.

They agreed glumly with my assessment. I said it was like the Wright Brothers at Kitty Hawk, saying, "Let's skip this motorized box-kite thing and shoot for a 747 instead."

So they were all very happily surprised when I concluded the meeting by hiring them to go forward with the project! Some while afterward, Gerry told me that when I left that afternoon, they sat around the table nearly overwhelmed; they hadn't for a moment truly dared to hope that anyone in the world would take on so much risk. And to this day I believe that I was the only person who would have done so.

But why not? I had spent my career managing high-tech high risk; there should be a way to "put the risk up front" in this project too. The essence of the program I had in mind was testing, both with models and with computer simulations.

Among the first priorities was to decide if it was worth proceeding with the existing hull. I thought it beautiful, and it would save time if we could use it, but a hull—though requiring at least a year to build—represents only about five percent of the value of a finished yacht. It's important to be sure that it's the right one, and the hull is not the place to save money. Also, the hull was constructed in steel; maybe aluminum might be better, as that metal is much lighter. So Gerry undertook a towing tank test on an accurate model of the hull at Delft University's naval architectural center, the place from which he had graduated, and began to think about hull materials.

When the model was ready I tagged along to the towing tank to watch. It's interesting to see how the waves the model creates at various speeds and heeling angles are examined and how the resistance is measured and studied. Gerry and the experts decided that the hull shape would serve extremely well with some straightforward modifications—the rudder should be given a deeper draft and moved aft by two meters and the keel should be deepened by 1.8 meters to accommodate some additional lead ballast: one hundred tons more. As to aluminum versus steel, the latter was the clear winner. That's because steel is both much stronger and also completely fireproof. The safety regulations require so much fire insulation to be added to an aluminum hull (of over five hundred tons gross displacement) that virtually all that lighter metal's weight savings are voided by the weight of the extra fireproofing material. Finally, Gerry said, "Tom, if I were ever going to be in the Southern Ocean on a yacht like this, I'd want the strength of steel." So if I were to proceed, the existing hull would serve admirably.

The next tests all had to do with the DynaRig itself. Dijkstra and his team needed to verify and update the German wind tunnel work. I had decided that the original research was sufficiently thorough, and that we could accept the basic conclusion: that of all the possible shapes and curves tested, the yards should have a twelve percent chord. (If the length of the yard is one hundred, the height of the arc, measured from tip to tip, is twelve—since the yards are of three different lengths, this means that there are three different radiuses of curvature for the spars.) So starting from this premise, we needed to determine the coefficients of driving force, and resistance, in order to know what sort of sailing performance we might achieve. This can only be done using a wind tunnel.

The foremost expert in these measurements is Ian Campbell at the Wolfson Unit at Southampton University. Ian has worked with most of the teams for the America's Cup over the years, and his measurements are highly refined. His team made a model of the hull and superstructure from the water line upward, and Jeroen de Vos, a young Dijkstra partner, made the model masts, yards, and sails to go onto the hull in the wind tunnel. The finished model had remotely controlled rotating masts, so that the rig could be "tuned" for optimum performance at the changing wind angles in the tunnel, just as the full-sized yacht would be trimmed in the ocean breezes.

The model in the tunnel was fascinating; it looked very good "sailing" with the masts moving and seeming to be alive. I spent some time there and followed the tests. The results were so encouraging that Ian repeated a number of them, simply to be certain that these great numbers were real. I played with a smoke wand--a thin stream of smoke that permits one to study the air flow minutely. We could see readily that the wind "loved" the twelve percent curves. The breeze clung to the surfaces of the sails with no turbulence evident, and the turbulence from the mast was well clear of the sails. Ian told me that I was the first owner ever to come to the facility to witness his testing.

Working with the combined towing tank and wind tunnel results, Gerry and Jeroen were able to make a velocity prediction for all the yacht's points of sail including upwind, beam-wind, and downwind, the so-called "polars." I was enormously encouraged by these projections; if properly carried to fruition, this clipper yacht would be the fastest all-around big yacht in the world. The numbers are the happy result of a long waterline length, and a large sail area,

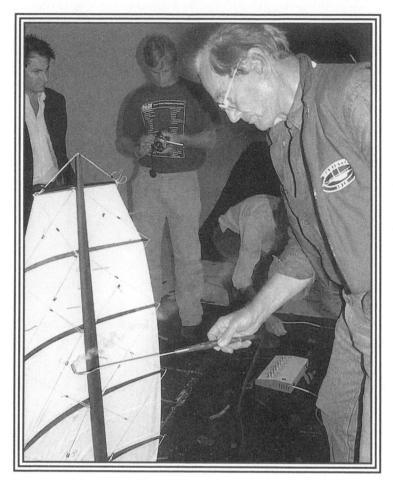

Perkins in the Wolfson wind tunnel
using a "smoke wand" to visualize air flow
over a model of the Falcon's *rig*

made extra efficient by the DynaRig concept. If we could keep the weight of the interior under control, within our "weight budget," the real yacht would achieve everything predicted.

The Dijkstra partners had yet another model to build and test. Gerry was worried that in a three-mast configuration the DynaRig might be difficult to tack. Sometimes the old clippers had trouble with this maneuver in which the bow is moved through the wind onto the new course—clippers had no trouble in "wearing around," that is, gybing with the stern to the wind. So Eric, one of the younger guys, built a radio-controlled model, about six feet in length, to try on the canal. The model tacked and gybed perfectly; the full-sized yacht would do just as well. Interestingly, a fellow with a conventionally rigged model of the same size and sail area showed up—the DynaRig model looked to be about twice as fast in the impromptu competition.

Behind the models was a program of computer simulation. The subcontracting experts in this field did a finite element analysis of the forces both in bending and torque on the proposed rigs to achieve a design of the strength required to see the yacht safely through anything that the seven seas might have in store. It's worth noting that without computer-aided design, a project of the immense complexity of this yacht simply would not have been possible.

Around this point I had a social evening in the beautiful Edwardian saloon aboard *Mariette* with Gerry and his wife, Loontje. Over dinner I mused, "I wonder why no one else has ever tried the DynaRig for a yacht." Before Gerry could answer, Loontje said, "You are about to find out!" After the laughter subsided, his laconic response—"You are supposed to assist my retirement, not cause it!"—was perfect. This interchange highlighted the experimental aspect, but still I remained confident in the calculations.

Though not yet fully committed to the project, the next step was to create the design, in broad brush at least, for the exterior and interior so that Perini might have enough information to prepare a bid.

Designer Ken Freivokh and his partner Liz Windsor had done a superb job for me in the reconstruction of my motorboat *Atlantide*, a classic from 1930, re-creating an Art Deco interior to my sketches. So I turned to Ken to consider this clipper yacht. We agreed that the existing aluminum superstructure was hideously ugly. He said, "Take a chain saw to it." I did. It was simply eliminated, literally thrown away onto the scrap metal pile. The exterior and interior "look" I wanted was to be "luxury high-tech machine." I had in mind the feeling one gets with a top-end sports car, a Ferrari, for example. The interior shows plenty of the underpinning technology, the carbon, the steel, the aluminum, but there is an overlay of softening wood, leather, wool, and finishing of hand craftsman's quality.

I had the basic layout of the interior in mind. A staircase would wrap around the central mast to create a glass-floored atrium as the centerpiece of the yacht. There would be just a few rooms. I wanted to avoid the "Mystery House Syndrome" of the famous San Jose mansion built for Mrs. Winchester, widow of the rifle manufacturer of that name. The poor woman was under the influence of a spiritualist who persuaded her that she would live on and on, for as long as she added rooms to the house. The corridors leading to nowhere, the rooms within rooms, and the duplications of rooms which resulted, remind me of the interior of today's typical large motor yacht. These boring gin palaces are usually designed by committees, and there is something for everyone.

But I too had a gin palace feature in mind. I thought that the bar should be circular, seating about twelve people, and that it should be bisected by sliding glass doors so that in fine weather they could be opened and the salon and aft deck would thereby become one huge area. Also, I wanted a cabin on the upper deck handy to the wheelhouse. I called this the "passage cabin" because during long voyages, for example a trade wind passage, that's where I would live, wanting always to be close to the action. And in the wheelhouse itself I specified two distinct stations: one for everything to do with the engines, and one exclusively for control of the sails. Ken was delighted with this challenging design and got going right away. I was able to turn back to the high-risk aspects of the program.

Gerry and I decided to make a one-sixth-scale DynaRig section consisting of a single sail mounted on a mast section and with two curved yards. We needed to prove that the original German ideas could be made to work on a larger scale than the one the inventors had used in the tunnel. A Dutch wood craftsman was hired to fabricate this mock-up. We learned a lot from this model. After considerable tinkering Jeroen got it to work repeatedly, unfurling the sail from its housing inside the mast and furling back again into the mast, by means of a hand crank. Along the way he perfected the double bolt rope, a key to the final design. In the beginning the rig was tested inside a warehouse with a big fan blowing—we had to be sure that the sail could be stowed even with the wind in the wrong direction—with nature being what is, this would eventually occur in the real world.

After the warehouse, the rig was mounted on a little boat and sailed in the canal outside the office. With the model's yards of about sixteen feet length, the sail was plenty big enough to prove feasibility. The guys were able to tack, reach, and gybe, as the real vessel would eventually need to do, very satisfactorily. One afternoon they were arrested by the water police; it's against the law to sail in the Amsterdam canals. But the cops were so intrigued by the experimental design that they were let off the hook. (I had something of the same experience once with a state police officer, when caught speeding in a new Bugatti EB 110—a tour of the alloy engine with its sixty valves and 620 horsepower engine was enough for him to let me go.)

Before the yacht could possibly become a real project with serious money flowing in, the problem of where and how to build the carbon spars (masts and yards) had to be solved. Gerry recommended a company in Spain, on the island of Mallorca, called Carbospars. They had built some AeroRigs in the material, and while not remotely like the DynaRig, those masts were at least free-standing, and their skills might translate into our needs. The other serious mast builder with carbon experience was in New Zealand—too far away to be practical. I visited Carbospars in their factory on the outskirts of Palma. The president, Damon Roberts, from the U.K., was an engineer's engineer. His knowledge of composite materials was awesome. He showed me an AeroRig mast under construction which was as tall as ours were proposed to be, although it was round in shape, and not as complicated as our elliptically shaped and compound curved design. I was very encouraged. After some discussion I agreed to supply some money for Carbospars to start to do the research necessary for a contract to be drawn up for the eventual construction of the rigs.

A few weeks later, I was unable to contact Damon. Carbospars was failing! Fortunately, I got my money back before they closed down, but my spars seemed to be in jeopardy. Perini Navi had made it abundantly clear that they were not able to undertake the whole project. If I was to proceed, it would be with me carrying the prime responsibility—I would have to be the customer, the manufacturer, and the project manager. I decided that would be okay. I would have to track Damon down and hire him. But he had joined a start-up company called Insensys which he was cofounding with a business partner.

They planned to pioneer in using fiber-optic sensors in composite structures like wind turbine blades and oil drilling rigs to measure stress and strain. I got together with them and it was obvious that we could help each other out. I could hire the new company to manufacture my spars—that would give them a big order to get the business started, and they could incorporate their proprietary optical techniques into the rigs. Why not add yet another new unproven technology into this equation? We worked out a time and materials contract with a profit incentive aspect. But the question of where to build these enormous structures was still open.

Meanwhile, Ken had finished his preliminary plans, and I submitted them to Perini Navi. A completely new superstructure in aluminum was specified; it looked both high-tech and very sleek. Ken incorporated all the contemporary art I have accumulated, much of which was chosen on advice from my daughter, a professional artist. Some of the paintings are huge, so the colors in the room had to be coordinated with them. All the art is challenging—it sort of grabs you—many find it disturbing, Judith Regan decided that it's homoerotic. No one is without an opinion, which is the result I desired.

The time was coming to negotiate a contract with Perini Navi to build the yacht. As this would be my third boat from them, we knew each other very well. I would be their first client to undertake a third project; the yacht would be the largest in the world; the technology would be revolutionary and if we, together, pulled all this off it would give Perini huge publicity and prestige. I kept telling them to "sharpen their pencils," that is, make me a very good deal. Before our meeting to draw up a contract I sent them, via FedEx, a battery-operated pencil sharpener to make my point. The rule of thumb for a big yacht is a million euros per meter. I hoped to bring her in under that, but the experimental rig complicated matters.

Finally, we reached an agreement for both the yacht and for the manufacture of the spars; the agreement proved to benefit all three parties, Perkins, Perini, and Insensys. Perini would make a big shed available, rent free, in their yard in Tuzla, adjacent to the build hall for the yacht, and they would help hire a work force whose wages I would pay (carbon fiber projects are hand-labor intensive); Insensys would provide the know-how and the management; I would supply the specialized capital equipment, ovens, vacuum systems, and impregnating machines. Upon completion, I would have my spars and Perini would inherit a running facility, with my equipment gratis. As in any good deal, it had to be fair to all parties. With these decisions made, Giancarlo and I inked a contract. I signed the arrangement with Insensys as well. The yacht was now officially underway after more than a year of testing and planning.

But the major test, making a one-to-one scale test rig for the development of the unique sail handling systems, remained before us. I was hoping to have this proof of principle in hand before the major flow if money into the build program was fully underway. I couldn't wait for the Turkish spar factory to be up and running to begin making the two huge yards—each seventy-five feet in length—so Insensys hired a subcontractor in England to do the work.

Carbon parts are made in molds which are derived from a two-step process. First a wooden plug in the shape of the finished piece is made. Strips of beautiful spruce were used; the finished plug was smoothed to the finish of a fine piece of furniture. Then a fiberglass "female" mold is taken from this wooden replica. Finally, the layers of carbon cloth are impregnated with resin and laid into this mold. After every fifteen layers (and hundreds of layers are required in the thicker places) a vacuum is applied to squeeze the excess resin away, and the layers are baked at 100 degrees Celsius (212 degrees

Fahrenheit) for about twelve hours to cure the material. It is a slow process, but when completed the carbon fiber has a strength per weight ratio exceeding anything else. And it never suffers fatigue.

We ordered the carbon thread from Toray Industries in Japan; hundreds of thousands of miles of thread wound onto large bobbins. It's a very high-tech and costly material. I believe that my order was the largest ever placed for the stuff, excepting probably the buying sprees of the U.S. Air Force for their bomber building habit. Anyway, it was a big enough order for the chairman of Toray to call to give me a personal thank-you, and would I be ordering more soon?

The thread was delivered to a small specialized weaving company in Manchester, England, where it was woven into cloth about eight inches wide and several hundred feet in length. These rolls of carbon cloth were then eventually exported to Tuzla—we had a little problem getting the export permit from the British government for this military grade cloth but we persuaded the officials, finally, that we weren't building missiles in that Muslim country.

The construction of the test rig was the single most important part of the build program. Damon had made a one-sixth-scale model of a mast section, which he twisted and bent until it failed, explosively, to test the accuracy of the computer model—the piece survived about fifteen percent more torture than predicted. But until we could make a sail automatically deploy and refurl, we had nothing.

At this point, about two years into the project, Fabio Perini got personally involved. I had already hired a small team of engineers in the U.K. to design and build the mechanical side of the sail system. I planned to use variable speed motors, computer controlled. Each sail requires five motors, one for each corner to pull the sail out along the yards from the inside of the mast, and another motor to turn the mandrel upon which the sail is rewound. With the fifteen sails on the yacht, seventy-five motors in total are needed. Fabio had been thinking about this yacht, which would carry his name as the builder. He was famous for inventing the first automatic sailing systems and now this boat, the biggest of all, wouldn't be using his technology.

Over the course of a dinner aboard *Atlantide*, he made his pitch.

If I would give him carte blanche to do the mechanical side of all the sail systems, he wouldn't charge me for the engineering, just for the out-of-pocket materials cost. Also, he proposed to use the company that did all his paper machinery computers to design the yacht's sail control systems, operating from my own logic flow diagrams. I felt a bit like Br'er Rabbit pleading with the Fox; I very much wished for Fabio to help me and to guide me through this technical briar patch. So after pretending some reluctance in surrendering control, I did so with a big inner smile.

I was commuting to Europe or to Turkey roughly every six weeks to manage the project, but I needed an on-site manager. I picked Chris Gartner, then captain of *Mariette*, to run the project in my absence and to be captain of the finished boat. At the time Chris, an American from Golden and a graduate of the University of Colorado, had been working for me for thirteen years. I had total confidence in his judgment, and he jumped at the opportunity. I leased a house in Mercan—a nice community near the seaside and close to the yard—to accommodate the growing number of people working directly for me on the build. Eventually we had three houses and fifteen persons; we called it the "Perkins neighborhood."

The test rig came together when the two yards arrived from England. We mounted the rig, with its trestlelike temporary mast, on a strong cement dock where it would be exposed to a variety of winds. The rig could be rotated to face any direction, and we had it well instrumented so that we could gather as much data as possible. Fabio invented a new kind of spiral winch to accommodate the bolt ropes, and most ingeniously, he eliminated the need for variable speed motors and all the electronics and costs they entailed. His motto was: "*Stupido è Meglio*": "stupid is better." I ordered a test sail from Doyle Sailmakers in Marblehead, Massachusetts; Robbie Doyle has a degree in physics from Harvard and is up to trying new ideas. Eventually he was to make all the sails, and his son, Tyler, wrote a PhD thesis paper on the DynaRig airflow.

Unfortunately, when we tried the system for the first time it tore the sail badly. It tore the sail over and over again during the next few

months. This was the single most difficult period of the entire project. Money was flowing in to the build, on a number of fronts, at an
alarming rate and we didn't have a system that worked. Chris, engineer Jed White, and I spent hours and hours up in the test rig study-
ing alternative solutions. Very gradually the small inventions we
added, nearly everywhere, began to work. When we finally had the
system operating flawlessly in thirty knots of wind during a snow-
storm, I began to believe that we were home safe.

Meanwhile "my" thirty-five young Turks were making huge
progress in the mast facility. Also, the yacht itself was really beginning to take shape. Every day some two hundred workers climbed
aboard to work hard, long hours. All the Dijkstra hull modifications
had been made, and the ducting, piping, and electrical wiring were
well under way. During the build we weighed the boat several times,
using hydraulic lifting jacks, and we kept well within our weight
budget of 1,240 metric tons (1,364 U.S. tons).

At this point I made a major decision which had a big impact on
the outcome. The longtime manager of the Perini Tuzla yard (called
Yildiz: Turkish for "star," the emblem of Perini Navi) is a retired
captain from the Turkish navy named Baki Gökbayrak. Baki-Bey, to
use the Turkish honorific meaning "sir," has a degree in naval architecture from the University of Michigan and many years' experience
running shipyards prior to joining Perini. The normal practice is for
Yildiz to build about sixty percent of a yacht, and then send it back
to Perini's yard in Viareggio, Italy, for finishing.

The Perini reputation for quality is excellent, and is attributed in
part to this practice. But my boat was too big and too deep to enter
Viareggio, so an alternative site had to be found. Baki proposed to
me that he be permitted to do the entire job, one hundred percent,
in his yard in Turkey. He simply said: "If you give me this honor, I
will deliver to you the finest yacht in the world." He had never carried such a project to completion; no yard in Turkey had ever done
a big sailing yacht; and my boat was the biggest sailboat on earth.

But I remembered my experience with the Turks all those decades ago when the pilots put their hearts into the job and won the
competition. There was something in Baki's personality that was

very assuring. I decided to gamble on his promise: I said yes. From that day forward one could feel a change in the attitude of nearly every worker. This was going to be their yacht—it would be the pride of their country. Though never before even remotely shoddy in any way, still, there was a noticeable new attention to detail. Jobs that might before have been called finished were now sometimes done over again to achieve a higher standard. Third-party contractors, like the paint experts from DuPont, began to comment that the Yildiz yard was working to the quality level of the best yards in Holland, a rare compliment indeed.

Ken's designs were wonderfully beautiful and elegant, and extremely challenging to build. His simplicity of line was in some ways deceptive of the inner complexity—I am sure every contractor for a Frank Lloyd Wright house had the same reaction. We selected Sinnex in Germany to build the owner's areas and the guest accommodations. They are a precision outfit who were brilliant in execution. The crew areas were given to Ulutas, a local Turkish finisher. Hasan Ulutas is a lover of complex woodworking machinery. Perhaps unexpectedly, he relied more on high-tech machines than low-cost hourly labor to complete his portion. The interior space comprised some eleven thousand square feet (312 square meters) of living area. That's the interior space for a big house; but we weren't just building a house. A yacht is more similar to building a town; we have our own waterworks, our own sewage system, electricity, heating, telecommunications, and so forth.

A project like this seems to become stalled, though steady progress is being made. During every visit to the yard the same wires seem to be hanging down from the overhead, the same paint crew seems to be sandpapering the topsides in the same places; sometimes I wondered if the boat would ever be finished. Eventually the project accumulated over one million three hundred thousand man-hours of work—and that's not counting any man-hours in purchased items, like radars and engines.

Along the way I decided that the boat would need a home port and I bought a berth in a new marina being created in Malta, a beautiful spot in the heart of the old city of Valletta. With such a home port I thought the yacht should be named *The Maltese Falcon*: the falcon is, indeed, the symbol of the country. The name was available and so it became official. The two fast speed boats lodged upon the foredeck were named *Brigid O'Shaughnessy* and *Iva Archer*, after the two primary female characters in the famous book of that name, and the crew work boat was named *Effie Perine*, after Sam Spade's Girl Friday in the story. Similarly, the big wide Hobbie Cat carried aboard got tagged *The Fat Man* and the two jet skis were named *Joel* and *Wilmer* after the heavies in the story. While still on a roll, we named the four tiny laser sailboats carried aboard: *Terrible Talon, Cruel Claw, Baneful Beak*, and *Ravenous Raptor*.

Although glaciers move slowly, they do move. Finally in early 2006 the masts were nearing completion and the boat was nearly ready to be launched. The spars were enormous, each over fifty-eight meters in length, which would be some 192 feet from the flagpole top to the water. The eighteen yards took a tremendous amount of space—they looked a bit like tusks from prehistoric mastodons and their storage shed was called the "bone yard."

When the day came to pull the *Falcon* out of her build shed, hundreds of workers assembled to watch. It was done in the old-fashioned way, using greased skids, a slow and time-consuming process. Just before she inched out of the hall, the timbers groaning under her weight, I shouted for the procedure to stop. I told Baki-Bey that a Turkish flag had to be mounted on the flagstaff at the stern before the yacht saw the sunlight for the first time. A big flag was found and the hauling was resumed, with not a few tears in many Turkish workers' eyes as the white star and crescent on the red background emerged, gleaming in the bright light. All were brimming with deserved pride. A week or so later, I gave every single hourly worker a big solid silver coin, especially made, to commemorate the build.

After the *Falcon* was floating alongside her dock, the difficult operation of installing her masts commenced; but not before three Turkish gold coins were attached to their bases—the traditional offering to Poseidon. A crane with a lift of 250 feet was rented and the mainmast was the first to be installed. All the yards, winches, and

sails were already mounted and the total weight was some twenty-
five metric tons—it hung from a single carbon tang built into the
mast top for this purpose. The mast base with the hundreds of electrical wires installed in their carrier cleared the opening in the
yacht's top deck by only one centimeter; but by going slowly, all
went well. The rigger, who had overseen the lifting, was hoisted aloft
to detach the sling from the crane. When he returned to the deck, I
had a crew member hoist me to the top—I had wanted to be the first
up the mast, but had to settle for being second. The view from eighteen stories in the air was spectacular, and the gentle flexing of the
spar in the light breeze added to the thrill. Everyone saw this and for
days later I got "thumbs up" from many grinning Turkish workers.

The remaining two masts also went in smoothly, but a near disaster occurred the following day, a Saturday.

We had just launched our new man-overboard rescue boat to
test its motor when we heard shouting from the big shipyard neigh-
boring Perini's Yildiz location, in the very industrial Tuzla harbor. A
large chemical tanker, which must have weighed at least fifty thousand tons, was being maneuvered toward the dock immediately opposite the *Falcon* by two tugs. In the process, the ship's third officer
somehow got caught by the hawser (the towing line) of one of the
tugs and he was pulled by the rope through an elliptical aperture on
the upper deck, called a "Panama," not much larger than himself. I
saw him being catapulted from four decks height into the water. He
was obviously very seriously injured if not dead. By a miracle of good
luck our rescue boat fired up immediately and five of my crew were
able to rescue the man and get him to shore. They returned covered
in his blood.

But with the towing line and the line handler out of action, the
tug pilot must have panicked and in an effort to save the situation
started to push the ship, with the bow of the tug against the ship's
rudder. While under full throttle, the bow slipped off the narrow
edge, and the tug crashed into the ship's stern. This smashed the
tug's little wheelhouse and possibly killed the pilot as well. There
was a strong wind blowing and, to our horror, slowly but inexorably,
the giant ship began to drift down toward us aboard the *Falcon*. All

three masts had been rotated so that our yards were thwart-ship and sticking about fifteen feet over the side. We had no power running and it was not possible to rotate them back fore and aft into a safe position. With the ship looming over us, and with no more than ten feet of clearance remaining, the second tug began successfully to pull the giant clear. Our rig, representing years of work and millions of dollars' investment, was thus saved by a very narrow margin. Had the monster settled down on us, the spars would have become huge worthless shards of carbon fiber. We learned a week later that both the ship's officer and the pilot, though each badly injured, survived. The shipyard owner came by and thanked my guys for their part in the rescue.

As mentioned at the beginning, *Falcon*'s sea trials, both power and sail, went extremely well. I had budgeted three days for the latter, anticipating a variety of problems for such a radically new system, but in the event, only three hours were needed to prove that everything was, essentially, perfect.

And so my yacht sailed away from Istanbul, where Perini had hosted a reception for bigwigs of the Turkish government, and onto the front cover of virtually every yachting magazine in the world. She has universally been hailed as a breakthrough. Some editors have said that she is the most important development in yachting in the past century. The *International Herald Tribune* said that I had achieved that rarest of all honors: a place in history. Most agree with me that she is stunningly beautiful, and that the luxury machine look of the interior is a triumph for Ken, the designer.

I am aboard the *Falcon* now as I write these words. We are about one thousand miles from our destination, St. Barts in the Caribbean—my favorite island. The yacht has just passed her ten thousand mile mark since leaving Turkey, and most of those miles have been under sail. We have been in very strong winds, over sixty-five knots in a Mistral in the Golfe du Lion, and everything was fine aboard. So far our top speed has been twenty-five knots under sail, but I believe that we can do better still. We have entered one regatta, and it was an important one, the Perini Cup races. We won first place, beating fifteen other Perini yachts, many of which were previously considered to be very fast. The participants seemed amazed that the "Big Bird" (as the crew fondly calls her) tacked, gybed, pointed high on the wind, and generally handled as easily as a dinghy.

On this passage, our first ocean crossing, the wind hasn't been strong enough during the nights for us to beat *Cutty Sark*'s record 363 nautical miles in twenty-four hours—so far our best is 319—but we will get there. The sun is shining, the trade winds are a moderate twenty-three knots, and with all our beautiful sails set we are making eighteen knots through the water.

The Maltese Falcon is my crowning achievement.

I hope that my education is sufficiently complete now for me to enjoy it and not feel compelled to push on to something else.

Any bets?

A Final Word

And so, Dear Reader, having stuck with me through all these tales in which I promised to present "the truth as I see it, unvarnished, and as beautiful or as ugly as you may find it," I hope that you may have discovered a rose here and there among all the thorns. The venture chapter profited from the invaluable review of partners Brook Byers and John Doerr, whom I thank for their help.

Henry Adams, who wrote in the third person, nevertheless ultimately revealed everything about himself. That takes some courage. But he lived in an age before the Internet. Now, an author gets nearly instant feedback from readers posting their "reviews" online. To save you the effort of looking, I'll present some likely ones in advance:

> "His reputation will survive everything, except his autobiography." —Narinder

> "A good read, sometimes amusing—I wonder who wrote it for him?" —Tony

> "Self-aggrandizing drivel from a misogynistic, narcissistic egomaniac, who inadvertently makes it clear why he has more enemies than friends!" —Patricia

*"I deeply believe that before acceptance must come trust. . . .
I have searched the Web and there is absolutely no article by
Natasha Steinmetz or for that matter a magazine called
Celebrity Wire. They do not exist! Perkins made it all up!!!!
I wonder if poor Danielle Steel knows this?"* —Carleton

■　　■　　■

Anyway, I would like to thank Bill Shinker and Lauren Marino at
Gotham Books, my publisher and editor, who actually do exist, for
their faith and help, and Fred Hill, my agent, for his continuing advice and skill.

　　　—T. P.

Index

Note: Page numbers in *italics* refer to illustrations.

Abbott, Bill, 80
Acuson
    and Abbott, 80
    and Maslak, 139
    Perkins' role at, 10
    products, 112, 133
Adams, Henry, xi, 21, 69, 275
AeroRigs, 263
Agilent, 76
AGM car rallies, 90–92
Altair, 28, 30, 31
Amazon, 133, 236
American Civil Liberties Union
    (ACLU), 39
American President Lines, 53
American Research and
    Development, 50, 51, 102
Anderson family, 107
Andromeda la Dea, 195, 240, 241–
    44, 253
Antarctica voyage, 195
Ariel, 247–48

army, 47–48
artwork, 264
Astra, 28
Atlantic Challenge 1997, 167–80,
    168
    change in captains, 169–70
    conditions, 173–74, 175–76
    crew, 172, 174–75, 176, 179
    forfeit, 179–80
    navigator/meteorologist, 170,
        171, 172–73, 176, 177, 179
    preparations, 170–71
    provisions, 167, 173, 176, 178–
        79
    race, 167–68, 171–79
Atlantide, 253, 261, 266–67
automobiles, 89–97
    Buccialli TAV 12, 93–95
    Bugattis, 90, *90*, 93, 96, 263
    car rallies, 90–92
    collection of, 89–90, 92–95, 96
    Ferrari, 79, 89

automobiles (*cont.*)
  McLaren F-1, 209–10, 217
  and Perkins' father, 45

Babbio, Larry, 15
Bagley, Al, 80
Balanchine, George, 156, 161
ballooning, 91–92
Baneful Beak, 270
Barr, Charlie, 167
Bartiromo, Maria, 231
Baryshnikov, Mikhail, 154
Baskins, Ann, 13, 15, 17
Bechtolsheim, Andy, 141
Bell Labs, 72, 104, 204
Belvedere, California, 219–22
biotechnology, 117–23, 132–33
Boonstra, Cor, 205
Booz Allen Hamilton, 55
Boston Consulting Group (BCG),
    82–83
Boyer, Herb, 119–23, 124
Brigid O'Shaughnessy, 270
Brin, Sergey, 141
British Admiralty, 244
Brown, Dan, 227
Bruhn, Erik, 151, 153, 154, 160
Bryan, John, 102
Bugatti Atlantic Elektron, 90
Bugatti EB 110, 263
business career, origins of, 50
business plans, writing, 135
BusinessWeek, 6, 19
Busiri-Vici chapel, 27–28
Byers, Brook
  acknowledgement of, 275
  and Hybritech, 132, 138–39
  and KPC & B, *130*, 131, 134,
    142

and Swanson, 117
and Tandem, 112

Caen, Herb, 148, 153, 157
calculators, 74, 106
Cambridge University, 132
Campbell, Ian, 259
Candida, 28, 31, 32
Cape, Ronald, 117, 119
Cape Formentor, 244
Capellas, Michael, 3–4
carbon fiber, 257, 265–66
Carbospars, 263–64
Caremark, 133
Caufield, Frank
  on investment bankers, 114
  and KPC & B, *130*, 131, 134,
    142
Celebrity Wire, 183–201. *See also*
    Steel, Danielle
Cetus, 117–18, 124
Charlie Rose Show, 231
Chiron Corp., 119
City of Hope Medical Research
    Foundation, 122, 123
Clark, Jim, 133–34
Classic Supercharged Sports Cars
    (Perkins), 90
Claude, Andrei, 233–34, 235
Clay, Roy, 79, 80
clipper ships, 247–48, 256, 260–61
CNET.com, 12, 14
Cohen, Stan, 119, 120
color translating radiography, 61
The Committee for the Ballet, 153,
    155
Compaq
  and HP merger, 1–4, 9
  and KPC & B, 133, 135

and Philips N.V., 206
and Tandem, 113
Compton, Kevin, 132
Computed Sonography, 112
computer-aided design (CAD), 261
computer business, 110–14. *See also* Tandem Computers
congressional hearings, 18
consultant, Perkins as, 55, 81
Cook, Paul, 131
Corning Glass, 205
Crisp, Peter, 102, 106
Cruel Claw, 270
Cummings, Ross, 93
Cupertino, California, 81
Cutty Sark, 247, 248

Davidow, Bill, 80, 111
Davies, Ellen, 53–54
Davies Symphony Hall, 53, 147
Davis and Rock, 102, 104
Davis Skaggs, 66
Delacorte, 190
Delft University, 258
Dell, 3
diabetes, 121, 123
DialGrade product line, 67
Digital Equipment Corporation (DEC), 50, 74–75, 112
Dijkstra, Gerard
    design, 254–55, 256, 257, 258, 268
    dinner with Perkins, 261
    on DynaRig technology, 256
    testing models, 258–59, 260–61
    testing the *Falcon*, 252
Dijkstra, Loontje, 261
DNA, 119, 120

Doerr, John
    acknowledgement of, 275
    enthusiasm, 134
    and Google, 141
    and KPC & B, 132, 142
    as marketing strategist, 135
Dom Kirke project, 23–25
Doriot, Georges, 50–51, 74, 102
Doyle, Robbie, 267
Doyle Sailmakers, 267
Draguignan, France, 36
Draper, Bill, 109
Draper Gaither and Anderson (DG&A), 56, 61, 102
drugs, recreational, 206
Dunn, Pattie, 7
    challenges to, 13–14
    criminal indictments, 17, 19
    and Perkins, 9–11, 13–14
    and press leaks, 12–13, 14–17
    reaction to *Zillionaire*, 11
    recruitment of CEO, 6–9
Dwight, Herb, 109
DynaRig technology, 255–59, 262–63, 267–68

Edex Corporation, 104
The Education of Henry Adams (Adams), 21
education of Perkins
    MBA, 48, 49–51, 52–53
    undergraduate studies, 46–47, 49
Edwards, Bill, 102
Effie Perine, 270
Eindhoven, Netherlands, 203–6
Eldred, Noel, 54, 76–77, 78
Enron, 15
Eskisehir, Turkey, 48–49

exorcisms, 165–66
*Experiments in Physical Optics
Using Continuous Laser Light*
(Perkins), 58

Fabio, 232
Fairchild Semiconductor
Company, 104
Falk, Kathryn, 230, 232, 234, 235
Farley, Peter, 117, 119
The Fat Man, 270
Ferrari, 79
fiber optics, 56–57, 212
Fife, William, 28
Fifth Force, 209–17
compiler issue, 212, 216–17
demonstration, 213–14
marketing plans, 214–15
proposal, 211–13
Fiorina, Carly, 2
and board of directors, 5–6, 13
and Compaq-HP merger, 1–4, 9
criticism of Perkins, 18
dismissal of, 6, 12, 18–19
management style, 4
memoir, 18, 180
fire department volunteers, 219–22
Food and Drug Administration
(FDA), 60, 124
Fortune, 6
Fox and Friends, 231
Freivokh, Ken, 261–62, 264, 269,
272

Gare, Simon d'la, 129–30
Gartner, Chris, *169*, 170, 176, 267,
268
Gates, Bill, 48–49

Genentech
leadership of, 139–40
origins, 117–25
and Packard, 142–43
Perkins' role on board, 10
products, 133
General Radio Company (GR),
51
gene splicing, 119, 120
Gerard Dijkstra and Partners, 254–
55. *See also* Dijkstra, Gerard
Giancarlo, 254, 255–56, 265
Glaser, Donald, 118–19
"Glass Cathedral," 23–26, *25*
Gogh, Vincent van, 95
Gökbayrak, Baki, 268–69
Golfe du Lion, 241, 272
Google, 114–15, 133, 141
Grad, Doug, 229
Great Ocean Race of 1905, 167
Green, Mike, 110–11
Greene, Ted, 138–39

Hackborn, Dick, 12
Hamar, Norway, 23–25
Hambrecht, Bill, 115, 124
Hambrecht and Quist, 68
Hamburg University, 255
Hammond, Steve, 30
Harlan, Neil, 148, 149–50
HarperCollins, 228–29
Harrah, Bill, 92
Harry and David, 55
Harvard Business School, 48, 49–
51, 53
Harvard University, 46, 232
heart murmur of Perkins, 48
helium-neon continuous gas laser,
57–58

Herreshoff, Halsey, 170–71, 173,
    176, 177
Herreshoff, Nat, 26, 170
Herreshoff Museum, 170
Hewlett, Bill, 73
    ambition, 71–72
    on calculators, 74
    and computer business, 77–78
    family, 3
    and HP Labs, 74
    management style, 71, 81, 82
    and OTI, 55–56
    and Packard's Washington
        sabbatical, 80
    Perkins' interview, 51–52
    and San Philippe Ranch, 54
Hewlett, Walter, 3
Hewlett-Packard
    board (see Hewlett-Packard
        Board of Directors)
    and Boston Consulting Group,
        82–83
    company culture, 71–72, 79
    Compaq merger, 1–4, 9
    competition, 11
    computer business, 74–79
    congressional hearing on, 18
    Corporate Development
        position, 81–84
    early employment at, 52–53, 54–
        55, 62, 68
    general managers, 71, 72
    growth in, 71
    HP Model 2116, 75–76
    HP Model 35 calculator, 74, 106
    HP Labs, 72–75, 76
    innovation, 72
    interview, 51–52
    marketing and advertising, 76–
        79
    organizational chart, 4
    and Packard, 142–43
    Palo Alto division, 75
    patent and intellectual property
        portfolio, 4
    personnel department, 52
    printer division, 72, 74
    relationships of Perkins, 78, 79–
        80
    stock price, 3, 9
    and Tandem, 112, 113
Hewlett-Packard Board of Directors
    accomplishments, 4–5
    chairmanship, 6–7, 13 (see also
        Dunn, Pattie)
    compliance focus, 10–11
    Dunn's clashes with Perkins, 9–
        11
    and Fiorina, 5–6
    nominating and governance
        committee, 18
    Perkins' resignation from, 16
    Perkins' role on, 1, 5, 10
    press leaks, 6, 9, 12, 14–17
    and pretexting issue, 18
    recruitment of CEO, 7–9
    resignations from, 6, 16
    role of, 6
    surveillance of, 14–17, 19
    technology committee, 2, 4, 11
    tensions on, 11–12
Hill, Fred, 227–28
Hillman, Henry, 106, 131–32,
    140–41
Holiday Inn, 92
Holland, 203–6
Holmes, David, 55
Home Health Care of America,
    133
Hornblower books, 248

hot air balloons, 91–92
Howard, Charles, 96
Hughes Research, 58
Hurd, Mark, 8–9, 12, 13, 17
Hybritech, 132–33, 138

I Am Charlotte Simmons (Wolfe), 47
IBM, 78, 112
Insensys, 264, 265
insulin, 121, 123
Intel, 104, 108
International One Design (IOD), 63
investment bankers, 113–15
Irresistible Forces (Steele), 186, 187–88
Iva Archer, 270

Jaenicke, Dick
  employment of, 61
  laser development, 62, 65
  and OTI, 66
  retirement, 68
Janklow, Mort, 190
Japan, 95, 97
Javan, Ali, 57–58
Jewett, Fritz, 152–53
Jewett, Lucy, 152–53
Joel, 270
Johnson, Franklin "Pitch," 102, 112, 131
Junior Common Stock, 124
justice system, U.S., 38–39

Kapany, Narinder, 56–57, 60–61, 62–68

Kaplan, David, 18
Katzman, Jim, 110–11
Keyworth, Jay
  on Dunn and board, 14
  and press leaks, 12, 14–17, 18
  recruitment of CEO, 6–9
Khosla, Vinod, 132
The Kiss (Steele), 186
Kleiner, Eugene, *103*
  background, 102–4
  death, 132
  and investment of capital, 116–17
  Kleiner's First Law, 108, 115
  and KPC & B, *130*, 131, 142
  raising capital, 101, 105–8, 112
Kleiner & Perkins (K&P), 101–25
  and Cetus, 117–18, 124
  and Compaq-HP merger, 1
  established, 108
  and Genentech, 117–23
  and investment bankers, 113–15
  investment of capital, 115–17
  investors, 104, 105, 112, 125
  personality struggles in, 138–40
  profits, 105
  prospectus, 104–5
  raising capital, 101–2, 105–8, 125
  search for ventures, 108–10
  standards, 105
  and Tandem, 110–14, 123, 125
Kleiner Perkins Caufield & Byers (KPC & B), 129–43
  decision process, 134–36
  and d'la Gare performance, 129–30
  established, 131–32
  and Hybritech, 132–33
  management of, 134–35, 142
  New Industries Fund, 140–41

partnerships, 107, 133, 134
  and "Tony," 136–38
The Klone and I (Steele), 188–89
Korean War, 47–48
Kraft, Mikel, 248–49
Kramer, Buzz, 59
Kvamme, Floyd, 132

Lacob, Joe, 132
Lally, Jim, 132
Lane, Ray, 132, 142
lasers
  advances in technology, 57–58
  advertisement, 65
  applications, 60, 61, 67
  development of, 43–44
  patent wars, 58
  See also University Laboratories,
    Inc. (ULI)
Lasertron, 63–64, 112
Lauren, Ralph, 96
LeBlond, Richard, 147, 150–51,
  158–59
Lee, Ralph, 78–79, 80, 81
Lincoln, Abraham, 46
Loma Prieta earthquake, 142–43
The Long Road Home (Steele), 197
Loustaunou, Jack, 108, 112
LSI Logic, 133
Lubbock, Basil, 248
Lucas, Don, 56, 61

MacKenzie, Doug, 132
Maiman, Ted, 58
Makarova, Natalia, 154
Malta, 269–70
Maltese Falcon, 251–73, 252
  auxiliary watercraft, 270

berth, 269–70
construction, 264–70
costs, 265
design, 254–57, 261–64
DynaRig technology, 255–59,
  262–63, 267–68
experimental nature of, 265
hull, 256, 258, 268
interior, 262, 264, 269, 272
maneuverability, 260–61
manufacturers, 263–64
named, 270
and Perini, 253
Poseidon's offering, 270
proposal, 253–54
regatta, 272–73
risks involved, 257–58
sails, 254–55, 256, 259, 262–63,
  266–68
sea trials, 251–52, 272
spars, 254, 256–57, 259, 262–64,
  265–66, 268, 270, 271
success of, 201, 272
tanker encounter, 271–72
testing models, 255, 258–61,
  260, 263
velocity predictions, 259–60
weight, 271
management consulting, 55, 81
Mann, Bruce, 116–17
manslaughter charges, 33, 36–38
Mariette, 168
  acquisition of, 26–27
  damage to, 175–76
  and Perkins' fleet, 253
  regattas, 28–34, 168, 272–73 (*see
    also* Atlantic Challenge 1997;
    Nioulargue Regatta in St.
    Tropez)
  Tom (captain), 30, 31, 36, 38

Maslak, Sam, 139
MBA of Perkins, 52–53
McLaren F-1, 209–10, 217
media. *See* press
Melchor, Jack, 76, 77
Mercan, Turkey, 267
Mercedes-Benz, 89
microprocessors, 5
Microsoft, 49
Middleton, Fred, 124
Mistral winds, 241, 272
MIT (Massachusetts Institute of
    Technology), 46–47, 49, 57,
    58
Monterey Bay Aquarium, 143
Moore, Gordon, 107
Morgan Stanley, 140
"Mr. Romantic Times" contest,
    233, 234
Mullis, Kary, 119
Murdoch, Rupert, 215, 216, 229–
    30
Murdoch, Wendi, 230
Myers, Gerry, 115–16

NatLab, 204
NATO gunnery competition, 48, 49
NCR (formerly National Cash
    Register company), 8, 9
Neary, Patricia, 157–58
Neely, Norman B., 54
Nelson, Horatio, 248
Netscape, 133
NewsCorp, 13, 215
Newsweek, 18
New York Times, 50
New York Yacht Club, 167, 171
Nioulargue Regatta in St. Tropez,
    29–36

accidental death, 32–36
manslaughter charges, 33, 36–38
race, 29–32
race committee's jury, 33–34, 38
Nomura Securities, 95
nonstop kernel, development of,
    111
Noyce, Bob, 107

O'Brian, Mary, 241, 242, 243
O'Brian, Patrick, 239–49, 240
    book tour, 240
    characters, 239
    cruise with Perkins, 239–40,
        241–44
    dinner with Perkins, 192, 240–
        41, 245
    formality of, 241, 243
    Greenwich Naval College
        dinner, 246
    lecture, 240
    personal life, 243
    on women, 245
    writing of, 229, 239, 244
Oliver, Bernard, 72–73
Ollard, Richard, 242, 243
O'Neal, Stan, 11
"Operation Hickory Stake," 5
Optic Technology Inc. (OTI), 56–
    62, 65–66
Owsley, Augustus Stanley, III, 43

Packard, Dave, 73
    ambition, 71–72
    and computer business, 75–76,
        77–78
    family, 3
    and Genentech, 124

and HP Labs, 74–75
and Loma Prieta earthquake,
    142–43
management style, 71, 81, 82
mentorship of Perkins, 52–53
and OTI, 55–56, 61
Perkins' interview, 51–52
on personnel departments, 52
and San Philippe Ranch, 54
and University Laboratories,
    Inc., 62–63
Washington sabbatical, 80, 83–
    84
Page, Jimmy, 163
Page, Larry, 141
Paine, John, 229
parents of Perkins, 44–46
Pebble Beach Concourse, 93
Perini, Fabio, 253, 266–67
Perini Cup races, 272–73
Perini Navi, 253, 254, 264
Perkins, Elizabeth, 44
Perkins, Tom, *44*
    and car rallies, *90*
    children, 44, 61
    education, 46–47, 48, 49–51,
        52–53
    heart murmur, 48
    and KPC & B, *130*
    optimism, 21, 23
    parents, 44–46
    at Plumpton Place, *164*
    pretexting issue, 17–18
    sailing, *184, 260*
    wives (*see* Steel, Danielle;
        Thune-Ellefsen, Gerd)
    youth, 44–46
Perkins, Tor, 61
Philips N.V., 203–6, 211
physics, 46, 49–50

Physics Today, 64
picture telephones, 214, 215
Pieper, Ricka, 213, 214, 217
Pieper, Roel, *210*
    attempted murder of, 217
    background, 210–11
    compiler issue, 212, 216–17
    demonstration, 213–14
    marketing plans, 214–15
    proposal, 209, 211–13
Plumpton Place, 163–66, 245
polymerase chain reaction (PCR),
    119
Poseidon, 270
press
    and HP board, 6, 9, 12–13, 14–
        17, 18
    and San Francisco Ballet, 147,
        148, 150, 153, 154, 155, 157,
        160, 161–62
    See also specific newspapers
pretexting issue, 17–18
Pui-Wing Tam, 231

Quist, George, 68
Qume, 109

Ravenous Raptor, 270
Raychem, 131
Raytheon, 104
read-only memory, 74
reality-television series proposal,
    223–24
Redmond, Andrea, 8
Regan, Judith, 228–29, 264
Regatta Royale, Cannes, France,
    28
Reilly, Phil, 93, 95

Rhodes, Henry, 63, 66, 67
Robb, Kirk, 139–40
Roberts, Damon, 263–64, 266
Robertson, Sandy, 102, 106
Rockefeller family, 102, 105, 106
Romantic Times, 230, 232–33
ROTC (Reserve Officer Training
    Corps), 47
Royal Clipper, 248
ruby laser photocoagulator, 60
Russell Reynolds, 8

sailing
    boats owned by Perkins, 63 (*see
        also specific boats*)
    clipper ships, 247–48, 256, 260–
        61
    with Danielle, *184*
    with Gerd, 59, 253
    square-rigged sailing vessels, 249
        (see also *Maltese Falcon*)
    See also Atlantic Challenge
        1997; Nioulargue Regatta in
        St. Tropez
Salhaney, Lucie, 14, 15
San Francisco Ballet, 147–62
    board, 147–49, 150, 153
    and Committee for the Ballet,
        153, 155
    dancers, 153–54, 159
    new director search, 150–59,
        161–62
    press coverage, 161–62 (see also
        San Francisco Chronicle)
    Smuin controversy, 147–49
San Francisco Chronicle
    performance review, 161–62
    on Perkins' board role, 150
    Smuin bias of, 153, 154

    on tensions at Ballet, 147, 148,
        155
San Francisco Examiner, 153
San Philippe Ranch, 54
Saoutchik, 94
Sarbanes-Oxley Act ("SOX"), 10–
    11, 16
satellites, 136, 214, 215
Schmidt, Eric, 141
Schmidt, Oscar, 93
Securities and Exchange
    Commission (SEC), 18, 113,
    114, 124
Sentry Insurance, 107
September 11 terrorist attacks, 222
sewage pipe installation, 67
Sex and the Single Zillionaire
    (Perkins), 223–36
    agents, 227–28
    book proposal, 224–25
    cover, *230*
    Dunn's reaction to, 11
    editing, 226, 229
    and Nobel Prize, 201
    promotion of, 229–30, 231, 232–
        33, 234–35
    publication, 230–31
    reviews, 236
    rewriting of, 228, 229
    as romantic novel, 185
    royalties, 232
    sales, 231–32
    writing process, 225–26
Seydoux, Michel, 90, 91, 92
Shannon, Claude, 72
Shockley, William, 104
Shockley Semiconductor, 104
"The Short Happy Life of Francis
    Macomber" (Hemingway), 217
shorting stocks, 114

Simpson, O. J., 229
Sinnex, 269
60 Minutes, 18
Sloot, Jan
  business agreement, 214
  death, 215, 217
  demonstration, 213–14
  invention, 211–12
  precautions with compiler, 212,
    215–16
Smuin, Michael
  contract, 159–60
  controversy surrounding, 147–49
  and dancers, 153–54
  and LeBlond, 151
  personality, 150
  and press, 150, 153
  and search for director, 157
  and Tomasson, 160
Snow-Job, 109–10
Sonsini, Larry, 136
Spanish Coast Guard, 243
Sparks, Sparky, 135
Spectra Physics, 68, 79, 109
Sperry Gyroscope Company, 48–49
square-rigged sailing vessels, 249
Stanford Research Institute, 74
Stanford University, 115, 123
Star Clipper sailing cruise ships, 248
Steel, Danielle
  and Atlantic Challenge (1997),
    167, 171
  charitable giving, 184–85
  childhood, 197, 199, 201
  critics, 192
  death of son, 193–95
  empathy, 199
  family life, 196–98
  interview given by Perkins, 183–
    201, 276

  and manslaughter trial, 36, 37–38
  and O'Brian, 241, 246
  Perkins' relationship with, 192–
    97, 198, 200–201
  personalities, 183–85, 201
  religious convictions, 185
  reviews, 236
  sailing, *184*
  sales, 185, 245
  staff, 200
  writing career, 185–90, *189*,
    190–92
  and *Zillionaire*, 224–25, 226,
    227, 231
Steinmetz, Natasha, 183–201
Stevens Point, Wisconsin, 101
Stoft, Paul, 75
Stone, Bob, 171
St. Tropez, France, 29–36, 248
Stumpers (professor), 204
Sun Flowers (Van Gogh), 95
Sun Microsystems, 133
Sutter Hill, 66, 102, 109
Swanson, Bob, 117–23, *118*, 131,
  139–40
swimming, 46, 47

Taeping, 247–48
Tandem Computers
  and Kleiner & Perkins, 125
  and KPC & B, 133
  origins, 110–14
  Perkins' role at, 10, 123
  and Pieper, 210–11
telephones, 214, 215
television video storage, 211–17
Tenenbaum, L. J., 152, 154, 156,
  158, 159
tennis shoes, resoling of, 109

Terrible Talon, 270

Thendara, 28

Thune-Ellefsen, Arild, 25–26

Thune-Ellefsen, Gerd, *24*
 cancer, 23–25
 and car rallies, 90, 91, 92
 children, 44
 death, 25
 early relationship, 59–60
 marriage, 60
 memorial, 23–26
 miracle in Busiri-Vici chapel,
   27–28
 mourning of Perkins for, 27–28,
   192, 195
 and Perkins as fireman, 222
 at Plumpton Place, 163–66, *164*
 receptions, 80
 sailing, 253
 and San Francisco Ballet, 147,
   149, 156
 and University Laboratories,
   Inc., 62

Time, 132

time-share computers, 78

Tokyo Stock Index, 95

Tomasson, Helgi, *151*
 appointment of, 160–61
 death threat, 161
 final performance of, 158
 negotiations with, 159
 performance review, 161–62
 pursuit of, 151, 154–57

Tomasson, Marlene, 154, 155, 156,
   161

Toray Industries, 266

Torrini Trophy, 28

Tough Choices (Fiorina), 18, 180

Traina, John, 192, 195, 241

Traina, Nick, 193–95, 199

Tread-Two, 109

Treybig, Jimmy
 and Compaq merger, 139, 210–11
 and Kleiner & Perkins, 108, 110,
   117
 and Tandem, *111*, 112

Turkey
 and *Falcon*, 254, 267, 268–69, 270
 NATO gunnery competition,
   48–49, 268–69

Ulutas, Hasan, 269

University Laboratories, Inc. (ULI)
 acquired by Spectra Physics, 68,
   79
 advertisement, 65
 DialGrade product line, 67
 and HP, 76
 laser development, 62–68
 success of, 101
 venture capital, 66

University of California Medical
   School, 119, 123

UNIX operating system, 210

U.S. Air Force, 257

U.S. Army, 47–48

venture capital, 85, 101–2, 131. *See
   also* Kleiner & Perkins; Kleiner
   Perkins Caufield & Byers

Vernebygget, 23–26, *25*

Vietnam War, 84

Vos, Jeroen de, 259

Wall Street, 3

Wall Street Journal, 6, 18, 84, 231

Watergate scandal, 84

Wausau Insurance, 107
Wayman, Bob, 6
Westchester County, New York, 46
White, Jed, 268
White Plains High School, 46
Wilmer, 270
Wilson (high school instructor), 46
windjammers, 247–48
Windsor, Liz, 261
Wolfe, Tom, 228
Wolfson Unit at Southampton
    University, 259
Wright (cook/butler), 164

X-rays, 61

The Yellow Admiral (O'Brian),
    244
Yildiz yard, 268–69
Young, John, 80, 83–84, 143
youth of Perkins, 44–46

Zaremba, Ivan, 93
Ziekie (translator), 49